NEW TESTAMENT SERMONS

Robert Murray M'Cheyne

NEW TESTAMENT SERMONS

Edited by
Michael D. McMullen

THE BANNER OF TRUTH TRUST

THE BANNER OF TRUTH TRUST
3 Murrayfield Road, Edinburgh EH12 6EL, UK
P.O. Box 621, Carlisle, PA 17013, USA

*

© Banner of Truth Trust 2004

ISBN 0 85151 874 5

*

Typeset in 11/15 pt Goudy Old Style BT at
the Banner of Truth Trust, Edinburgh.
Printed and bound in Great Britain
at the University Press,
Cambridge

DEDICATION

I dedicate these volumes to three American Christian families that my wife and I met in Scotland and grew to love in Christ. In no order other than alphabetical, they are Roy and Marcelle Ciampa and their children; Thor and Li Madsen and their children; and Terry and Denise Wilder and their children. In the Lord's gracious plan, Drs Ciampa, Madsen, Wilder and I are all now serving Him as Seminary Professors in America.

MICHAEL D. MCMULLEN

Contents

Foreword   xi

1. The Marriage Feast (*Matt.* 22:1–14)   1
2. Jesus Took Bread (*Matt.* 26:26)   13
3. The Supper the Sweetest Ordinance (*Matt.* 26:26)   19
4. The Rent Veil (*Matt.* 27:51)   28
5. The Sabbath Made for Man (*Mark* 2:27)   35
6. Be Opened! (*Mark* 7:31–37)   42
7. Satan's Palace (*Luke* 11:21–22)   52
8. Lost Sheep (*Luke* 15:1–7)   65
9. Christ Weeping over Jerusalem (*Luke* 19:41)   76
10. The Grace of God Seen at Antioch (*Acts* 11:22–24)   89
11. Almost Persuaded (*Acts* 11:22–24)   95
12. The Work of the Spirit in the Heart (*Rom.* 5:5)   104
13. Baptized into Christ (*Rom.* 6:3–4)   115

NEW TESTAMENT SERMONS

14. Dead to the Law by Christ (*Rom.* 7:4)   124
15. I Am Persuaded (*Rom.* 8:38–39)   129
16. On Not Loving Christ (*1 Cor.* 16:22)   143
17. The Gospel Ministry (*2 Cor.* 4:1–6)   153
18. A New Creature in Understanding (*2 Cor.* 5:17) 160
19. A New Creature in Affections (*2 Cor.* 5:17)   171
20. Desiring to Depart and to Be with Christ (*Phil.* 1:23)   182
21. Peter the Apostle (*1 Pet.* 1:1–3)   196
22. Blessed Be God! (*1 Pet.* 1:3–4)   201
23. Kept by God's Power (*1 Pet.* 1:5)   207
24. Rejoicing in Affliction (*1 Pet.* 1:6–7)   210
25. The Trial of Faith (*1 Pet.* 1:7)   214
26. Loving Christ Unseen (*1 Pet.* 1:8–9)   218
27. Salvation Long Promised (*1 Pet.* 1:10–12)   224
28. Gird Up the Loins of Your Mind (*1 Pet.* 1:13)   226
29. Obedient Children (*1 Pet.* 1:14–15)   228
30. Calling on the Father (*1 Pet.* 1:17)   231
31. Redeemed with Precious Blood (*1 Pet.* 1:18–19)   235
32. Christ Foreordained and Manifest (*1 Pet.* 1:20–21) 240

Contents

33.	Obeying the Truth (1 Pet. 1:22)	243
34.	Born Again (1 Pet. 1:23–25)	247
35.	Tasting and Growing (1 Pet. 2:1–3)	252
36.	Built on the Foundation (1 Pet. 2:4–5)	258
37.	God's Foundation Stone (1 Pet. 2:6–7)	263
38.	Chosen (1 Pet. 2:9)	266
39.	The People of God (1 Pet. 2:10)	271
40.	Beseeching God's People (1 Pet. 2:11)	276
41.	Christian Behaviour (1 Pet. 2:12)	280
42.	Submit to Earthly Rulers (1 Pet. 2:13–16)	285
43.	Duties to God and Man (1 Pet. 2:17)	289
44.	Masters and Servants (1 Pet. 2:18–23)	295
45.	Christ Bore Our Sins (1 Pet. 2:24–25)	299
46.	Believing Wives (1 Pet. 3:1–6)	305
47.	Seeing the Unseen (1 Pet. 5:7–9)	308
48.	New Creatures in Christ (1 John 3:4–10)	313

Foreword

ROBERT MURRAY M'CHEYNE was one of the many spiritual giants whom God has used to bless Scotland, and the world. He was born on 21 May 1813. His older brother David, a very godly witness and example to him, spoke of the ministry as 'the most blessed work on earth'. When David died at a young age, Robert was profoundly affected. Not long afterwards he was converted. David's influence went further, for Robert trained for that 'most blessed work', and in July 1835 was licensed by the Presbytery of Annan. In November of the same year, M'Cheyne was appointed assistant to John Bonar, Minister at Larbert and Dunipace. Exactly a year later he was inducted into the new church of St Peter's in Dundee.

As he arrived in Dundee and surveyed his field of labour, M'Cheyne wrote in his diary, 'Perhaps the Lord will make this wilderness of chimney-tops to be green and beautiful as the garden of the Lord, a field which the Lord hath blessed.' This indeed the Lord did abundantly.

M'Cheyne's health was always delicate, but in 1838 he was so physically drained that his doctors insisted on 'a total cessation of his public work'. With deep regret, he left for Edinburgh. While there M'Cheyne was asked to take part in a preliminary fact-finding mission to Israel. He was very anxious about leaving his flock, but God provided for them through another man of God, William Chalmers Burns. As M'Cheyne and his companions toured North Africa, Israel and Europe, God moved mightily in awakening, among the people of Dundee. Many were brought to faith and repentance and many more were brought into a new relationship with their Lord.

NEW TESTAMENT SERMONS

M'Cheyne had sown the seed, Burns came and watered that seed, and God gave the increase.

Many Christians are familiar to some degree with Andrew Bonar's classic, the *Memoir and Remains of Robert Murray M'Cheyne* (1844; enlarged edition, 1892, reprinted London: Banner of Truth, 1966). It gives the church a glimpse of the life, preaching and passion of a young man utterly dedicated to the Lord, and remains a most challenging work. But it is equally true that 'the half has not been told', and that many of his writings and sermon notes have hitherto remained unpublished.

The vast majority of the sermons in this set of three volumes are taken directly from M'Cheyne's original handwritten sermon manuscripts. A few were published in the nineteenth century but never reprinted, some in *Revival Truth: Being Sermons Hitherto Unpublished*. This was a small volume published in 1860 and edited by William Reid. In Alexander Smellie's biography of M'Cheyne, published in 1913, we read of Smellie receiving an unexpected parcel from James Macdonald of Edinburgh. The parcel was, says Smellie, altogether priceless, containing as it did, numerous M'Cheyne manuscripts, including letters to and from his family and friends; notebooks (several of which have been used in these volumes); sermons (some appear here); and documents of different kinds. Smellie was lent this material in preparation for a volume that later became his biography of M'Cheyne. Macdonald had purchased the box and contents from William Scott of Thornhill, at that time one of the few surviving relatives of the M'Cheynes. Macdonald proposed to give the contents to the Jewish Committee of the United Free Church of Scotland, to be preserved in the Library of New College, Edinburgh, and this is where they are today.

The sermons have been only lightly edited to make them more suitable for publication. Some, including the series on 1 Peter in this volume, have been slightly expanded by quoting texts in full or stating more extensively what was only indicated in note form. In several cases there were two sets of notes on the same passage,

Foreword

and these have been combined to make one sermon. In all cases, M'Cheyne's own words have been preserved.

In my work on M'Cheyne I have been blessed by the friendship of David Haslam, the dedicated man behind a wonderful website devoted exclusively to Robert Murray M'Cheyne. I would highly recommend this site: http://web.ukonline.co.uk/d.haslam/.

These sermons are presented not to show M'Cheyne's skill at sermon construction, nor as a piece of nineteenth-century history, but as a testimony to what God can do with a surrendered life, and to affirm that what God has done, He can do again. M'Cheyne died at the relatively young age of 29, but in his few short years he lived closer to God than most believers would, had they several lifetimes. He wrote, 'Live so as to be missed.' What a challenge this remains!

MICHAEL D. MCMULLEN
(www.Christian-history.org)
Associate Professor of Church History
Midwestern Baptist Theological Seminary
Kansas City, Missouri, USA

May 2004

1

The Marriage Feast[1]

And Jesus answered and spake unto them again by parables, and said, The kingdom of heaven is like unto a certain king, which made a marriage for his son, And sent forth his servants to call them that were bidden to the wedding: and they would not come. Again, he sent forth other servants, saying, Tell them which are bidden, Behold, I have prepared my dinner: my oxen and my fatlings are killed, and all things are ready: come unto the marriage. But they made light of it, and went their ways, one to his farm, another to his merchandise: And the remnant took his servants, and intreated them spitefully, and slew them. But when the king heard thereof, he was wroth: and he sent forth his armies, and destroyed those murderers, and burned up their city. Then saith he to his servants, The wedding is ready, but they which were bidden were not worthy. Go ye therefore into the highways, and as many as ye shall find, bid to the marriage. So those servants went out into the highways, and gathered together all as many as they found, both bad and good: and the wedding was furnished with guests.

And when the king came in to see the guests, he saw there a man which had not on a wedding garment: And he saith unto him, Friend, how camest thou in hither not having a wedding garment? And he was speechless. Then said the king to the servants, Bind him hand and foot,

---

[1] Preached in Larbert (August 1836), in Dunipace, and in St Peter's, Dundee, April 1837.

and take him away, and cast him into outer darkness; there shall be weeping and gnashing of teeth. For many are called, but few are chosen (Matt. 22:1–14).

THIS PARABLE DESCRIBES to us briefly and vividly God's sending of the gospel, first of all to the Jews, and then to the Gentiles, and the different receptions which it received from each of them. Let us go over the different parts of it.

1. ALL MEN ARE INVITED TO A MARRIAGE FEAST.

The first lesson which this parable teaches us is that it is a marriage and a marriage-feast to which God has all along been inviting men. 'The kingdom of heaven is like unto a certain king, which made a marriage for his son, and sent forth his servants to call them that were bidden to the wedding: and they would not come. Again, he sent forth other servants, saying, Tell them which are bidden, Behold, I have prepared my dinner: my oxen and my fatlings are killed, and all things are ready: come unto the marriage' (*Matt.* 22: 2–4). This was the very message which all the prophets and apostles of old were commissioned to carry to God's chosen people of the Jewish nation. This was the very message which Christ Himself brought with Him, for He came not to destroy men's lives, but to save them, and He it is who spoke this parable; and this is the very message which we now bring to you.

First of all, observe that it is a marriage that you are invited to. Men in all ages, have been naked, and poor, and penniless, not only without any righteousness, but lying under the curse of God's wrath, infinitely sinful and abominable in his sight, yet the delights of the Lord Jesus, the King's Son, have been ever with the children of men; and He condescends to choose out of them those whom He will take as His bride, that they may be with Him eternally where He is,

The Marriage Supper

to behold and share His glory: and just as the husband becomes liable for all the debts of his wife, He agreed to bear all the iniquities of His bride in His own body on the tree. And just as all the honour and merit of the husband is given to the wife, so His own merit and loveliness shall be a garment to clothe His bride.

He hath sent forth His messengers accordingly to invite all sinners to become one with Him, and their word is, 'Hearken, O daughter, and consider, and incline thine ear; forget also thine own people and thy father's house.' And the clothing He offers to bring them in is of 'wrought gold', with 'raiment of needlework.' And to this day, my friends, our anxious desire is to espouse you to that one husband, that you may be 'members of his body, of his flesh, and of his bones'. Oh! what infinite honour that the Son of God should leave the bosom of the Father and propose so close, so mysterious, so blessed a union as this, with base and sinful worms, 'whose cottages are of clay, and who are crushed before the moth'. Oh! if there is one thing more wonderful in the whole world than this, it is that any one of us, base-born worms of a day, should refuse a union of such unspeakable grace!

But it is a feast that all are invited unto. 'Behold I have prepared my dinner', verse 4. At every wedding there is a feast, and so it is here. The blessings of the gospel have all along been set forth to men as a feast. Solomon set them forth as a feast in Proverbs 9, where he speaks of Wisdom having, 'builded her house, and hewn out her seven pillars: she hath killed her beasts; she hath mingled her wine; she hath also furnished her table. Come, eat of my bread, and drink of the wine which I have mingled'.

Isaiah set them forth as a feast in chapter 25, where he says, 'In this mountain shall the Lord of hosts make unto all people a feast of fat things, a feast of wines on the lees, of fat things full of marrow, of wines on the lees well refined.' And, again, in chapter 55, where he invites all, saying, 'Ho, every one that thirsteth, come ye to the waters, and he that hath no money, come ye, buy and eat; yea, come, buy wine and milk (the richest parts of every feast) without money, and without price. Wherefore do ye spend money for that which is not bread? and your labour for that which satisfieth not? Hearken diligently unto me, and eat ye that which is good, and let your soul delight itself in fatness.' Did not Christ set the gospel blessings forth as a feast, when He said, 'He that cometh unto me shall never hunger, and he that believeth on me shall never thirst. For my flesh is meat indeed, and my blood is drink indeed'? And, again, doth He not set them forth as a feast, in the holy ordinance of the supper, where bread and wine are offered you, to picture forth the blessings of redemption?

Oh yes, my friends, we have utterly failed in our preaching of Jesus, if we have not set Him forth to you as 'a feast of fat things, of wines on the lees well refined'. And you have utterly misunderstood every sermon that you ever heard, if you think that we have been inviting you to anything but a feast of peace and love, of joy and eternal life. Yes, the message we are commissioned to bring is not one of wrath, but of love and joy. 'Tell them which are bidden, Behold, I have prepared my dinner: my oxen and my fatlings are killed, and all things are ready: come unto the marriage', verse 4. I beseech you to mark that we do not invite you to come and make a feast for yourselves, to bring your own provisions with you. No, we invite you to a ready-prepared feast. 'All things are ready.' The oxen and the fatlings are killed; the wine is poured out; the garments are waiting your acceptance; all things are ready; not one thing is unprovided.

Pardon of all your sins is ready. God has provided 'the ram for the burnt-offering'. You have not to bring anything with you to blot out your sins before you come. No! Pardon of sin is one of the dishes of the feast. One of the ancients says, 'A good conscience is a continual feast', and so it is, but who has it? He only that has partaken of the Lamb of God that taketh away the sin of the world. He has a conscience void of offence, not because he never sinned, but because his sin is all taken away.

A garment of righteousness is ready. Christ has provided wedding garments for all the guests, as it was customary in the East to do. You cannot say, 'Wait till I have made myself worthy to come', for this garment is part of the feast. All things are ready: come to the marriage.

The oil of the Holy Spirit is ready. At all feasts, the guests were anointed with the most precious ointments; and so now in the East precious oils are sprinkled upon every guest. So Jesus has provided this promise of the Father. You cannot say, 'Stop till I have changed my heart', for that is one of the good things of the feast. All things are ready: come unto the marriage.

Ah, my friends, if you keep away from the feast after such an invitation as this, the only reason is, that you are too proud to come to a feast where you provide nothing. Be sure, then, if you do not come to the real feast in the gospel, that you do not come to the image of it in the Lord's Supper, lest you eat and drink judgment! Will you perform such a mockery on your own soul, such a mockery on God, as to refuse to partake of the true feast this day, and yet to sit down at that which is an image of it another day? First take, as we freely offer you, the true feast, and then what is any man that he should forbid you the bread and wine at the table of the Lord?

2. HOW THE JEWS TREATED THE INVITATION.

The second lesson which we learn from this parable is, the treatment which the Jews gave to the message, verses 3–6. Three kinds of refusal are given to the message.

First, they would not come. This was the way in which simple souls treated the message. It seems never to have reached their understanding. Perhaps they were asleep before the messenger got to the end of his message. They have no reason to give, but just that they will not come. Oh! how many such are there among us! Simple souls, who never yet could understand that the Bible message was addressed to them. Oh! how many will not so much as give a hearing to the messenger of Christ! Will not come the length of the church to hear the invitation.

How many have the Bible lying by them, and do not read, or even if they do, do not hear it speaking to them! Or if they do come to the house of God, it is for custom's sake, or to while away the tedious hours of the drowsy Sabbath-day. Oh! poor simple souls, loving their simplicity, who live and die in their ignorance! All that can be said of you, when you are sinking into hell, and begin then for the first time to awake and cry, all that can be said then is, Jesus would often have gathered you, but you would not.

The second class of refusers are far more intelligent men, and they treat religion with far greater respect. They give the Word, and the ministers of the Word, a full and patient hearing – they hear the description of the feast, and try to understand it; but weighing all that they hear in the one scale, and their farm and their merchandise in the other scale, they make light of the message. These are the thorny-ground hearers over again. Oh, how many such there were among the Jews! Oh, how many such there are among you! How many of you have set your whole mind on business, and say to us in your inmost heart, There is something in what you say, and, when I have a convenient season, I will call for you!

When Lot tried to warn his sons-in-law, he seemed to them as one that mocked. And so, when we stand here inviting you, Sabbath after Sabbath, you treat us as idle tale-bearers. Oh! it is enough to

The Marriage Supper

make an angel weep to see such spirits as yours, which, if redeemed and sanctified, might rejoice more loudly than angels before the throne, grovelling all your days without one thought higher than your farm or your merchandise!

The third set of refusers are those who, in verse 6, took his servants and entreated them spitefully. These formed a large class among the Jews, so large, that Christ called Jerusalem, 'Thou that killest the prophets, and stonest them which are sent unto thee.' And Stephen asked them the question, 'Which of the prophets have not your fathers persecuted?' And, again, we find Christ warning His disciples that they would be used in the same way, 'Behold, I send you forth as sheep in the midst of wolves, and ye shall be hated of all men for My name's sake.' 'If ye were of the world, the world would love his own: but because ye are not of the world, but I have chosen you out of the world, therefore the world hateth you.'

And it is so to this day, yea, peculiarly so in our day. If there is in any place a faithful and godly minister, be well assured some have hated and spoken ill of him for his message's sake. When an ardent preacher of Christ comes first into the work of the ministry, he is so conscious in his own bosom of having no motive but love for perishing souls, that he thinks it impossible but all will receive him with open arms.

Alas! he should have read more deeply how unconverted men treated the Master. If they called Him Beelzebub, what will they not call His servants? 'It is enough for the disciple that he be as His master.' Ah, yes! the sooner the romance of life is broken up the better. The sooner he comes to know that there are many who will love him the less because he loves them the more, so much the better. Search and try your own hearts, my friends, and if you feel disgusted by my plainness, if you turn away with dislike from my pointedness, think on your way home how much you resemble those who mocked the disciples, saying, These men are full of new wine; how like you are in spirit to those who took the servants, and entreated them spitefully, and slew them.

3. THE GOSPEL IS SENT TO THE GENTILES.

The third lesson which we learn from this parable is how God regarded the unbelieving Jews, and how he sent the gospel message to the Gentiles. Observe God's judgment on the unbelieving Jews. He was wroth, and sent forth His armies. The armies which destroyed Jerusalem were the heathen armies of Rome, under the command of the heathen emperor Titus, and yet there they are called His armies.

Does not this show that all power is God's, in heaven and on earth, that He is the governor among the nations; that, just as the Assyrian and his armies were but a rod in God's hand, an axe and a saw, though 'he meaneth not so, neither doth his heart think so; but it is in his heart to destroy and cut off nations not a few' (Isa. 10:5–7), so all armies are under His control, wars, famines, plagues, all fulfil His counsel? 'None can stay His hand or say to Him, What doest thou?'

Oh, believers, why should you fear any evil tidings? Let your heart be fixed, trusting in the Lord. If He be for you, who can be against you? They are more that be with us than they that be with them. And you who turn away from the invitations of Christ just in the same way as the Jews did, those who will not come just because they will not, you who make light of it, and prefer your farm and your merchandise, you who treat His servants despitefully in your hearts, loving them all the less because they love you the more, take heed.

Oh! bethink you that God is an unchangeable God! That He is a God of principle, not of association! That He acts from principles as fixed and sure in the world of grace as He does in the world of nature! If, then, He did not spare the Jews, do you think He will spare you? If He burned up their city, will He not burn up your city? As surely as Jerusalem is at this day trodden under foot of the Gentiles, and the highly favoured nation are now strangers and wanderers, a taunt, a proverb, and a curse, in every nation of the globe, so surely shall you, if you persist in turning away from this message, be vagabonds and outcasts in a miserable eternity.

Observe, again, how God sends the message to the Gentiles, verses 9–10. Before this refusal, the disciples were to go only to the lost sheep of the house of Israel. But now the message is, 'Go ye into all the world', and, accordingly, we go to every door, we carry the message to every bosom. And the effect of the call is just as Christ represents it. We gather together all as many as we find, both bad and good. The parable of the tares shows plainly that in the professing church we are to expect bad and good together. And the parable of the net shows the same thing, that the time of separation will be the last day. These three parables seem to teach us the impossibility of ever having what has been called a pure communion of the faithful on this side of eternity.

There is but one assembly and one feast, where the unclean cannot enter, and that is the general assembly and church of the first-born whose names are written in heaven. Remember, then, it is no sure test that you are a Christian that you partake of the Lord's Supper with Christians. Both bad and good will be found sitting at that table. The blood, the garment, the peace, the witness – these are the only true tests that you are a Christian indeed.

4. THE JUDGMENT IS COMING.

But I hasten to the fourth and last lesson which we learn from this parable, that there is a day of separation and judgment coming. 'And when the king came in to see the guests, he saw there a man which had not on a wedding garment: and he saith unto him, Friend, how camest thou in hither, not having a wedding garment? And he was speechless. Then said the king to the servants, Bind him hand and foot, and take him away, and cast him into outer darkness; there shall be weeping and gnashing of teeth. For many are called, but few are chosen' (verses 11–14).

From this we learn that, however much unconverted men may mingle with the godly upon earth, they shall be at once detected in the judgment. The tares are in this world growing up with the wheat in the same families, in the same congregations. The good fish and the bad fish are drawn to shore in the same net. Nay, those who have put on the righteousness of Jesus, and those who are dressed in the filthy rags of their own righteousness, sit down together at the same gospel-feast, and at the table of the Lord.

And however much godly ministers may warn, and strive, and beseech the unconverted not to come to the Lord's Table until they come to Christ, yet still it ever will be so. In our congregations the bad and the good grow together till the harvest, but no longer! The king comes in to see the guests, the King of kings, the searcher of all hearts, who searches Jerusalem as with candles.

His saints are all a goodly company, sitting with Abraham, Isaac, and Jacob, all dressed in spotless white garments; for the white linen is the righteousness of saints. In themselves, they are naked and vile, altogether unworthy of the presence of a king, and their best righteousnesses were as filthy rags.

But they heard the word of the message, 'All things are ready', and they came, standing in need of every thing, and they put on Christ's white raiment, even the righteousness of God, a more comely raiment than that of angels. They obeyed the word of Christ, 'Put on thy beautiful garments, O Jerusalem.'

But the Christless soul, oh, how naked and vile shall he be in that day! On the earth he was unnoticed, perhaps, lived on in decency and worldliness, waited on ordinances, and partook of sacraments. But in the judgment, how naked and deformed, how vile and polluted does he seem, in the midst of the redeemed, all clothed with the righteousness of God. Like an ugly toad crawling in some lovely garden, like Satan, when he appears in the ranks of the holy angels, so shall the Christless soul appear in that day, when he shall hear the awful words, 'Friend, how camest thou in hither, not having a wedding garment.' Oh, my friends, it is easy to pass current for decent religious men among your neighbours, it is easy to deceive ministers, and to deceive the world, it is easy to join yourselves with the people of God, and to sit down with them at the same sacrament, but there is one whom you cannot deceive. There is one eye upon you at the feast that knows at a glance whether or not you have put on the righteousness of God, which is Christ's wedding garment.

And if at the ensuing solemnity you venture to sit down at that feast to which none but believers are invited, not having this garment, nor caring anything about it, it is true He may suffer you to sit quietly and unchallenged here, but the day is at hand – yea, to many of you, 'at the very doors' – when the King shall say to you, 'Friend, how camest thou in hither, not having a wedding garment?'

Learn that every Christless soul will condemn itself: 'And he was speechless.' So, my friends will it be with you. It may be there is not one Christless soul before me this day that is not ready to give a thousand excuses why he is as he is. Nay, I dare say, not one Christless soul shall sit down at the sacrament that shall not have some kind of defence of so unreasonable and so unmeaning a profanation. But in that day you will be speechless, you will condemn yourselves. Think what blushes shall cover you when you have not a word to say.

You that are stout-hearted and boasters, think how you shall be quashed and silenced. And will it not be the hardest part of your condemnation that you must condemn yourselves? If you could cry out, and say, 'It is unjust', that would be some relief, but to feel that it is just condemnation, this is the very hell of hell!

Learn that outer darkness will be the home of such souls. He thought to enjoy the brilliancy and joy of the feast, and, lo, he is cast into outer darkness, how much darker because of his former light! How dismal will your change be, you that sit down at our sacraments here, and think to sit down in heaven, who have no wedding garment! Oh, ye lovers of darkness, how just that outer darkness should be your portion!

Finally, remember that many are called, but few chosen. When we speak to the unconverted, we speak to the many. You are all called this day, and all things are ready. Are you of the many or of the few? Oh, how sad to think that most of you will not heed; most of you will not turn; most of you will go away to your 'farm' and your 'merchandise' and will finally stand 'speechless' before the throne?

But oh, little flock, whose hearts the Lord has touched, who have put on the wedding garment, welcome to the feast of love! Take it as a pledge of your Father's love, and that you shall never want any good thing. 'Fear not, little flock, for it is your Father's good pleasure to give you the kingdom.' Amen.

2

Jesus Took Bread

And as they were eating, Jesus took bread, and blessed it, and brake it, and gave it to the disciples, and said, Take, eat; this is my body (Matt. 26:26).

LET US CONSIDER the actions of Jesus and of His disciples at the Supper:

1. THE ACTIONS OF JESUS.

i. JESUS TOOK BREAD.

What did this action represent? It represented *Christ's taking upon Himself the great work of substitution for sinners.*

Without doubt He was the fittest person of the Godhead to do this work. He is the ransom for our souls: 'I have found a ransom' (*Job* 33:24). In the mystery of the Godhead, the Father held the rights of the Godhead in His hand, the sword of justice, and the Spirit's work is to persuade souls to close with Christ. The Son was chosen as our Substitute, and we may rest on that.

He was fitter than all creatures for this work. The highest, holiest angel would not have done. There is no infinite distance between one creature and another creature. The angel was not so much higher than man as the Son was higher than both. Both angels and men are the breath of God's mouth. The substitution of an angel would not have honoured God's law.

God did not choose a man, for every man had his own hell to bear. There is none righteous, for all have sinned; and what was needed was a sinless man. God calls Him, 'Mine elect' (*Isa.* 42:1)! Is he *your* Chosen One? God has desired Him! Do you? God has provided Him, saying, 'They will reverence my Son' (*Luke* 20:13). Do *you* reverence Him?

Jesus taking bread also represented *the incarnation of Christ*. It is plain that this typified Christ on earth, just as the manna on the ground represented Christ come down from heaven. He was to be the foundation stone, laid on the ground. This is the fountain of our salvation: 'God was manifest in the flesh' (*1 Tim.* 3:16). Behold, the great mystery of godliness! He is a root out of the dry ground. Behold the wisdom of God, and the power of God unto salvation!

ii. He Blessed It.

This represented the Father fitting the Saviour with all fitness for the work. He was anointed (*Isa.* 61:1). The Father held Him by the hand. He filled Him with the Spirit. He sanctified and sent Him into the world. God prepared a body for Him (*Heb.* 10:5). Now He has received gifts for men (*Eph.* 4:8). The oil on the head of the Anointed comes down to all the members of His body (*Psa.* 133:2).

iii. He Broke It.

This speaks of the sufferings of Christ. It pleased the Father to bruise Him (*Isa.* 53:10).

a. *The source of His sufferings*. It was the just wrath of God that fell on Him, in our place. 'Thou hast brought me into the dust of death' (*Psa.* 22:15). He cried, 'Why hast thou forsaken me?'

b. *The dreadfulness of His sufferings.* The bread was broken, not merely wounded. The wine was poured out. He poured out His soul unto death (Isa. 53:12).

iv. He Gave It.

He handed the bread and wine to the disciples. This plainly signifies the making over of His blood, His righteousness, His all, to His own.

a. *Christ is freely offered to all.* He is offered to you, O man. 'Look unto me . . . all the ends of the earth.' 'Him that cometh to me I will in no wise cast out.' 'Whosoever will, let him come.' The brazen serpent is free to all. The Ark is open, and yet there is room. The cities of refuge are there to be entered into.

b. But yet, note that *this bread is only given to his disciples.*

2. THE ACTIONS OF THE COMMUNICANTS.

i. They Receive the Bread and the Wine.

They thankfully receive what is offered.

i. This implies that *they do receive a broken Saviour.* Christ is made of God unto them righteousness. They do close with Him. They feel that they cannot justify themselves. They firmly believe that He has done all and suffered all and is free to them. They close with Him. They cleave to Him. They come to Him. They take this broken Saviour to be their Surety.

ii. *They take a whole Saviour.*

Most that generally come should keep away from the holy Table. Many know that they were never convinced of sin, were never made to pray, were never brought to close savingly with Christ. Many say, I hope to turn yet before I die. Ah! this shows you are not closing with Christ. You should not come to this holy Table. Would you lie unto God? Many know they have had their convictions of sin, but they passed away. They should not come to this holy Table.

But there are also many of you who have become discouraged in trying to find out whether you have ever believed. Believe now, and so come! The only fitness required is to feel your need of Him!

ii. They Eat and Drink.

It is no sacrament if it be only taken. It must be eaten and drunk. Bread is the staff of life. Wine is very nourishing to those that have 'often infirmities' (1 Tim. 5:23). Both are the greatest nutritious blessings of man. The body is strengthened, upheld, refreshed, like a traveller for a journey. So we feed on Jesus our strength. We draw our nourishment and strength from Him. Our soul leans on Him, feeds on Him. We come under His wings and are satisfied with the goodness of His house. We drink of the river of His pleasures (Psa. 36:8).

Taking represents justifying faith. Eating and drinking represent adoption and sanctification. As this bread and wine feeds my body, so a risen Saviour feeds my soul. He is my bread. He is my wine. I am like a weary traveller. He is the Good Samaritan. He upholds my goings.

You should examine yourselves on these points. Do you desire nourishment from Christ? Are you a branch receiving sap from him? Because he lives, do you live also? Are you a member of Christ? Most of you know that you are not! Most know that you are not born again, that you are dead! You are a dead branch. Though you seem to be joined to the living Vine, you are dead.

If any is living in avowed sin, winking at sin in his children, breaking the Sabbath, absenting himself from ordinances, swearing, drinking, working wickedness, you may know that this is not the mind that was in Christ. Keep back, lest when the bread is in your mouth the wrath of God come on you to the uttermost.

But I would say by way of encouragement to others, if the source of your trembling is that you feel so wicked in your heart, so weak, and yet you hate all sin, and wish the whole image of God to be restored in you, come. The Supper is for you.

iii. THEY GIVE TO OTHERS.

This speaks of love to the brethren, and a desire that all Christ's children should be found with you. Just as vine branch passes the rich juice to the smaller twigs and tendrils, so you would have every gift and grace shared by all. Examine whether you love Christians as Christians. If you dislike Christians, the Supper is not for you. If you oppose their schemes of godliness and usefulness, it is not for you.

But to others I would say, Some of you love the brethren. Come and show it!

One great want of success in ministry is the monstrous abuse connected with the Lord's Supper. I have felt ever since I came among you that nothing stood more in the way of the conversion of your souls than the profanation of God's holy Sacrament. God is provoked to withdraw, your own consciences are seared, and that which should be a day of Christ's triumph is turned into a day of blinding to perdition.

Many come who know that they are living in open and positive sin. Many come who know that they are Christless. Many come who have never enquired about their souls.

If you would not pass the hot iron over your conscience and sear it against all feeling, attend while I shall explain the actions in this holy ordinance.

Christ is indeed free to all. He is the Ark, the brazen serpent, the cities of refuge. He says, 'Look unto me', to all the ends of the earth. As the angels said, these glad tidings of great joy are unto all people. Him that cometh, He will not cast out. There is still room. Whosoever will, let him come. He is not not willing that any should perish.

Taking broken bread and wine means that I do accept of the Saviour as my Surety. Like Noah, I enter into the Ark. Like the sacrificer, I lay my hand on the head of the lamb. I am like the man fleeing into the Refuge City, or the woman touching the hem of His garment. In the Song of Solomon, the bride held him and would not let him go. It is like taking an earnest penny as a token, like taking a ring in marriage, or accepting the right hand. So Christ stretches out His right hand. We have been sent to woo you long. We have told you His personal beauty, His rich clothing, His rich inheritance. Here, in the Lord's Supper, He stretches out His hand. If you do heartily consent, then you are welcome.

As to the actions of the communicants, eating and drinking express feeding on Christ, deriving strength for the family, for work, for the sick soul from Him. It is like the bride leaning on her beloved. Each branch of the vine gets nourishment. A member of the body gets nourishment and strength under His wings. He is the olive tree feeding the lamps (*Zech.* 4:2–3). It is to flourish like the palm tree, or like a cedar in Lebanon (*Psa.* 92:12). It is like Israel feeding on the manna for forty years.

But if in your heart you persecute the people of God, if your tongue is like a razor, or like sharp arrows, if you oppose the schemes of true Christians, ridicule them, and hate to hear them speak, the ordinance is not for you.

3

The Supper the Sweetest Ordinance[1]

And as they were eating, Jesus took bread, and blessed it, and brake it, and gave it to the disciples, and said, Take, eat; this is my body (Matt. 26:26).

THE LORD'S SUPPER is the sweetest of all ordinances:

1. *Because of the time when it was instituted.*
On the darkest night that ever was in this world, the night in which He was betrayed, the night in which His love was put to the test: on that night Jesus took bread, blessed it, brake it, and gave it to His disciples.

2. *Because it is the believer's ordinance.*
It is the duty of all men to pray. God hears even the ravens when they cry (*Psa.* 147:9), and so He often hears the prayers of unawakened men. It is the duty of all men to hear the preached gospel, 'Unto you, O men, I call; and my voice is to the sons of man' (*Prov.* 8:4). But the Supper is the children's bread. It is intended only for those who know and love the Saviour.

[1] Preached before the Lord's Supper in St Peter's, Dundee, 28 October 1838.

3. *Because Christ is the beginning and middle and end of it.*

'This do in remembrance of me', we are told. 'Ye do show the Lord's death till he come.' There are many sermons in which Christ is not from beginning to end. There are many books where you cannot find the Saviour. But there cannot be a Sacrament where Christ is not in it from beginning to end. It is all Christ and him crucified. This gives a peculiar sweetness to the Lord's Table.

Let us look, then, at the actions of our Saviour.

1. JESUS TOOK BREAD.

This represented two things:

i. THE CHOOSING OF CHRIST TO THE GREAT WORK OF SUBSTITUTION.

'Behold my servant whom I uphold; mine elect, in whom my soul delighteth' (*Isa.* 42:1). God chose His own Son to undertake the work. There can be no doubt that Christ was the only being in all the universe that would have done for this mighty work. It seems likely that no other person of the Godhead would have done. The Father held the sword of justice in His hand; the Spirit undertook the work of winning and drawing souls to Christ. The Son was chosen to undertake the work of substitution. 'I have found a ransom' (*Job* 33:24).

It is plain that none of the holy angels would have done. God looked round all the holy angels, 'ten thousand times ten thousand and thousands of thousands', angels and principalities and powers. Each is crying, 'Holy, holy, holy, Lord God Almighty.' But He saw at once that they could never stand in the stead of sinners. No creature could bear the Creator's wrath. They are sweet messengers of mercy, but oh! they could not bear the wrath of God, their beauty would fade.

The Supper the Sweetest Ordinance

It is plain that no mere man could have done. 'The LORD looked down from heaven upon the children of men, to see if there were any that did understand, and seek God. They are all gone aside, they are all together become filthy: there is none that doeth good, no, not one' (*Psa.* 14:2–3). Every man had his own hell to bear. Every man's sins were heavier than he could bear. No man could give a ransom for himself, much less for his brother.

God looked into His own bosom. He found One there that was sinless, without spot and blameless; One that was equal with God; One that had the same infinite compassion toward hell-deserving sinners; One that could bear the Creator's wrath, and yet live. He cried, 'I have found a ransom. I will send my beloved Son. It may be they will reverence my Son.'

Learn what a fitting Saviour Christ is. He is the very Saviour that you need. He is God's choice, 'Mine elect'. Now God knew all our sins, He knew the weight of wrath that was due to our sins. He knew the infinite fitness of Christ to bear all. He chose His Son. Flee to Him, awakened sinners. Just as the Ark was strong enough to resist the floods breaking up from beneath, and the torrents coming down from the sky – not a timber was cracked, for it was God's providing – so Christ is of God's choosing, the very Saviour you need. Flee into Him. Not one wave of sorrow will reach your soul, not one drop of wrath will fall upon you.

ii. THE INCARNATION OF CHRIST.

I have often observed to you that when the Saviour was going to make a memorial of Himself, He did not take silver or gold or jewels or fine paintings or marble statuary, but bread, plain bread. Why? Because He did not want to set forth His original glory but His humiliation. He did not want to paint the Son in the bosom of the Father, or the King of Glory on his throne, but Christ on earth, God clothed in flesh, Immanuel, God with us. Just so, He was represented by the manna, 'a small white thing upon the ground, as small as hoar frost'. He is spoken of as a Foundation stone, a thing laid down upon the ground. He is spoken of as a Fountain opened, which comes out of the ground. He is spoken of in Isaiah as the 'root out of a dry ground', 'He hath no form nor comeliness'. He says of Himself, 'I am the rose of Sharon, and the lily of the valleys' (*Song of Sol.* 2:1), growing low down in the valley of this fallen world. In all these the Son of God is set forth, not in His glory, but in His emptiness, not on the throne but as the footstool. So is the bread of the Lord's Supper.

Ah! draw near and see this great sight, God manifest in the flesh, represented in a bit of homely bread. Oh! what a sweet truth that bit of bread can tell. It was wonderful when God came down and dwelt within curtains, when He filled the tabernacle with his presence so that the priests could not stand to minister. But oh! how much more wonderful is this, when a Divine Person comes down and dwells in flesh. When He that hung the earth upon nothing becomes, 'a worm and no man' upon the earth. When He that formed man of the dust of the ground Himself takes a body, a frail body, is hungry, thirsty, weary, sleepy, sweats, groans, bleeds, dies. Oh! believers, meditate on this mystery of godliness when you behold that bread.

2. HE BLESSED IT.

This represents the Father fitting the Son with all fitness for His work.

i. GOD PREPARED A BODY.

'Sacrifice and offering thou wouldest not desire, but a body hast thou prepared me' (*Heb.* 10:5). Just as God gave Moses a pattern of the tabernacle in the Mount, so He prepared the body in which the Son of God should dwell.

ii. He Anointed Him.

When Jesus was baptized in Jordan, the heavens were opened and the Spirit descended on Him like a dove and abode upon Him; and so when He began to preach in Nazareth He said, 'The Spirit of the Lord is upon me, because he hath anointed me to preach the gospel to the poor' (*Luke* 4:18). Although He was God in Himself, yet so great was the work given Him to do that the Spirit was given to Him without measure.

iii. He Gave Him the Tongue of the Learned.

'The Lord God hath given me the tongue of the learned, that I should know how to speak a word in season to him that is weary' (*Isa.* 50:4). God furnished Him as a preacher.

iv. He Held Him by the Hand.

'I the Lord have called thee in righteousness, and will hold thine hand, and will keep thee, and give thee for a covenant of the people' (*Isa.* 42:6). Not only was He upheld by His own divinity and by the Spirit abiding in Him but God the Father too held up His hand. You find Him looking to this in the hour of His bitter agony, 'Behold, the hour cometh, yea, is now come, that ye shall be scattered every man to his own, and shall leave me alone: and yet I am not alone, because the Father is with me' (*John* 16:32).

Learn, believers, a sweet lesson of confidence in Jesus from the simple ceremony of blessing the bread. He is not only chosen of the Father but blessed and furnished by the Father for the work given Him to do. Ah! how this should raise up our confidence in Jesus, how it should lead us calmly to repose our souls in Him. When we learn that God has chosen a Champion to fight for us against the enemy, this gives us joy, but when we learn that He hath given Him the armour of heaven, the choicest weapons, yea, that the hand of God the Father is holding Him up, our confidence may well increase, we may rest our souls in His work.

When we tell you that God has chosen a High Priest to make atonement for our sins, this is great rest. But when we learn that he has furnished Him, anointed Him, provided the Lamb for the burnt offering, then you may sweetly repose upon His finished work.

3. HE BRAKE IT.

This is my body broken for you. There can be no doubt that this simple action represents the sufferings of the Son of God in the stead of sinners.

Learn:
i. THE SOURCE OF THESE SUFFERINGS.

'He brake it.' When you look at the agonies of the cross, you are generally too much taken up with the mere instruments engaged in that awful scene. You see the four soldiers driving in the nails that pierced His hands and feet. You see the priests shooting out the lip; the passers-by wagging the head; the crucified thieves reviling Him.

There is quite another way of looking at the scene. If we would look more deeply, I believe you would see only two Persons present at that awful moment. 'It pleased the Father to bruise Him. Thou hast put Him to grief. Thou wilt make His soul an offering for sin.' In this view you lose sight of the bloody soldiers, you forget the distorted faces of the raging priests, you cease to hear the blasphemies of the crowd, you see only the Father bruising Him;

The Supper the Sweetest Ordinance

the holy, holy, holy God pouring out His wrath upon the sin-bearing Lamb. So it was with the Saviour Himself. I have no doubt He felt the nails, for He says, 'They pierced my hands and my feet.' He saw the raging of his cruel enemies, for He says, 'Many bulls have compassed me: strong bulls of Bashan have beset me round about. Dogs have compassed me, the assembly of the wicked have enclosed me.' He felt the thirst for He says, 'My tongue cleaveth to my jaws', for thirst. He even observed the soldiers parting His raiment, 'They parted my garments among them, and cast lots upon my vesture.' But He saw them as if He did not see them. He heeded not: a far more dreadful object was in his view, an angry God. 'My God, my God, why hast Thou forsaken me,' and again, 'Thou hast brought me into the dust of death.' Oh! what a sweet lesson this is, for it shows that His wrath has all fallen already. Hide there, sinner, and you are safe!

ii. How Great His sufferings.

The bread is broken. It is not merely bruised, but broken. The wine is poured out. This plainly shows the infinite sufferings of the Lamb of God. He was broken for us. He poured out His soul unto death.

Oh! learn the greatness of God's wrath against sin. If you had been present at the Flood, if you had seen the fountains of the great deep broken open, the rocky base of the earth broken open by the hand of God, you would have said, This is indeed the wrath of God. Or if you were to be present at the Second Coming of the Saviour, when the heavens shall depart away like a scroll, when the elements shall melt with fervent heat, you would cry, Ah! this is the wrath of God.

But there is one picture more awful than either. It is the broken bread and poured out wine. In that simple bread and wine you may see the breaking of His spirit who was God with us, the pouring out of the blood of the Son of God. How will you bear that wrath when it comes on you? Oh, the deep waters, and you are not a divine Person, you have no Holy Spirit given you, you have no God holding your hand. How will you wade through that bottomless, shoreless sea of divine anger? How will you bear the bruisings and breaking of God's hell? Oh! flee now from the wrath to come!

4. HE GAVE IT.

The giving of the bread and wine denotes the free offer of the broken Saviour to hell-deserving sinners. Oh! there is not a sweeter truth in the Bible than that Christ is freely offered to all the world. This is the anchor of our peace.

ii. Did Not All the Types Set Him forth as a Free Saviour?

The ark with its huge empty chambers cried loud in the ears of sinners, Yet there is room! So it is with Christ. The brazen serpent lifted up invited all to look and be healed. So Christ is lifted up in your sight. The refuge cities elevated on the tops of hills with their gates open night and day seemed to have a tongue crying, 'Flee from the wrath to come.' So Christ is open night and day.

ii. Did He Not Speak in the Old Testament?

'Unto you, O men, I call; and my voice is to the sons of men' (*Prov.* 8:4). Again, 'Look unto me, and be ye saved, all the ends of the earth' (*Isa.* 45:22).

iii. Does Not the Gospel Speak Yet More Clearly?

Did not the angel say, 'I bring you good tidings of great joy, which shall be to all people'? Did not Christ say, 'Him that cometh to me

The Supper the Sweetest Ordinance

I will in no wise cast out'? Did not Jesus, when He bade farewell to the world, say, 'Go ye into all the world and preach the gospel to every creature'? And is not the last solemn invitation of the Bible, 'Whosoever will, let him take the water of life freely'?

A Word to Christians.

You are often disturbed at this time by the question, 'But what if I never believed? What if all has been delusion?' Now here is an answer. Suppose it *has* been all delusion, Christ is free to you today! With all His benefits, the glorious Surety of sinners, He is free to you because you are sinners. Believe on the Lord Jesus Christ, and thou shalt be saved. Oh, this Word is enough to die upon – 'Him that cometh to Me I will in no wise cast out.'

A Word to the World.

Oh! my friends, the Saviour is free to you. You are often angry when we tell you that the bread at the Lord's Table is not free to you; but here is something better: the Saviour Himself is free to you! There is not one of you to whom we do not offer Him, with all His benefits, His blood and righteousness. 'Unto you, O men, I call; and my voice is to the sons of men.'

My friends, the Saviour of the world is walking through the midst of you this day. He is seeking the lost. Happy are those of you that lay hold of Him!

4

The Rent Veil

And, behold, the veil of the temple was rent (Matt. 27:51).

THE DOCTRINE WHICH IS TO BE SEEN in the incident of the rending of the veil of the temple when Jesus died is this: By the death of Jesus the way is opened up to God, so that the chiefest of sinners may go in. I will seek to answer three questions: 1. When was the veil rent? When Jesus died. 2. To what extent was the veil rent? From top to bottom. 3. How is this seen in the Lord's Supper?

1. THE VEIL WAS RENT WHEN CHRIST DIED.
Before Christ came, the veil was complete. This showed that the way into the Holiest was not yet made manifest (*Heb.* 9:8). No sinners could come near to God. All were guilty in His sight. No flesh living could be justified.

When the Surety came, the moment He had paid the debt, the bond was torn. The moment He had fulfilled all obedience and borne the sufferings due to sinners, that moment the veil was rent! Now the way is open to the Father. Any of you who are convinced of sin feel as if a veil was between you and God, and that your iniquities have separated between you and your God. As long as

The Rent Veil

you look at the Law, at the holiness of God, at your own life and heart, you will find this to be the case. Your misery will be deeper and deeper. The clearer your view, the deeper your misery, the thicker the veil.

How will peace come? God leads you to the cross, leads you back to that event. Learn that it is the Son of God upon the tree. He is bearing the sins of the world in His own body on the tree. That darkness shows that God has forsaken Him. Listen to His dying sigh, 'Father, into thy hands I commend my Spirit.' God leads you then to the temple. Behold! The veil is rent. Ah! it is a sight of Christ that rends the veil.

2. IT WAS RENT FROM TOP TO BOTTOM.

The greatest sinner may enter in. Every sinner may enter in. There is room for all. 'Yet there is room' (*Luke* 14:22).

Now it is possible to draw near to God, to claim Him as our God. Within the veil in the old tabernacle were several things that spoke of salvation in Christ. There was the ark of the covenant with the mercy-seat, which spoke of Christ with the law in His heart, our justifying righteousness. There was Aaron's rod that worked wonders in the wilderness, the rod that smote the rock, so that the waters might flow out to sinners. There was the pot that had manna, representing Christ as the food of His people. But we cannot speak of these things in particular now.

3. THE RENT VEIL IS SEEN IN THE LORD'S SUPPER.

It is represented in the bread being broken, quite broken. So Christ is dead, quite dead. The veil was rent, quite rent. Come, sinner by Jesus to the Father.

i. The Supper Shows that Jesus Suffered.

He suffered in every respect; in all His offices; in all parts of His body. 'They pierced my hands and my feet.' 'I gave my back to the smiter and my cheeks to them that plucked off the hair. I hid not my face.' His head was hurt with a crown of thorns, and smitten with the reed. His side was pierced.

He suffered in His outward goods. They took even his clothes. He suffered in all of His five senses. He suffered in His soul.

Jesus suffered from men, and from all ranks of men, from priests, passers-by, soldiers and thieves; from those He saved; from His own disciples; from devils; and finally from heaven.

Christ was a Surety in being forsaken by God. He was a Surety when He said, 'My God, my God, why hast thou forsaken me?' (*Psa.* 22:1). How exquisitely this sets forth the depth of His sufferings. He had been from all eternity in the bosom of the Father, and was infinitely happy there. Before anything was created, He rejoiced there (*Prov.* 8:22–31). His sense of partaking in the Father's love was infinite; yet for our sake, He was forsaken; without any of the comforts of God; with no sense of being accepted, no sense of being in His love. Yea, worse, He had a feeling that God did justly put Him away. Ah! I am a child; I cannot speak of these things. This was the same punishment as the lost, to whom it will be said, 'Depart from me ye cursed!' He was made a curse for us, as if punished with everlasting destruction from the presence of the Lord.

Then look to Him and mourn. Many people cannot feel that their sins are worthy of hell. Look here, believing, and you will feel it. Dear Christians, in the broken bread behold a forsaken Saviour and mourn.

But also, look to Him and rejoice. Nothing will give you peace but looking to Him. If He was forsaken, if He is your Surety, then you will never be forsaken. Oh, simple truth revealed unto babes! It matters not whether your sins have been many or few. Here is infinite anger. One infinitely dear to God, who had tokens of God's love from all eternity, bearing that anger. He was One who had an infinite relish for God; therefore being forsaken was an infinite loss to Him.

ii. LEARN THE COMPLETENESS OF HIS OBEDIENCE.

From His cry, 'My God, my God, why hast thou frsaken me', learn the greatness of His faith and love. I have often explained that Christ came to be a Surety, not only in suffering for sinners, but in obeying also, obeying inwardly and outwardly the law of His Father. He came not only to suffer everything that we should have suffered, but to do everything that we should have done. He is a doing and a dying Saviour!

Look at Him, then, as a man obeying His God. See with what infinite perfection He did it. God said, Become a worm and no man. He obeys. God said, Love me with all Thy heart. He did always the things that please Him. God said, Love thy neighbour as Thyself. He loved them better, He laid down His life. He went about doing good continually. God said, Lay down Thy life for sinners. He did it. 'I came down from heaven, not to do mine own will', He said, 'but the will of him that sent me' (*John* 6:38).

See here His faith. How He trusted in God. Even when forsaken He said, 'My God, my God', twice over to show how sure He was that God was His God. 'Though he slay me, yet will I trust in him.' David had great faith when he said in Psalm 42, 'Deep calleth unto deep . . . yet the LORD will command his lovingkindness . . . Why art thou cast down, O my soul?' (*Psa.* 42:7–8, 11). Jonah had great faith too: 'All thy billows and thy waves passed over me . . . yet I will look again toward thy holy temple' (*Jon.* 2:3–4). But ah! here is far greater faith. A soul in hell; forsaken of His God; a greater than Jonah is here. Yet He believes the Word of God, that God would not leave His soul in hell. Against all that He feels and sees and thinks, He believes. He believes the Word of God.

See here His submission and His love. Such great love is here. He loved the God that had forsaken Him, 'My God, my God.' It is repeated with the deliberation of affection. If He had felt it unjust, or if He had lost His love for His Father, He would have cried, 'Unjust Judge!' He would have cried, 'Cruel tyrant!' But no, He cries with all the affection of His bosom, 'My God, my God.'

Believer, this is thy Surety! You who are unbelieving and without love perish in fulness, not believing any more than you can see or feel. But behold thy Surety! How fully He obeyed in your stead. Ah! cling you to Him and all the merit of His holy obedience is yours. You are complete in Him.

But if He submitted so entirely, how is His cry of dereliction to be explained? What does the 'Why?' mean?

Perhaps it was *a question of mere agony*. When a person submits to an operation, during the time of the agony they cry out, 'Oh why do you use me thus?' Not that they do not submit, but it is just the cry of utter agony.

Perhaps *His mind was darkened*, that He could not see clearly the reasons of His agony.

Perhaps with dying breath *He would show his innocence*. 'Father, this cannot be for my own sins. Why me, who never sinned?'

Perhaps *for our own use and comfort*, that we might plead it.

'Why me?' said the holy Lamb. 'Either Thee or them.' 'Why forsake me?' 'Because Thou standest for them. Thou hast their sins laid to thy charge. Thou consentedst. Thou didst so love *them*, that heaven and all in it would not help thee. Thou knewest what it would be before, and yet Thou didst undertake it.'

The Rent Veil

May we not, then, reverently give these answers, as from the heart of God, to the 'Why?'

a. *Because thou art in the room of sinners.*

'Thou hast put thy breast between. Thou hast passed over and covered them; therefore, though thou art dear to Me as Myself, I must forsake Thee.' Ah! learn the holiness of God. Ah, sinners, are you abiding under His wrath? Do you think He will not punish sin in you when He punished it in His own Son? Learn the love of Jesus. He did not turn back; He set His face steadfastly to go to the cross.

b. *Because I will never forsake them that cleave to Thee.*

'If I pour out all my wrath on Thee, not a drop will come on them.' Ah! glorious 'Why?' The blood of Christ still speaks, and it cries, 'Why hast Thou forsaken me?' If God were to think of destroying a soul that clings to Christ, that blood would cry so loud that God would not do it. Every soul that is saved is an answer and will be to the end of the world; every soul that heartily cleaves to Jesus. Sinner, go and tell the Saviour why. 'It was for me, in my room and place!' Oh! Dear believers, in taking the bread and wine this day, you do cleave to Jesus as your own and you answer His dying cry, 'Why me?', 'That *we* might never be forsaken.'

Why was He forsaken?

1. *Because sins were laid upon Him.*

Whenever God sees sin, He cannot but forsake. His wrath must fall. When God saw sin upon Christ His anger fell. God heard Him as a sinner, therefore there was no answer, no angel to help Him.

2. *Because it was Christ's free choice.*

'I delight to do thy will', He said. He had power to lay His life down. He voluntarily 'gave up the ghost'.

3. *Because He was the Surety of sinners.*

He agreed with His Father. 'Why?' He had bargained for it. He had set His face to it. God had set down the cup, and He had taken it up. He rushed on to it. His love set Him on it. 'Why?' Because He loved sinners. Either He or all the world had to suffer. 'Why?' Because it was either He or they!

5

The Sabbath Made for Man[1]

The sabbath was made for man (Mark 2:27).

CARNAL MEN CANNOT COMPREHEND the Sabbath day. They fall into two errors. Some are willing to keep it superstitiously. The Pharisees forbade the disciples to pluck the ears of corn; and they were enraged at Jesus for healing on the Sabbath day. Others run into the opposite extreme, and would abolish the Sabbath altogether. Both classes are equally ignorant of this divine truth, that 'the sabbath was made for man'.

As the golden sun, which pours a flood of light and heat round the world, was made for man; as the silver moon, the mild lamp of night, was made for man; as all cattle, and trees, and flowers, were made for man – so the Sabbath was made for man. It was made for his good, to lead him to his God. It was made for his happiness, to lead him to the fountain of joy. It was not made for the Jew only, nor for the Gentile only, it was made for man. It was not made for one nation, nor for one country, nor for one generation; it was made for the whole human race. As the sun and the moon were made for man to light him through the world, so the Sabbath was made for man, to lead him to heaven.

---

[1] Preached in St Peter's, Dundee, 26 December 1841.

I would now prove that the Sabbath was made for the whole human race.

1. PROOF FROM REASON

I do not often speak of what is according to mere reason, because our great work is to interpret Scripture, not to teach philosophy. It is very common to hear infidels talk of the unreasonableness of keeping a strict and holy Sabbath day, and yet I engage to prove the necessity of a Sabbath to the body, the mind, the soul of man, even without the aid of Scripture.

1. The Body

In the evidence taken before the House of Commons on the subject of the Sabbath, it was distinctly stated and proved by some of the most eminent medical men in England that to retain the body in its full vigour, there must be an entire rest one day in seven; that the bones and muscles, both of men and animals, require a total cessation from labour at least one day in every seven. Those who make use of horses know quite well that if a horse is to be kept in full strength and vigour, it must be allowed to rest one entire day in seven. This proves that the Sabbath was made for man.

2. The Mind

What is true of the body is equally true of the mind. If the human mind is to work with power, it requires not only occasional rests, but to be lifted away entirely from the subject upon which it is working, that it may be refreshed, to recover its life and tone. A body that is always kept bent loses its spring, and so does the mind of man without a Sabbath.

3. The Soul

If there be a God, and if there be a church of redeemed men, it is surely reasonable that these men should worship God with the utmost engagedness of heart and soul. But if our whole heart is to be engaged in this, we must needs have a certain time set apart for this purpose. Reason cannot discover how long that time should be, or how often it should recur. But reason plainly teaches that such a time should be. So that even the dim light of reason bears witness to this truth.

Men of 'reason' would fain have us believe that they have a new light which other eyes do not see. And they look down with pity on the priest-ridden multitude who love a well-spent Sabbath day. But there is a day coming when the whole world will see that the light that was in them was darkness; and how great is that darkness!

2. PROOF FROM THE EXAMPLE OF GOD

When God created the world, He did it in six days. 'And on the seventh day God ended his work which he had made; and he rested on the seventh day from all his work which he had made. And God blessed the seventh day, and sanctified it' (*Gen.* 2:2–3).

Now God's resting on the Sabbath day was not for His own sake. 'The everlasting God, the LORD, the Creator of the ends of the earth, fainteth not, neither is weary' (*Isa.* 40:28). It was for our sakes He rested, that He might set an example to man.

It was not for the sake of the Jews only. The Jews did not exist for two thousand years after. It was for the sake of man, the whole human race, from the first man to the last. The Sabbath was made for man. The enemies of the Sabbath generally say that the Sabbath was a Jewish ceremony. But they altogether forget that the first Sabbath dawned on a sinless world. Even in paradise man needed a Sabbath.

Our Sabbath-breakers seem to think that man is better now than before he fell. Even in Eden, God gave to man a Sabbath, a day devoted to God from morn to even. How much more now does poor guilty man, with a nature so contrary to God, and a heart that cleaveth to the dust, require a Sabbath. How awfully does God keeping a Sabbath in the beginning rebuke the folly of Sabbath-breakers now. Are you wiser than God? Do you know better what is good for man? Do you know better what suits his nature? What is needful to his wants?

3. PROOF FROM THE COMMAND OF GOD

'Remember the sabbath day, to keep it holy' (*Exod.* 20:8). When God took Israel to be a peculiar people to Himself, He revived, in a very clear and terrible manner, the holy law which was written on man's heart in the day of his creation. He spoke the law with His own voice from the flaming top of Sinai. He wrote it twice with His own finger upon tables of stone, to show that it was perpetual; and in the bosom of this law we find, 'Remember the sabbath day, to keep it holy.' It is not given as a new command, but it is an old one revived. All the other nine commandments are binding upon all men, so that there cannot be the shadow of a doubt that the fourth commandment is also binding upon all.

Christ says expressly, 'I am not come to destroy [the law, or the prophets], but to fulfil' (*Matt.* 5:17). And therefore He did not come to destroy the fourth commandment. In the new covenant, God says, 'I will put my law in their inward parts, and write it in their hearts' (*Jer.* 31:33). In the old covenant, He wrote the law upon stones.

The change is in the tablet, not in the law. God says, as it were, 'I will no more write the law on tablets of stone; I will write it in their hearts.' Still, it is the same law which He wrote upon stone. In like manner, the new creature says, 'I delight in the law of God after the inward man' (*Rom.* 7:22). It is the same law the new heart loves which God gave on Sinai; and this shows that the Sabbath was made for man.

4. ALL GOD'S CHILDREN LOVE THE SABBATH DAY.

'Verily my sabbaths ye shall keep: for it is a sign between me and you throughout your generations' (*Exod.* 31:13; *Ezek.* 20:12). As long as Israel kept their holy Sabbaths, they were known to be the Lord's people. It was a mark upon their forehead, pointing them out as a peculiar people.

It is still a sign between God and believers. Believers have many marks, but this is one of the simplest. David says, 'This is the day which the LORD hath made; we will rejoice and be glad in it' (*Psa.* 118:24); and John says, 'I was in the Spirit on the Lord's day' (*Rev.* 1:10). Did you ever meet with a holy minister who did not hold the sanctification of the entire Sabbath day? Or did you ever meet with a child of God, one who bore the image of Christ, who did not love to spend a holy Sabbath day?

Noah in the ark, Moses in the wilderness, David on the throne, Isaiah among a people of unclean lips, and John an exile in Patmos, all called the Sabbath a delight, and all God's children now have the same taste and relish for a well-spent Sabbath. It is the day when they get nearest to Christ, when they get most of His Spirit, and enter deepest into His joy. Does not this show that the Sabbath was made for man?

I do not mean to say that God's children are infallible, or that their tastes and feelings are to be the rule of life. But is it to be believed that God would put this peculiar taste and relish in to the hearts of all His children, in accordance with His own Word, if it were not His desire that we should love the Sabbath day? God's children are the reflections of Himself; they are made after His image. His law is written in their hearts, so that this peculiar love for the Sabbath is truly divine. So the Sabbath was made for man. Have you this peculiar taste for the Sabbath day? Do you love a well-spent Sabbath? If so, you have one mark that you are passed from death to life. How plainly may most of you know that you are not God's children, and that you are not travelling to the Sabbath above.

5. ALL GOD'S ENEMIES HATE THE SABBATH DAY.

The unbelieving Israelites in the desert could not comprehend it. They went out on the seventh day to gather manna, and they found none (*Exod.* 16:27). Ezekiel charges it against Israel, as one of their chiefest sins, 'My sabbaths they greatly polluted' (*Ezek.* 20:13). Amos describes the ungodly of his day as saying, 'When will the new moon be gone, that we may sell corn? and the sabbath, that we may set forth wheat?' (*Amos* 8:5). For Sabbath-breaking, Israel were carried away captive to Babylon, and the land rested and enjoyed its Sabbaths. Jeremiah complains that the adversaries of Jerusalem did mock at her Sabbath (*Lam.* 1:7).

So it is with ungodly men still. A whole day spent with God they cannot bear. They hate secret prayer because it brings them near to God. An hour with God would be a kind of hell to a carnal mind. For the same reason they cannot bear a holy Sabbath-day. They would not mind devoting a whole day every week to pleasure, or to the worship of an idol, but to spend a day with God is a kind of hell to a natural man. It brings him in mind of God and of Christ, and of the law, and of eternity, and this the natural man cannot bear. Does not this show that the Sabbath was made for man, as truly as the gospel was made for man?

The Sabbath Made for Man

Men do not like the gospel. It is foolishness unto them, and yet it is the only way of saving men. They do not like the Sabbath day, and yet it is the market-day of grace to men. If the Sabbath were of the world, the world would love its own. But because it is not of the world, but the gift of a holy God, therefore the world hate it, and the more they hate it, and rage against it, the more plain it is that the Sabbath was made for man.

Learn, then, first, not to wonder at the opposition made to the Sabbath day. It is an old quarrel between the seed of the serpent and the seed of the woman. They hated Christ Himself, and it is little wonder if they hate His holy day. Do not be surprised at the torrent of Sabbath-breakers that seems about to burst out upon Britain. They hated the Sabbath all along, because they hate Him whose day it is. 'He that sitteth in the heavens shall laugh: the Lord shall have them in derision.' They may triumph now, but it will be for a short time.

Second, try whether you are a child of God by this. Do you love a holy Sabbath day? I do not ask if you love the *externals* of the Sabbath day, the exciting sermon, the meeting with friends, the singing of praises. But do you love the *internals* of a holy Sabbath? The communion with God; the delighting in Him; loving, adoring, admiring Him. Do you love a Sabbath like a Sabbath above, and do you remember a time when it was not so? Do you now love the Sabbath better than you ever loved the pleasures of vanity? Then I trust you are passed from death to life.

Third, you that love not a Sabbath here, learn that you will never enjoy a Sabbath in eternity. You that spend the Sabbath in the alehouse over the newspaper, or in idle company, will never be in heaven. Hell is your portion. There are no Sabbaths there.

6

Be Opened![1]

And again, departing from the coasts of Tyre and Sidon, he came unto the sea of Galilee, through the midst of the coasts of Decapolis. And they bring unto him one that was deaf, and had an impediment in his speech; and they beseech him to put his hand upon him. And he took him aside from the multitude, and put his fingers into his ears, and he spit, and touched his tongue; And looking up to heaven, he sighed, and saith unto him, Ephphatha, that is, Be opened. And straightway his ears were opened, and the string of his tongue was loosed, and he spake plain. And he charged them that they should tell no man: but the more he charged them, so much the more a great deal they published it; and were beyond measure astonished, saying, He hath done all things well: he maketh both the deaf to hear, and the dumb to speak (Mark 7:31–37).

IN THIS CURE of a man that was deaf and dumb we have a type of the way in which Jesus saves a poor sinner. Unconverted souls are both deaf and dumb.

1. UNCONVERTED SOULS ARE DEAF.

i. THEY HEAR NOT THE VOICE OF GOD'S WRATH.

If the loudest thunder were rolling over a man's head and he paid

---

[1] Preached in St Peter's, Dundee, 3 December 1837.

no attention, you would say, He is deaf, he hears not. Or if a man were walking on the brink of a precipice where the dashing waves of an angry sea were roaring beneath, and yet if he walked on and did not take any notice, you would say, He is deaf, he does not hear. Just such is the case of unconverted souls.

The thunder of God's anger is rolling over their heads; they are condemned already; but they pay no attention; they do not care however loud and dreadful it be. They have ears, but hear not. They are walking on the brink of an undone eternity. The tossing wave of God's anger is rolling beneath, yet they walk on, they heed not, they are deaf.

ii. THEY HEAR NOT THE VOICE OF THE SAVIOUR.

If a man were walking in a storm and you opened the door of a safe refuge and said, 'Come in here', if he went on to meet the storm, you would say, 'He is deaf.' So is it with unconverted souls. Jesus is a strong tower and He cries to all weary sinners, 'Come in hither; whosoever will, let him come.' But sinners will not come, they are deaf.

Christ speaks of His love, how He loved the lost and came not to destroy but to save. They have no ear for this melody. They are deaf, they cannot hear. Christ speaks of His blood, how it is precious, how it blots out sins; though they be as scarlet, they shall be white as snow. Sinners will not listen to this. They heed not. They hear not.

Christt speaks of His Spirit, how He will change the heart that cleaves to Him, and give the victory over the world. Sinners care not for all this. They have ears, but they hear not. They are deaf. Oh! this is the secret of all deafness. Woe is me! How many deaf ears are now listening to me. Oh, brethren, pray for the hearing ear!

2. UNCONVERTED SOULS ARE DUMB.

They have an impediment in their speech:

i. THEY DO NOT PRAY.

Many of them do not even try to pray. Many of them speak words, but they do not speak to God. They hold no converse or communion with God. If there were no beings in the universe but God, an unconverted man would never disturb Him. They are dumb.

ii. THEY DO NOT PRAISE.

They ask no blessing over their food; they eat unblessed meals. They do not feel that God has done anything for their souls, whereof they should be glad. They never think of praising God upon their knees. They do not sing Psalms. They may join in the outward melody but the heart sings not. They are dumb.

iii. THEY DO NOT SPEAK A WORD FOR CHRIST.

How many thousand words an unconverted man speaks, and yet not one of them is spoken for Christ. They do not commend Christ to the ignorant, to poor perishing souls. Their lips cannot frame the Name of Jesus. They love not to speak often one to another concerning Jesus. They talk loud when other things are spoken of but when Jesus is spoken of they are dumb, not one word in His praise.

Oh! it is sad when such men are found in ministry. 'These are dumb dogs that cannot bark.' Are there not some hearing me who know that they have always been dumb; some who know that they have never prayed; that they never heartily praised God for anything; some who have spoken millions of words, many hard words, many kind words, but not one word for Christ. Ah! be awakened this day to mourn over your sad case, deaf and dumb, and blind and perishing.

3. THE CURE

i. They Came to Him.

It is very interesting to see that the poor deaf and dumb man felt no want and asked for no cure. He did not feel that he wanted anything. He did not know and did not care about the power of Jesus. He made no sign that he needed help, but his kind friends brought him to Jesus and they besought Jesus to lay His hand upon him. So is it often with unconverted souls. They feel no want and ask no cure. They do not care to hear about the power and love of Jesus. Why? Because they say, 'I am rich, and increased with goods, and have need need of nothing.' Ah! this accounts for so much indifference and coldness in hearing of the world. How many make no sign that they want help from Jesus, no uplifted eye, no heaving sigh to show that they wish the Saviour's help. But his friends beseech Jesus to put His hand upon him.

Learn from this, my Christian friends, to beseech Jesus for your friends. Ah! do not weary in this. He will be inquired of to do this thing. Carry your friends on your heart to Jesus. Once four carried one in a bed; so do you.

Learn from this, unconverted friends, how good a thing it is to have praying friends. It is thought a great thing to have friends who have interest with some saintly great man: they may speak for you in an hour of need. Ah! how much better to have friends who can beseech Jesus. Seek these. Keep these. There are brothers who are born for adversity.

ii. Jesus Took Him Aside from the Multitude.

Jesus could have cured him in the midst of the crowd, but He would not. Just as He once did with a blind man, 'He took him by the hand and led him out of the town.' So here, He took the deaf man aside from the crowd, led him away into some lonely place. So when Christ begins a work of grace in a soul He takes that soul aside from the multitude.

a. *He sometimes brings him into loneliness by His providence.*

As long as a man is in the midst of a merry crew of wicked companions he cannot hear the still small voice of Jesus. The jarring strife of the political discussion or the giddy laugh of wanton revelry often drowns altogether the Word of Jesus, so that when He visits a soul in mercy He draws it aside from the multitude. By some sickness He brings the soul into the loneliness and gloom of a sick room. Or He brings in the hand of death, and the bereaved soul sits alone and in silence. Lover and friend are put far from him and his acquaintance into darkness.

This world is like a busy auction room, crowded in every part. One thing after another is put up for sale, every eye is fixed. One bids, and then another bids higher, all is noise and bustle and confusion. If you would talk to a man you must take him out of the sale room. You say, 'Come aside with me. I have somewhat to say to thee.' Just so does Jesus. Unconverted souls are plagued in the busy bustling sale-room of the world. All eyes are fixed on worldly goods, all voices raised to bid for them.

But Jesus draws some men aside and says, 'Come aside with Me. I have somewhat to say unto thee.' Christ has done this with some of you. You have been drawn aside, some of you have been brought into the loneliness of the sick room, some into the chamber of death. You have been alone with Christ. Now I have a question to ask you: What has Christ said to you in your loneliness? And what have you said to Him? If a king were to knock at your door and take you aside into a lonely place, surely it would be to say something strange. Now Christ has been at your door. He has drawn you aside from the multitude. What has He said to you?

Be Opened!

b. *He takes us aside by grace.*

When Christ is going to save a soul He insulates him; that is, He makes him feel alone under the Word. In general, when unconverted men hear the Word, they say, 'This word is addressed to us, and we ought to attend to these things!' The hearer comes no nearer to himself than 'us' and 'we', he buries himself in the crowd. When some sin is spoken of he says, 'This applies well to such and such a neighbour.' In this way the soul keeps himself in a multitude.

When Christ begins a work of grace He takes the soul aside from this multitude. The soul begins to feel alone under the preached Word. He says, 'This is addressed to *me*.' He is convinced of all, he is judged of all. Just as in hunting, the first thing that is done is to separate one deer from the herd, and then to pierce it through with many arrows, so is it in grace. God separates the soul from the herd when He is going to pierce it with the arrows of conviction.

Some have never been taken aside from the multitude. You do not know what we mean. You are still sheltering yourself in a crowd. A work of grace has not been begun in you. May the Lord find you out with some arrow. Some are now taken aside by Jesus. You know what we mean, for you feel it. You feel alone under the preaching of the Word. Do not seek to join the crowd again. It is easy to drown convictions in the noise and bustle of the world. Take heed. Do not lose your convictions. Listen to the voice of Christ more than to the voice of men.

iii. JESUS POINTED OUT HIS SAD CASE TO HIM.

He 'put his fingers into his ears, and he spit, and touched his tongue; and looking up to heaven, he sighed'. Jesus here convinced the poor man of his miserable case by means of signs. He put His fingers into his ears, as if to say, 'Alas, how deaf you are. You cannot hear the voice of melody, you need your ears unstopped.' He touched his tongue, as if to say, 'Alas, your tongue is tied, you cannot speak. You need this tongue to be unloosed.' Then looking up into heaven He sighed, as if to say, 'Alas, no man can help you. You are undone if you be left to man. From heaven alone your help can come.'

a. *Learn from this that Jesus pities afflicted bodies.*

They cost Him many a tear and many a sigh. He looked to heaven and sighed. He never saw the sick, the diseased, the lame, but He had compassion on them. Whenever they applied to Him, He healed them all. There is not one instance in the Bible where a sick person came to Jesus and was not made whole. Christians, be like Christ in this. Be tenderly compassionate to the afflicted bodies of men. You cannot heal, but you can provide the means of healing. Show this day that you are like Christ. Oh! how happy it is to have such an opportunity of showing that we are like Christ.

b. *Learn from this how Christ convinces the soul of sin.*

He points to his deaf ears, to his silent tongue, looks up to heaven and sighs. Has Christ done this for you? Has He convinced you that you are deaf and dumb, and poor and blind and naked? That only from heaven above your help can come? Are you convinced that Christ sighs over you?

c. *Let this show you the misery of your case.*

Christ sees the whole of your case. He knows the greatness of your sins, the depravity of your heart, and He sighs. You see but little of your true condition. He sees all and sighs. This shows you must be very bad. When a skilful physician looks sad and shakes his head at the sight of some patient, it is a bad sign of his case. So

Be Opened!

is it with you. Jesus sees both worlds, heaven and hell, and He sighs over you. Be sure it is a sigh from the bosom of Christ.

d. *But this shows that Christ is willing to be a Saviour to you.*
He pities you. He wishes to be a Saviour to you. You that never heard any melody in the name of Jesus. You that never spoke a word to His glory, you think that Christ is all vengeance against you. See here! He is all a sigh. He grieves over you. 'Oh, that you had hearkened unto my commandment. Then had your peace been like a river and your righteousness like the waves of the sea. How often would I have gathered you as a hen gathers its chickens under its wings and ye would not!' Oh! weary soul, look to a sighing Saviour, with His inmost heart He desires to be your Saviour and Lord.

iv. Jesus Cured Him by a Word.
'He saith unto him, Ephphatha, that is, Be opened. And straightway . . . !' How simply Jesus speaks and it is done. It was His voice that said, 'Let there be light', and there was light. So here He says, 'Ephphatha, Be opened', and it is done. So is it with the soul when Christ brings a soul aside and convinces it of sin. That soul may be very anxious, but it is quite shut. The ear is shut to the glad tidings of the Saviour. The ear cannot take it in. The eye is shut to the beauty of Christ. It cannot look believingly at the Lamb of God. The heart is shut to the excellency of Jesus. It cannot embrace him.

Though Jesus knocks and presses for an entrance, the heart remains quite shut. But oh, what a change when Christ says, 'Ephphatha, Be opened!' Then the ear is opened, and could listen for ever to the truth of the finished work of Jesus. The eye is opened and could look for ever on the altogether lovely Saviour. The heart is opened and embraces Christ, receives Him as a Surety, a Ransom, a Righteousness, a Portion for the soul.

a. *Learn how simple a thing salvation is.*

It is the opening of the ear, the eye, the heart to Jesus. Ah! most of you are far too wise. He hides these things from the wise and prudent and reveals them unto babes. 'What shall we do, that we might work the work of God? . . . This is the work of God, that ye believe on Him whom He hath sent' (*John* 6:28–29)!

b. *Learn that Christ alone can bring you to peace.*

His voice alone can say, 'Ephphatha'. Ministers try to open your eyes, try to open your ears, but ah, how vain our work! Except Christ speak the Word by His Spirit, 'Ephphatha'. Remember you must wait on Christ for this. 'O God, I beseech thee, deliver my soul!'

4. THE BEHAVIOUR OF THE MAN'S FRIENDS.

They 'were beyond measure astonished, saying, he hath done all things well: he maketh both the deaf to hear and the dumb to speak'. So is it when Christ converts a soul.

i. MEN ARE ASTONISHED.

a. *The world is astonished.*

Their old friends wonder what has happened. Are there none of you who have been thus astonished, and yet remain yourselves unconverted? Ah, it is sad to see other brands plucked out and to remain in the burning yourselves.

b. *Their praying friends are astonished.*

Yes, even Christians are astonished when a soul is saved. It is a wonderful work, a work of grace. Oh! who would not wonder and adore the hand of Christ in such a work?

Be Opened!

ii. They Said, 'He Hath Done All Things Well.'

They give the glory all to Christ. So must we. Oh! my friends, I see plainly that if there is any work of grace done in the midst of us, any souls to be saved, Christ must get all the praise of it. We must lay aside entirely all dependence on man and give the glory all to Him, to whom alone all the glory is due. Has Christ saved any of you? Come, let us join and praise Him, saying, 'He hath done all things well.'

One word more: Learn submission to the hand of Christ. We often complain that more souls are not saved, that this soul is not awakened and that soul is not comforted. Now this is wrong. He will do all things well. Leave the work more in Christ's hand. Trust Him with his own work and be sure that when this world is burned up and we stand in glory with Christ and happy angels, we will lay down our crowns at the feet of Jesus and say, 'He hath done all things well!'

7

Satan's Palace

> *When a strong man armed keepeth his palace, his goods are in peace: but when a stronger than he shall come upon him, and overcome him, he taketh from him all his armour wherein he trusted, and divideth his spoils* (Luke 11:21–22).

WE ARE TOLD, IN THE PRECEDING VERSES, that Jesus was casting out a dumb spirit. Some of the people who beheld the miracle said that He did it by 'Beelzebub, the chief of the devils'. Jesus showed them plainly that Satan was not so foolish as to cast out his own servants, and that, therefore, it must be that 'the finger of God' was in the matter. 'If I with the finger of God cast out devils, no doubt the kingdom of God is come upon you. When a strong man armed keepeth his palace, his goods are in peace: but when a stronger than he shall come upon him, and overcome him, he taketh from him all his armour wherein he trusted, and divideth his spoils.'

In these words, we have a vivid description of the conversion of a poor lost sinner. First of all, we find him like a palace guarded by an armed giant; all his goods in peace, his conscience, his affections, his will, all quiet and undisturbed. Suddenly there comes One stronger than the giant. His form is like the Son of God. He is 'the Lord strong and mighty, the Lord Mighty in battle'. As David overcame the Philistine Goliath, so He overcomes the strong one, takes his armour away, enters into the soul, and takes possession of all that is there. This has been the happy history of all of you that are this day God's children. May God grant that it may speedily be the history of many more!

1. THE DESCRIPTION OF SATAN

Consider, firstly, the description of Satan which is here given: 'The strong man armed.' He is the strong one. This will appear from many things. He is often spoken of singly in the Bible. We often read of devils in the Bible, of the angels that kept not their first estate, of the angels that fell; but we read still more often of one single being who is above them all. He is called Satan the Devil, Beelzebub, Lucifer, the Dragon, the Old Serpent, the Wicked One, the Tempter, the Adversary. He is spoken of as the great enemy of God, of Christ, and of believers. 'I will put enmity between thee and the woman, and between thy seed and her seed; it shall bruise thy head, and thou shalt bruise his heel' (Gen. 3:15).

He is called a 'prince', and even a 'god'. Jesus three times called him, 'the prince of this world'. In the Epistle of Paul to the Ephesians, he is called 'the Prince of the power of the air, the spirit that now worketh in the children of disobedience'; and in 2 Corinthians, 'the god of this world'. This shows that his power is very great, that his usurped yet real dominion is as wide as the air, and, indeed, a rule extending over the whole world.

From the beasts he is compared to, it appears that he is 'the strong one'. He is compared, to the *Serpent*, because of its excelling all animals in cunning. 'Now the serpent was more subtle than all the beasts of the field.' He is compared to the *Lion*, 'the king of the forest'. 'Save me from the lion's mouth'. 'Your adversary the devil, as a roaring lion, goeth about seeking whom he may devour.' Some have thought that *Behemoth*, in Job, was a type of him, 'the chief of the ways of God'. Some have thought *Leviathan* also a type of him. He is 'a king over all the children of pride'.

From his being over all other devils he appears to be rightly termed, 'the strong one'. In Matthew chapter 25, it is said, 'Depart, ye cursed, into everlasting fire, prepared for the devil and his angels.' The devils are his, his servants, his miserable slaves. In Revelation 12:3 it is said, 'There was war in heaven; Michael and his angels fought against the dragon; and the dragon fought, and his angels.'

From his being called Lucifer, he appears to be 'the strong one'. 'How art thou fallen from heaven, O Lucifer, son of the morning!' (*Isa.* 14:12). Lucifer, or the morning star, is the brightest of all the stars, last in the train of night, if it does not rather belong to the dawn. From all this, it would seem, that Satan before his sin and expulsion from heaven, was the very brightest angel in heaven; that he outshone them all, as 'the morning star' does all the train of night, that he stood nearest the throne of God, as 'the morning star' shines nearest the sun. But now he is fallen. He is the great enemy of God, the great enemy of souls. Some people are ready to smile when we speak of Satan. Some think he is only an old wife's fable with which to frighten children; but you who are the children of God will receive the Word of God and believe in the real personality and power of Satan, for you see his doings in the world as plainly as you see the light of the morning star. 'To the law and to the testimony! If they speak not according to this word, it is because there is no light in them.' 'Be ye not mockers, lest your bands be made strong.' Satan is not only the strong one, but the strong one armed. Just as Goliath of Gath, the great champion of the ancient Philistines, was fully armed; so Satan is armed 'from top to toe'. He is fully supplied with weapons of offence and defence.

He has *a hot iron,* for the conscience of the unconverted: 'Having their conscience seared with a hot iron' (*1 Tim.* 4:2). This is a dreadful piece of Satan's armour. Are there none hearing me who have felt its power? A seared conscience is worth a thousand shields of brass in repelling the arrows of God's Word. Often we try to convince you of sin. We even lay our finger on your besetting sin. We show you from the Bible that they that commit such things shall not inherit the kingdom of God. Your ears hear the words, your understanding comprehends them, your judgment is convinced, surely your conscience will be awakened, and lead the way to repentance. Ah, no! The 'hot iron' has been over it. It is 'past feeling', it is 'seared', it is dead!

He has *a blinding veil.* 'The god of this world hath blinded the minds of them that believe not, lest the light of the glorious Gospel of Christ, who is the image of God, should shine unto them' (*2 Cor.* 4:4). Again, 'the veil is upon their heart'. It is said that a soft cotton substance will turn the edge of a sabre more completely than a coat of mail. So it is with the veil of Satan, it turns away the edge of the sword of the Spirit, while it keeps the deluded soul in gross spiritual darkness.

We often set forth Immanuel, the Surety of perishing sinners. We endeavour to declare His original glory, to tell of His love, His taking our nature, His suffering and dying in the stead of the guilty, and His freeness to every sinner who will only come to him. His beauty shines. Your ears receive the words. You are surprised as you listen to the blessed gospel. Surely you will immediately turn your back upon the world and flee to Christ! Ah, no! You see 'no form nor comeliness' in him, for the 'veil is upon your heart'. 'The god of this world hath blinded your minds,' and you remain in his power!

And he has *chains* also to bind his miserable victims. You remember hearing of a woman who had a spirit of infirmity eighteen years, and was bowed together, and could in no wise lift up herself. Jesus said that Satan had bound her. So it is with unconverted souls. They are bound by Satan, kept bowed down, not for eighteen years only, but ever since they were born, they can by no means lift themselves up. Are there none hearing me who feel bound down to sin by an invisible chain? Are there none of you who can weep when you think how you are the miserable slaves of some powerful lust? You feel that it is destroying your body, and ruining your soul. It is ruining your character, your credit, everything that is dear to you. You resolve to reform. Surely you will keep your vows. Ah, no! The dog goes back to its own vomit again, and the sow that was washed to her wallowing in the mire. 'Can the Ethiopian change his skin, or the leopard his spots? Then may ye also do good, that are accustomed to do evil.'

Satan even employs *the sword of the Spirit*. 'If Thou be the Son of God, cast Thyself down from hence: for it is written; He shall give his angels charge over Thee.' This is the most dangerous of all Satan's weapons. He stole it from the armoury of God. Are there none hearing me who are so deceived by Satan that they make even the Bible keep them in their sins? Are there none hearing me who 'wrest the Scriptures to their own destruction'? 'If I am elected', you say, 'I shall be saved; if not, then I shall be lost; so I may as well just live on in my sins.'

In this way, many run on to destruction, by a false interpretation and application of the Bible. 'It is written, God is merciful and gracious, so I hope we shall be saved at last.' In this way, others neglect the 'great salvation', and bring upon themselves 'swift destruction'. Awake, dear souls and escape for your lives, for ye are deceived by a mighty one.

The prince of the power of the air is working in you, the children of disobedience, and deceiving you to your own eternal ruin!

2. THE STATE OF THE UNCONVERTED SOUL

Consider now the state of the unconverted soul. It is a palace. It is a noble mansion; formed out of the dust, but formed by the hand of God. He also breathed into man's nostrils the breath of life, and man became a living soul. He was formed in the image of God, and God once dwelt there. The understanding, the affections, yea, all the faculties of the soul were made for the entertainment of God; and even though become 'the cage of every unclean bird', the soul of man even in its dilapidated condition, is a palace still.

Oh, consider, sinner, the original dignity of your nature! Consider the chief design and end of all these noble faculties which you still possess. Would it not be a mournful spectacle to see all the ancient cathedrals of England, which were erected for the worship of God, turned into places of nettles and dens for wild beasts? How much more sad to see the human soul, which was made for the worship of God, turned into the dwelling-place of every evil passion, and become the very palace of Satan!

It is now his palace, and he keepeth it. 'The spirit that now worketh in the children of disobedience' dwells there. Satan lives in an unconverted soul as much as he pleases. He goes in and out, and brings in any guest he chooses, for he rules there! He does all he can to secure it to himself, and to fortify it against Christ. All the prejudices with which he hardens men's hearts against truth and holiness are the strongholds which he erects for the keeping of his palace. This palace is his 'garrison'. Oh, dear unconverted souls, this is your true condition. Is it not a melancholy one?

Christians are 'kept by the power of God', but you are kept by the power of Satan. Christians are dwelt in by the Holy Spirit of God, but you are dwelt in by the unclean spirit of the devil! See what you may become! He may bring any unclean spirits he pleases into your heart, and you will continue to open to him and bid him welcome. I know you will say, 'Is thy servant a dog, that he should do this thing?' But if you will consider one moment, you will see that there is no sin you may not be led into, since you are wholly in the power of the devil. Lusts you abhor at present may yet become pleasant, and you may be even led on from stage to stage till you finally despair of salvation, and end your miserable existence by self-murder. The unconverted soul is not safe one moment, for it is just what the devil pleases, and must submit to be ruled and led by him, and made to do his unholy will!

And his goods are 'in peace'. In his heart, which was fitted to be a habitation of God, the devil has 'his palace', and all the powers and faculties of the soul being employed by him in the service of sin, are his 'goods'. There is a kind of peace in the palace of an unconverted soul, while the devil as a strong man armed keepeth it. The sinner hath a good opinion of himself, is very secure and merry, has no doubt concerning the goodness of his state, nor any dread of the judgment to come. He flatters himself in his own eyes, and cries 'Peace' to himself. His conscience is perfectly tranquil. We may preach very plainly. You may come to the house of God as God's people come, and sit as his people sit; still, as long as Satan reigns within you, your conscience will be a 'dumb spirit'.

This explains why most of you feel nothing under the preached Word, and go away only harder than you came. Your consciences are at peace. Fatal peace! The affections are also at peace. They are all tied fast to your sins; and they do not move towards Christ and God. When a man is very heavily chained he cannot move. He is at perfect rest. So it is with Christless souls among you. Your heart is all in peace. Your very will is chained, and you are saying, 'Peace, peace,' when there is no peace! You sit still and are at ease. And is this a good state? Ah, no! Although it is a state of peace, it is the peace of the grave! It is the peace of dead men; and, besides, it will not last. 'I will search Jerusalem with candles, and punish the men who are settled on their lees.' The devil may keep you in peace now; but the time will come when you and he will be cast into the fire, and will there be peace there? Ah, no! Then there will not be a moment of peace, no rest, no relief not even a drop of water to cool the tongue. Oh, that the Prince of Peace would now break your false peace, and give you 'the peace of God' for the peace of Satan!

3. THE VISIT OF CHRIST

We come now, in the last place, to consider the visit of One who is stronger than the strong one armed (verse 22). In many ways it might be shown that Christ is stronger than he.

Christ is his Creator. 'By him were all things created that are in heaven and in earth.' Although Lucifer was the son of the morning, the highest and the brightest, yet he was not self-originated; he came from the creative hand of Christ. He was the creature of His hand. Just as Christ is greater than the Lion and the Serpent, and the Behemoth and Leviathan, for they are all the work of His hands, so is He greater than Satan! He said, 'Let them be', and they were! So Christ is greater than the devil, because He created him as an angel of light.

In dying, Christ was stronger than he. The dying hour of Christ was the hour and power of darkness. It was then that Satan exerted all his power, and yet he only bruised His heel. He entered into Judas to carry him on to the betraying of Christ. He stirred up the Jews to cry, 'Crucify him, Crucify him!' Strong bulls of Bashan beset him round. The dogs compassed him. Satan gaped upon him as a ravening, roaring lion, yet, even then, when apparently in the very depths of weakness, Christ was stronger than he. Even when he seemed to be 'a worm and no man', He was stronger than the strong one armed, for 'through death he destroyed him that had the power of death, that is, the devil.' He triumphed over him, even in His cross!

In conversion, Jesus appears stronger than Satan. He comes upon him by surprise, when his goods are in peace, and when the devil thinks it is all his own for ever, and overcomes him. And not only so, but He presently gives evidences of his victory over him. 'He taketh from him all his armour wherein he trusted.' When the power of sin and corruption in the soul is broken, when the mistakes are rectified, the eyes opened, the heart humbled and changed, and made serious and spiritual, then Satan's armour is taken away. Christ is stronger than he, for He not only overcomes him, but disarms him.

When Christ laid His hands upon the woman bowed down for eighteen years, all the power of Satan could not hold her down any longer. Satan had bound her long, but after Christ said to her, 'Thou art loosed from thine infirmity', he could not bind her another moment. So when Christ pierces a sinner's conscience, when He pours out the Spirit of grace and of supplications, the searing 'hot iron' can do no more to produce insensibility and indifference. The soul mourns. Its goods are no longer in peace. The awakened sinner cries, 'What must I do to be saved?'

Again, Christ tears away the veil, and reveals Himself to the soul, and says, 'I am Joseph your brother! I am thy Surety, thy Sin-Bearer! Him that cometh unto Me I will in no wise cast out.' No more can Satan blind the heart.

Again, Christ tears the chains away, and sets the prisoner free, and Satan cannot hinder him. He puts His Spirit into the heart, and 'where the Spirit of the Lord is, there is liberty'. 'If the Son make you free, you shall be free indeed.' Are there any of you brought to sit at the feet of Jesus, 'clothed and in your right mind'? Then you know and feel in your own happy experience that Jesus is stronger than Satan. Fear not, lest you should again be in bondage to Satan, for your Deliverer will prove Himself 'mighty to save'. He will overcome to the very end! Your enemy is strong and mighty, but Christ is stronger than he, for He is 'the Lord Almighty'. Greater is He that is for us than all that are against us. Satan is strong, busy, active, malicious. But Jesus is able to save to the uttermost all that come unto God by Him, from the devil as well as from sin, as well as from the world.

Let us possess our souls in patience. Jesus still lives, and will not let Satan pluck us out of His hand. Jesus still lives, and will soon come again to deliver us entirely from the fiery darts of the wicked one. The great chain is prepared (*Rev.* 20:1). Satan shall one day be bound. 'The God of peace shall bruise Satan under your feet shortly.'

Christ also divides the spoils. After a battle it was customary for the conquerors to gather all the spoils into one place and divide them. The meaning is that Christ will take possession of all. All the endowments of mind and body, the estate, power, interest, which before were made use of in the service of sin and Satan, are now converted to Christ's service, and employed for Him. Yet that is not all. He makes a distribution of them among His followers, and having conquered Satan, gives to all believers the benefit of that victory.

The great question, my friend, is this: has Christ taken full possession of your heart? Has He divided the spoils? You were once under the power of Satan. Have you changed masters? Happy those of you who can say, 'He sent from above, He took me; He drew me out of many waters. He delivered me from my strong enemy and from them that hated me: for they were too strong for me.'

When John Newton's eyes were dim, so that he could not read, an aged minister called. At family prayer a portion was read containing these words, 'By the grace of God I am what I am.' After the reading he paused, 'I am not what I ought to be; how imperfect and deficient! I am not what I wish to be; I abhor that which is evil, and cleave to that which is good. I am not what I hope to be; soon, soon I shall put off mortality, and with mortality all sin and imperfection. Yet, though I am not what I ought to be, nor what I wish to be, nor what I hope to be, I can truly say, I am not what I once was, the slave of sin and Satan. I can heartily join with the apostle and acknowledge, "By the grace of God I am what I am."'

Dear friend, have you an experience of the converting grace of God like that? Do you know anything of the superior power of Christ's almighty, victorious, and saving grace? Is Satan cast out by the converting power of Christ, or has he only walked out of his own accord to return at some future period, bringing with him 'seven other spirits more wicked than himself'? Here we have the condition of a formal hypocrite, his bright side and his dark side. His heart still remains the devil's house. He calls it his own, 'my house', and he retains his interest in it. And yet the unclean spirit is 'gone out'. He was not driven out by the power of converting grace; but he went out and withdrew for a time, so that the man seems not to be under the power of Satan as formerly, nor so followed with his temptations. Satan is gone, or has turned himself into an angel of light.

Moreover, the house is 'swept' from common pollutions by a forced confession of sin, as Pharaoh's, a feigned contrition for it, as Ahab's, and a partial reformation, as Herod's. There are those who have, 'escaped the pollutions of the world', and yet are still under the power of, 'the god of this world'. The house is, 'swept', but it is not, 'washed', and Christ has said, 'If I wash thee not, thou hast no part with Me.' The house, the heart, must be 'washed', or it is none of His. 'Sweeping', or outward reformation, takes off only the loose dirt, while the besetting, beloved sin is untouched. The life is swept from the sin that lies open to the eye of the world, but the heart is not searched and washed from secret filthiness.

Again the house is garnished with common gifts and graces. Simon Magus was garnished with faith, Balaam with good desires, Herod with a respect for John, the Pharisees with many external performances. The house is 'garnished', but the property is not altered. It was never surrendered to Christ, nor inhabited by the Spirit. Let us therefore take heed of resting in that which a man may have, yet come short!

The formal professor merges eventually into the final apostate. The devil, who goes out at pleasure, comes in at will, and brings seven other devils with him, worse than himself, and they enter the white-washed professor's heart, 'and dwell there; and the last state of that man is worse than the first'. Hypocrisy is the high road to apostasy! If the heart remains in the interest of sin and Satan, the fairest profession of godliness will come to nothing. Where secret haunts of sin are kept up under the cloak of good religious profession, the conscience is debauched, God is provoked to withdraw His restraining grace, and the close, formal hypocrite commonly proves an open apostate. The last state of such is worse than the first, in respect both of sin and punishment. Apostates are usually the worst of men, the most vain and profligate, the most bold and daring, their consciences are seared, and their sins, of all others, are the most aggravated.

God often sets marks of his displeasure upon them in this world, and in the other world they will receive the greater damnation. Let us, therefore, hear and fear, and hold fast our integrity. 'Be sober, be vigilant; because your adversary the devil, as a roaring lion, walketh about, seeking whom he may devour: whom resist steadfast in the faith.'

'Finally, my brethren, be strong in the Lord and in the power of his might. Put on the whole armour of God, that ye may be able to stand against the wiles of the devil' (*Eph.* 6:10–11).

8

Lost Sheep[1]

Then drew near unto him all the publicans and sinners for to hear him. And the Pharisees and scribes murmured, saying, This man receiveth sinners, and eateth with them. And he spake this parable unto them, saying, What man of you, having an hundred sheep, if he lose one of them, doth not leave the ninety and nine in the wilderness, and go after that which is lost, until he find it? And when he hath found it, he layeth it on his shoulders, rejoicing. And when he cometh home, he calleth together his friends and neighbours, saying unto them, Rejoice with me; for I have found my sheep which was lost. I say unto you, that likewise joy shall be in heaven over one sinner that repenteth, more than over ninety and nine just persons, which need no repentance (Luke 15:1–7).

FROM THE PRECEDING CHAPTER, we find that Jesus had just come from the house of one of the chief Pharisees, where He had been partaking of the Sabbath meal along with an invited company of Pharisees and lawyers, ever on the watch to entangle Him in His words. Several of these Pharisees seem to have a company with them and other travellers standing round Him, when multitudes of publicans and sinners of the lowest and most degraded character came pressing nearer and nearer to the Saviour.

[1] Preached 20 December 1835 in Dunipace; 24 January 1836 in Larbert.

These movements of increasing attention on the part of the crowd drew forth the murmurs of the Pharisees, indignant that such outcasts should find more interest in the message and a warmer reception in the manner of a teacher come from God than they themselves did. 'The Pharisees and scribes murmured saying, This man receiveth sinners and eateth with them' (*Luke* 15:2).

The answer of our Lord was conveyed in the Parable of the Lost Sheep, the object of which was evidently both to convince the Pharisees and to win the poor outcast publicans. How blessed a Saviour is Jesus! He hath a word in season to every man. Neither the proud Pharisee nor the degraded publican are overlooked by Him. Oh! that the same Jesus might be present here, to commend Himself to every one of your consciences, in this picture of kindness and tenderness, the Good Shepherd seeking the lost sheep. Let us go over the different parts of the Parable then with this object and may the Spirit open His own Word unto us.

1. IT IS A LOST SHEEP THE SHEPHERD GOES AFTER.

First of all, then, I observe that it is a lost sheep that the Shepherd goes after with so much trouble and fatigue, and not a sheep that never went astray.

i. It is not a sheep that has been carried off from the fold and left bleeding and torn upon the mountains, making the valleys resound with its sad bleatings, mourning over its sad condition so far from the Shepherd's shelter and the Shepherd's care.

ii. Nor is it even a sheep that is earnestly seeking the way back to the green pastures and the still waters.

iii. We are told nothing more than that it is a lost sheep, that has wandered so far from the fold and so far into the wilderness that it

Lost Sheep

is bewildered and lost. But the more dangerous the condition of the sheep is, so much the more anxious is the Shepherd.

Everything must be risked rather than certainly lose one sheep of his hundred. He leaves the ninety-nine in the wilderness and goes after the bewildered sheep. The Good Shepherd, who is not an hireling, seeks the lost sheep. Just so is it with the Saviour! He comes to seek and to save that which was lost.

He did not come to the earth to seek for angels. Nor for souls that have been carried off by force. Nor for those who were anxiously crying after Him. There was no cry of distress from this lost world. But he came for the lost soul.

The unfallen families in heaven seem, as it were, for a time to be forgotten and left behind whilst the Eternal Son steps down from the throne of the universe, leaving the bosom of the Father, and descends to this remote corner of His dominion where dwell so many who are lost, a world whose inhabitants like lost sheep have gone astray, turning every one to his own way. The unquenchable love of compassion burns in His bosom while He becomes a Man of sorrows and acquainted with grief. A love that many waters could not quench, a love stronger than death, for it moved Him to give His life for the sheep. Had He been in quest of the society of righteous spirits, why should He leave the mansions of glory where ten thousand righteous angels were His ministers?

When you see the Shepherd far separated from his flock, in pain and weariness clambering the mountains, in haste and anxiety penetrating far into the wilderness, need you ask whether he is in search of ease and pleasure or of the sheep that was lost? And just so when we find the Saviour in the villages of Judea, in weariness and painfulness, going from city to city. Need you ask whether He came to seek repose and satisfaction in the companionship of mortals, or to seek and to save that which was lost?

Doubtless there are some hearing me who are in the condition of the lost sheep. Doubtless there are some of you who know that every day of your life you have been wandering away from the great Shepherd of the world. Every day you have been wandering from the fold that God preserves. You know that you have turned into many a green and pleasant path, but it was your own way, not God's way. Again you have turned into many a rough and thorny walk, still it was your own way, not God's way. You are the lost sheep.

Doubtless some hearing me know that they have been all their life wandering from Christ, the Good Shepherd, that gave His life for the sheep. You know that instead of your crying after the Saviour, He has always cried after you, and cried in vain! You have never entered in by Christ into the sheepfold, neither have you been made to lie down in the green pastures, nor been led by the still waters. You then are the lost sheep. Think, then, I beseech you, that it is you that Jesus seeks. Christ left heaven for you. He is in search of you to this day! But you may be ready to object:

OBJECTION 1:
'I have been without God in the world, without caring about the Bible, or about Christ. It is impossible Christ can be seeking me.'

ANSWER:
Are you not all the more a lost sheep? It is the lost sheep He came to save. Christ died for the ungodly. It is the ungodly to whom He offers His blood and His righteousness.

OBJECTION 2:
'But I have lived without care for my soul, and even now I feel no anxiety about my soul. I have spoken against Christ and disobeyed the gospel.'

Lost Sheep

ANSWER:

Still you are just all the more a lost sheep; wherefore I take you to witness that I have warned you this day that the glorious Saviour is seeking you! 'I have stretched out my hands!', says He.

OBJECTION 3:

'I have sinned against light, against a clear knowledge of the Bible and the Law of God. I have sinned against the blood of Christ and the free offer of the Spirit.'

ANSWER:

Still, you are a lost sheep, and it is the lost sheep Christ is seeking. If you have wandered to the utmost distance from Christ that it is possible for a soul to go, then Christ seeks you most of all, for He seeks *most* the sheep that is *most lost*.

OBJECTION 4:

'I know that Christ has been always seeking me, but I have refused Him so long. I fear He will now laugh at my anxiety.'

ANSWER:

Still, you are a lost sheep, and therefore still does the Bible bid me say, Christ is seeking you!

Ah, brethren, what hard thoughts you have of God and of Jesus Christ! They are not taken from the Bible, but from your own wicked hearts. Oh, dear souls! If those of you who are so careless and indifferent about your own salvation, if you knew the anxiety with which the great and glorious Saviour has always been seeking you, surely your hearts, that are like iron, would be melted, surely your souls, that are like the nether millstone, would be broken!

'We are ambassadors for Christ, as though God did beseech you by us: we pray you in Christ's stead, be ye reconciled unto God' (*2 Cor.* 5:20)!

2. THE SHEPHERD FINDS THE LOST SHEEP, AND LAYS IT ON HIS SHOULDERS.

The second circumstance in the parable is that recorded in verse 5, 'And when he hath found it he layeth it on his shoulders rejoicing.'

This was the second good office that the kind Shepherd did for the bewildered sheep. He knew that, although he had found it, yet a poor sheep would never find its way back to the fold. It had wandered so far into the wilderness, over the mountains and down into the valleys, and through woods and thorny paths, that it never could find its way back. It would be caught in many a thicket, it might be lamed by the way, or faint through weariness, and therefore he lays it on his shoulders, rejoicing.

Often struggling, often restless and weary, still it is borne high above all entanglements till it is set down in the fold, or in the green pastures, and by the still waters. How kind is the good Shepherd, and how kind is the Saviour!

Just so it is with Him. Not only does He find the lost soul but He carries it back to the fold. He not only converts and justifies, but He sanctifies also. He knows well the entanglements and thorny paths that beset the returning soul. He knows that our hearts have wandered so far over the mountains of vanity and through the deep valleys of sin and across the scanty brooks of worldly pleasures and among the thorns and thickets of worldly cares and anxieties, that it would be quite impossible for us to find our way back to the green pastures of godliness and the still waters of grace.

Lost Sheep

We cannot sanctify ourselves, any more than we can justify ourselves, and therefore Jesus, of whom it was prophesied that He would 'gather the lambs with his arm, and carry them in his bosom' (*Isa.* 40:11), lays the lost sheep on his shoulder and carries it home. The soul leans upon the Beloved, coming up out of the wilderness. He is borne high above the entanglements of old temptations and old habits and old sins. He is borne as upon eagle's wings. He is led by the Spirit to the land of uprightness.

Here then is a second argument to move the most lost and bewildered sinner among you. Not only is Christ seeking you with as much anxiety as if there was not another sinner in the universe, but, behold, He is willing to carry you back to the ways of holiness, to make wisdom's ways pleasantness and peace to you. If you will only consent to be found of Christ, to use the shed blood and the justifying righteousness, to throw away your own good qualities for a righteousness, and to be complete in Christ, then you shall not only receive Jesus as a Saviour but Jesus as a Sanctifier. He will not only begin but will carry on the good work in your soul.

Oh, to be borne on the shoulders of the Good Shepherd, to be carried as a lamb in His bosom, so that none can pluck us out of His hand! What a completeness there is in Jesus' salvation! Nothing is left wanting. Will you not be persuaded to take this Saviour for your Saviour?

There may be some among you who have been found by the Good Shepherd but have never consented to be borne on His shoulders. There may be some of you walking in heaviness this day because you think you have believed and yet you find that you are not growing holier. You have been convinced that you have no righteousness and therefore you are willing to take Christ for your righteousness and to give Him all the glory of that; but then you may be looking to yourself for strength to walk holily, to walk back to the fold. Ah, proud heart! You wish to rob Jesus of half the honour of saving you, and many a weary step will you have to take in the vain attempt to walk heavenward without being carried. Your feet will be hurt by the thorns of the world, old temptations will be as a hidden pit in your path. Old affections will be a hedge in your way, and the beasts of the forest will prey on you. The lion is seeking to devour you.

Let this parable convince you that, as you must be justified by grace, so you must be sanctified by grace. When first you saw the Saviour He said, 'My blood is sufficient for thee.' And once you were justified He said, 'My grace is sufficient for thee.'

Yield yourself unto God. Consent to be borne on the shoulders of the Redeemer; and then you may sing in humble triumph, 'In the LORD have I righteousness and strength' (*Isa.* 45:24)!

3. THE SHEPHERD BRINGS THE LOST SHEEP HOME WITH REJOICING.

The last event in the parable is that in verse 6: When the Shepherd comes home, he calls his friends together to rejoice with him. Here is the only part of the parable interpreted by our Lord in verse 7.

If you compare verse 7 with verse 10, you will find a slight but not insignificant difference between Christ's explanations of the two parables. In the first it is said, 'Joy shall be *in heaven*', a phrase which occurs also in the Lord's Prayer and refers to the created inhabitants of heaven. But in verse 10 the joy is said to be 'in the presence of the angels of God', which can hardly mean anything else than that God who so loved the world, God who has no pleasure in the death of the wicked but rather that they turn and live, rejoices on the throne of heaven over every redeemed soul, and fills with new ecstasies the myriads of attending angels.

Nor is it unworthy of notice that, in the first, the joy is said to be future. 'Joy shall be' (verse 7); whereas in the second it is said to be present, 'There is joy' (verse 10), intimating the immediate knowledge which God has of the turning of the believing mind. No sooner is there the turning of the heart to embrace Jesus than there is joy in God. Jehovah smiles, and all the angels, whose blessedness it is to live in the light of His countenance and to reflect His image, cannot but partake in His beatific joy.

Now, brethren, here is a third argument to persuade you to be found this day by the Good Shepherd who gave His life for the sheep, that if you will this day take Him for your Saviour, being forgiven through His blood, and this day take Him for your Sanctifier, being sanctified through His Spirit and carried on His shoulders, then this day God the Saviour and all holy angels shall rejoice over you.

You will be beloved by the angels, and beloved of the Father. The angels will henceforth be your ministers through life, for are they not all ministering spirits? And none shall be able to pluck you out of the Father's hand, for He loves with an everlasting love. Aye, and when you die, not only shall you say, Though I walk through the valley of the shadow of death, I will fear no evil, for Thou, Lord Jesus, art with me; but the angels also shall bear you in their hands to the pearly gates of the New Jerusalem, and there shall all the lost sheep that have been found be gathered into one flock.

'They shall hunger no more, neither thirst any more; neither shall the sun light on them, nor any heat. For the Lamb which is in the midst of the throne shall feed them, and shall lead them unto living fountains of waters: and God shall wipe away all tears from their eyes' (*Rev.* 7:16–17).

But the very essence of the encouragement depends upon your marking accurately the kind of salvation which God and the angels rejoice over. Nothing can be plainer than that they would not rejoice over just any kind of salvation. For though I do not believe that God or a holy angel have any pleasure in the pain even of a worm simply for the pain's sake, as it is written in Ezekiel, 'I have no pleasure in the death of him that dieth', yet of this I am very sure, for the existence of an eternal hell bears awful testimony to the truth, that though they rejoice in the happiness of every creature, still the unstained honour of the Godhead is dearer to them than the happiness of worlds. The repentance which gives joy to angels and the God of angels is the repentance which gives all the glory to the Saviour.

The reason why God and the angels will rejoice this day so mightily over you if you will accept of Christ this day as your Saviour and Sanctifier is that by such a conversion a soul is saved and the Saviour is honoured. Just as you have seen two clear flowing rivers unite into one and roll on majestically to the ocean, so there are two elements which make up the full tide of the joy over a repenting sinner. There is joy that a soul and a body are rescued from the worm and the fire, and the weeping and wailing and gnashing of teeth, and there is a still higher joy that God's law is thereby magnified, that powers and principalities are spoiled of one victim more, that a soul is borne off in triumph on the shoulders of the Shepherd of Israel.

A word of awakening to self-righteous sinners, then, to those who think that duties, societies, regularities, church-going, Bible-reading – that these things from yourselves will do well enough for a righteousness in the sight of God and of angels, and who know nothing of being found as an utterly lost sheep, of being carried on the shoulders of Christ as a bewildered sheep.

Poor sinners, there is no rejoicing over you, the angels are weeping. Even if it were possible that you were admitted into heaven, the angels would look on you with horror and the angels of the presence would hide their faces from the awful darkness of Jehovah's frown. For what greater insult could be offered to the God and Father of our Lord and Saviour Jesus Christ, than thus proudly to enter the gates of Paradise proclaiming the uselessness of the blood of Jesus to justify and the uselessness of the Spirit to sanctify?

The Good Shepherd is seeking you, you have many a time put Him away, but still He seeks you, offering you forgiveness of sins, offering you His sanctifying power, offering you a place amid the happy angels. But if you will not be moved to accept of Christ, the day will come when that beseeching Saviour will laugh at your calamity and mock when your fear cometh. Aye, and when the smoke of your torment shall ascend up before God and the holy angels for ever and ever – those angels that would have rejoiced over your salvation. They shall say over your agony, 'Hallelujah, salvation and glory and honour and power be unto the Lord our God; for true and righteous are His judgments.'

9

Christ Weeping Over Jerusalem

And when he was come near, he beheld the city, and wept over it (Luke 19:41).

THE FIRST LESSON WHICH I LEARN from these words is that Christ was truly man. When He was come near and beheld the city, He wept over it. The whole Bible unites in declaring that Christ was truly God. In one place it tells us that He 'was with God and . . . was God' (*John* 1:1); in another place that He 'thought it not robbery to be equal with God' (*Phil.* 2:6); in another place, that He is 'over all, God blessed for ever' (*Rom.* 9:5).

1. CHRIST'S TRUE HUMANITY

But in this passage it is just as plainly proved to us that He is truly man. It appears from this, that He wept! It is altogether human to weep. There are no tears in heaven, for there, 'God wipes away tears from off all faces.' And though there be tears in hell, for, 'There shall be weeping and gnashing of teeth', yet still these are the tears not of pity, but of anguish and despair. The tear of pity belongs only to man.

It also appears from this, that He wept *at the sight of the object*. This is a sure mark of humanity. When you only *hear* of people being poor, then you feel but little compassion, and manifest but little sympathy; but when you go and visit them, when you enter their wretched room, and see how poorly it is furnished, when you see the straw bed, the sick mother, the pale, hungry children, then the eye affects the heart, and compassion is sure to flow and that is the reason why God bids you visit the fatherless and widows in their affliction. Just so it was with Paul at Athens; it was when he saw the whole city given over to idolatry that his spirit was stirred within him. Just so it was with Jesus at this time. 'When He was come near, he beheld the city, and wept over it' (*Luke* 19:41).

He had come from Bethany and Bethphage, two villages on the other side of Mount Olivet. He was riding on an ass's colt, covered with the garments of His disciples. The whole multitude of His disciples were rejoicing and praising God for the wonders they had seen. When they looked to their meek and lowly Master, they cried, 'Hosanna! Blessed is He that cometh in the name of the Lord!' And when they looked on the city of their fathers stretched beneath their feet, they felt the exulting Psalm rising within them: 'Jerusalem is builded as a city that is compact together . . . Pray for the peace of Jerusalem: they shall prosper that love thee. Peace be within thy walls, and prosperity within thy palaces' (*Psa.* 122:3, 6–7).

But Jesus – what was He doing? When Jesus beheld it, He wept over it. When He came to that part of the road down the Mount of Olivet which commands the fullest view of Jerusalem, He wept over it. When He saw the beautiful city of God, the dwelling-place of David and Solomon, the scene of so many types of Himself, the glorious Temple with its enormous pile of white stone rising into the air, its brazen gates and golden roof, where God had dwelt, where all the prophets had prophesied, where thousands of believers had worshipped; when He remembered how sinful they were; when He saw how they would, ere long, crucify Him, and despise and reject all His offers of mercy; when He saw the coming destruction of His people, and the eternal vengeance which was to follow, Jesus wept.

Oh, believers, this is your Saviour! How truly is your Immanuel your Elder Brother also; for we have not an High Priest which cannot be touched with a feeling of our infirmities, but One who was in all points tempted like as we are, yet without sin. In time of pain, believer, you should remember that Jesus knows that feeling, and feels along with you. In time of hunger, and thirst, and nakedness, believer, remember that Jesus knows that feeling, and has compassion for you. In time of weeping, remember that Jesus wept; He feels along with you, when the bursting tear starts forth and will not be restrained. In time of sorrow for your unconverted friends, remember Jesus felt that pain, and feels it again with you. In all your afflictions He is afflicted.

Little children, tell Him all your little sorrows, for Jesus was once a little child, and feels for them all.

Grown believers, tell all your human griefs to Jesus, for He is truly man. 'In every thing by prayer and supplication with thanksgiving let your requests be made known unto God', and then, but not till then, will 'the peace of God, which passeth all understanding . . . keep your hearts and minds through Christ Jesus' (*Phil.* 4:6–7).

2. THE GOSPEL CONTAINS THE THINGS WHICH BELONG TO OUR PEACE.

'If thou hadst known, even thou, at least in this thy day, the things which belong unto thy peace!' Peace of conscience can be found only by the receiving of this message. Worldly men have no true peace of conscience. It is quite true that many men, by continually sinning, have seared over the conscience as with a hot iron, so that it is dead and past feeling.

But even the most worldly men have their time when conscience smites them. With all their smiling faces, they have often withering glances at their past wickedness. Often, when laughing and talking, with sinful company, the recollection of some horrid sin, and the fear of God's vengeance, strikes through their heart like an arrow. 'There is no peace, saith my God, to the wicked.'

Conscience is often awakened to an awful power by the Spirit of God. When He reveals a man's true condition to him; shows him that all his natural life has been spent in sin and opposition to God; that he has been earning much wages, but the wages is death; oh, then, how great confusion and trouble there is in the conscience!

The most seared consciences are sometimes awakened to hideous power in a time of sickness, or on a death-bed. The business and fascinating pleasures, the dainties and delicacies, that amused and occupied the mind, now cease to engage or interest; the companions of life's merry hours are now removed, or, if admitted to the sick man's chamber, try in vain to raise a smile upon his cheek. God makes him see the bitterness which elicited that saying, 'Miserable comforters are ye all.'

Oh! it is strange to see the worldliest of men, those that all their life loathed the company of Christ's messengers, beseeching their minister to pray by their bedside. 'There is no peace, saith my God, to the wicked.'

After death, all seared consciences are awakened to a power that shall never end. The body returns to the dust as it was, and the spirit to God who gave it; and then begins the gnawing of the worm that cannot die. The sinner can never more forget his sin; he can no more sleep, or enjoy pleasures, so as to forget his sad condition.

'Their worm dieth not, and the fire is not quenched.' 'There is no peace . . . to the wicked.'

Now, the message which we bring is one of peace. It tells you how to find peace from the smitings of conscience; peace from the awakening of the Spirit; peace on a death-bed, and peace in eternity! If God open your heart to attend to the things which are spoken, if you would be persuaded to hear and to receive the Word which tells you of Christ having died in the stead of lost sinners, then that would give you immediate peace. And peace of heart can be found only from receiving this message.

As long as a man is unconverted, he can have no true peace of heart, because of the conflicting passions that are in his bosom. The grand passion in every natural heart is selfishness. It is seen in the child grasping and holding everything for itself. It is seen in the boy seeking nobody's pleasure but his own; always forgetting others and indulging himself. It is seen in grown men making haste to be rich, not caring what becomes of others, if they are helped forward; not caring who may want their food, if they have bread enough and to spare, and can only heap up wealth.

Or, if they give some superfluity to the poor, it is that they may have the sweet luxury of thinking themselves benevolent, or seeing their names in print.

Now if selfishness reigned alone, unconverted men would have some quietness in their bosoms; there would be the calm of a sordid bosom, like the Dead Sea, receiving all, but giving out nothing. But the other passions, when much used as servants, at length become masters, and dispute with selfishness the dominion of the heart. The love of money, the love of dress, the lust of the flesh, the lust of the eye, the pride of life, acquire such power that they overpower selfishness. The soul is led contrary to education, contrary to reason, contrary to self-interest. Oh! brethren, how many of you feel that your life is just a history of this war of diverse lusts and passions. 'There is no peace, saith my God, to the wicked.'

But the message we bring tells of the Spirit who makes a clean heart, and renews a right spirit within. Come to Jesus, and you will yet be seen sitting at His feet clothed, and in your right mind. Oh, there is no peace like that of a pure heart that loves God, and loves the Saviour! God is blessed, and He is pure; he has no tumult of passions within. Would you not like to be made like God; to have Him dwelling in you? Oh, that you would hearken to His commandments! 'Then had thy peace been as a river, and thy righteousness as the waves of the sea' (*Isa.* 48:18).

Peace as to the world is also found in the gospel message. As long as a man is unconverted, he must share in the inordinate cares and anxieties of the world. One day he is lifted up to heaven by the prospect of success in business, and is mightily elated with money-making. Again he is sunk into despondency by gloomy forebodings of failure, distress, poverty. At one time his family are in health, and he fears no danger, and calculates upon no distress. Again, sickness comes, and death, to blast his fairest hopes. Ah! there is not a straw upon the sea more at the mercy of winds and waves than is the peace of unconverted men at the mercy of every wind of providence that blows. Is that not the real truth, O unconverted man?

It is only in Christ that a poor soul can come to rest with regard even to this world. Christ is a complete Refuge in every storm of providence. Is my soul united to Christ? Then God is my Father, and He will be sure to supply all my need. Consider the birds of the air, for they neither sow nor reap; they neither have storehouse nor barn, and God feeds them, and will He not feed me? Consider the lilies, how they grow; they toil not, they spin not, and yet Solomon in all his glory was not arrayed like one of these. If then God so clothes the grass of the field, which today is, and tomorrow is cast into the oven, will He not much more clothe me, His ransomed child?

Oh, brethren, he is the richest man in all the world that feels in his heart that no storm can come near his dwelling, and that the Lord shall preserve his going out and coming in, from this time forth and for evermore. Oh, then, do not turn away from our message; it belongs to your peace for time and for eternity! Do not say that it is sad tidings we bring you; do not say of us that we are men who turn the world upside down. Yes, we are, but it is to turn it on its right side, that it may once more be a pleasant vessel full of 'the peace of God which passeth all understanding'.

The time is at hand – Oh, how near it may be to many of you! – when you shall feel with agony that the message of Christ is the only message of peace; that the ministers of Christ are your truest friends, the peacemakers whom Christ calls blessed.

3. CHRIST LONGS AFTER THE SALVATION OF THE CHIEF OF SINNERS.

'If thou hadst known, even thou . . .': Jerusalem was, in some respects, the wickedest city that ever was. It was very guilty, *because it sinned against greater light than other cities*. The temple of God was in the midst of it, the worship of God was constantly maintained in it. All that were godly in the land came up to worship there three times in a year; even godly foreigners, like the Ethiopian treasurer, came from afar to worship there. All the prophets had messages to Jerusalem, and yet we learn from the prophets that iniquity abounded in Jerusalem. 'How is the faithful city become an harlot! It was full of judgment; righteousness lodged in it, but now murderers' (*Isa.* 1:21). The light which God brought into Jerusalem only made the wicked inhabitants love the darkness more!

Christ Weeping Over Jerusalem

Jerusalem was a very guilty city, *because it persecuted the prophets.* God sent many messengers to Jerusalem, but all were persecuted there. Christ told His disciples to begin the preaching of the gospel at Jerusalem; yet there they were stoned and put to death; so that it seems to have been a proverb which Christ quoted, 'It cannot be that a prophet perish out of Jerusalem.' And Stephen spoke the truth, when he said, 'Which of the prophets have not your fathers persecuted?'

But Jerusalem reached the highest guilt *because it rejected Christ.* 'He came unto His own, and His own received Him not.' Brethren, this was the city over which Christ wept. It was not anything good in Jerusalem that moved His pity. He saw nothing but wickedness and coming misery. It was not the piteous cries of Jerusalem that moved His pity. Jerusalem was going on in its usual way, buying and selling, and getting gain. It was the guilt that was over Jerusalem that moved His pity. He saw that the storm of God's anger was over it, and its day of grace was past, that it would have the deepest place in hell; therefore He wept and sighed forth the broken wish, 'If thou hadst known, even thou . . . !'

Are there some here who have committed great sins? Are there some of you who can look back on deep stains and dark blots upon your history? Are there not some who have sins that cry to heaven? Sins against honesty, sins against purity, sins against sobriety? Behold, Christ longs after your salvation! He sees no beauty or goodness in you. He sees and listens to your sins. And oh, He sees your hell; and therefore He weeps over you, and says, 'Oh! that thou hadst known, even thou', poor sinner, the message that belongs to thy peace.

Are there some of you who have sinned against great light? Some who have had godly parents, who taught you to read the Bible and pray; who prayed for you and with you; and have you despised all their words and prayers? Have you shut your ears and run into the vice and sin of the world? Some of you have had godly ministers who cared much for your souls, who watched over you and instructed you when you were young, who took great pains with you in admitting you to the sacrament, who spoke to you by yourselves, and in public preached very faithfully to you. Have you had this great blessing, and yet trampled all under foot, broken through the good hopes of your minister, gone with wicked companions and plunged into sin? Ah! then, behold Christ weeps over you and seeks your salvation still, saying, 'If thou hadst known – Oh, that thou hadst known, even thou, poor sinner – the things that belong to thy peace!'

Are there some who feel that they have deliberately rejected Christ? That they have, like Jerusalem, crucified the Saviour and put Him to an open shame? Have you put away the outstretched arms of Christ, and would not have Him as a Saviour? Still, see how He weeps and says, 'If thou hadst known, even thou!' Ah! brethren, whatever you be, in whatever sin you lie, at whatever distance from God you now are, Christ is this day longing after your salvation. He has the same heart in heaven that He had on earth. His wounds are all healed now; but His heart bleeds still for poor sinners. Awake, then, poor godless unconverted souls! Will you trample all this bleeding love under your feet? 'If thou hadst known, even thou, the things which belong unto thy peace . . . !'

4. JERUSALEM HAD ITS DAY OF GRACE; SO HAVE WE.

'At least in this thy day . . .' The day of grace is like the day of nature. It has its dawn, its morning, its full noon, its twilight, and its midnight. Jerusalem had a long day of grace. That day was at its height during the three years that Christ taught in her streets, but soon the twilight came on, which ended in the blackest night, when these things were hid from her eyes. So it is with us.

Youth is a day of grace. If you intend to come to Jesus and be saved, there is no time so seasonable as the time of one's youth; but alas, how many permit it to pass by unimproved! In youth our hearts are soft, tender, and easily impressed. The conscience has not become seared by long continuance in sin, and its voice is still strong and clear. The understanding is not perverted and biased against the truth. The attention has not become engrossed with the business of the world and the cares of life; nor have the affections been rendered callous by the deceitfulness of the world, harassing trials, heavy sorrows, and repeated disappointments.

The youthful spirit is ever going forth on the wings of joyous fancy in quest of fresh enjoyments; and the heart is offering its richest treasures of love to every one who has the features of loveliness enstamped on the kindly countenance, or on the benignant course of a lovely life. The young resemble the juicy saplings, which are easily bent into any shape, or made to grow in any direction. But grown persons, who have become habituated to sin, are like the trees of centuries, whose massive trunks could not be moved by the strength of a thousand men.

Most people who are ever converted are converted in youth. Conviction of sin and conviction of righteousness are most easily wrought into the youthful mind. It is commonly observed that young people are readiest at learning languages. If the season of youth is let slip, it will hardly be possible to learn them afterwards. Now, although conversion be altogether a supernatural work, yet it is true of conversion also, that it is far oftener wrought in youth than afterwards. My young friends, this is your day of grace; remember, it quickly passes, the twilight is at hand; the night cometh when no man can believe. And, oh, how many of you are old and grey-headed, and yet unconverted? Oh, let us pray that Christ, and the things that belong to your peace, be not yet hid from your eyes!

A fruitful ministry is a day of grace. Most people that are ever converted are converted under a faithful ministry. It is seldom that God blesses the work of an unfaithful minister. Although conversion is wholly God's work, and depends not on the gifts and graces of any minister, yet it pleases God to work through His own instruments whom He hath chosen for Himself. A faithful ministry is a day of grace, and happy is that spot where it dawns. But that day has its twilight and its night. 'Your fathers, where are they? And the prophets, do they live for ever?' They were not suffered to continue by reason of death. Christ only hath an unchangeable priesthood. Often the burning and shining light is removed away. God takes away the candle, as well as the candlestick.

How often a barren cold ministry follows on the back of the liveliest and most fruitful! Brethren, how many of you have been under lively ministers whose tongues are now silent in the grave! Brethren, there are in this town and neighbourhood faithful men who preach the truth fully and faithfully. This, then, is your day. Be converted now, or else the ministers will be taken from you, and these things will be hid from your eyes!

When the Spirit strives, that is a day of grace. All that are converted are converted when the Spirit strives with them, but the Spirit will not always strive with men. When the heart is greatly moved under the reading of the Bible, or under the preaching of the Word, there is little doubt but the Spirit is striving with that heart. When the mind is led seriously to look back at the life it has led, or when the heart shrinks from some sin, there cannot be a doubt that the Spirit is striving. But if this be resisted, then He goes away, sometimes never to return. 'My Spirit shall not always strive.' Brethren, if you have any such awakenings in your heart, do not quench them. It is easy to quench the Spirit! Go back to the world and to the din of perpetual business, or plunge into sensual sin, and you will soon be rid of all awakenings! But remember Christ's Word, even of such as you, 'Oh, that thou hadst known!'

I would conclude with a word to the unconverted and a word to believers.

Learn from this the sureness of hell to the Christless! Christ wept over Jerusalem. Do you think He would have wept if there had been no hell? If you were sick, and did not know it, but the physician came to see you, and you saw him sigh, and shake the head; and if you saw all your friends becoming anxious, and beginning to sob aloud, would this not alarm you? Oh, then, poor sinner, think for a moment. You are quite happy and careless, longing to be away from the house of God that you may laugh and have silly talk once more. But see, Christ is weeping! Now Christ knows the whole of your case. He sees both worlds! Surely there must be a hell for such as you, else Christ would not weep.

Let believers learn from this to weep over perishing souls. Go near and see their case, and then weep over it. This was the main feature in Christ's character. If you would be like Him, be like Him in this. Not only love the world, as Christ did; not only be ready to suffer for them, as Christ was; not only pray for them, as Christ did; but weep over them, as Christ did. And do not join the world in its mirth, were it for no other reason but this. Would you deceive their souls?

If you were to mingle with poor unconverted souls in their God-forgetting companies, where they dance, drink, are gay and merry, singing their own songs, and enjoying themselves in their accustomed manner, what could you expect to do for their conversion?

You should weep over them, and seek their salvation, rather than let down your Christianity and join them in their worldliness, forgetfulness of God, carnal mirth, and giddy folly. If you would do them good, you must seek God's Holy Spirit to give you a heart to weep for them, rather than join with them in their melancholy ways of forgetting their guilt and danger.

Only think of the Saviour's tears when He looked down upon the perishing, and surely that will scare you from ever again forgetting your place and relationship to Him, and that will make you cherish for poor unconverted souls the bleeding heart and weeping eye. And never more go along with them in their soul-intoxicating mirth and hell-forgetting pleasures.

'Deliver me from blood-guiltiness, O God' (*Psa.* 51:14)!

10

The Grace of God Seen at Antioch

Then tidings of these things came unto the ears of the church which was in Jerusalem: and they sent forth Barnabas, that he should go as far as Antioch. Who, when he came, and had seen the grace of God, was glad, and exhorted them all, that with purpose of heart they would cleave unto the Lord. For he was a good man, and full of the Holy Ghost and of faith: and much people was added unto the Lord (Acts 11:22–24).

ANTIOCH WAS A VENERABLE TOWN where the believers were first called Christians (*Acts* 11:26). Persecution drove many believers there, so that God brought good out of evil. 'Out of the eater came forth meat, and out of the strong came forth sweetness' (*Judg.* 14:14). The church took a deep interest in the work and sent Barnabas. What he saw serves as an example to all Christian Churches.

1. WHAT BARNABAS SAW.
i. THE GRACE OF GOD.
The grace of God is the spiritual coming of Jesus into a place. He had come into Antioch and turned many to Himself, yet He could

not be seen. Neither is it meant that the Holy Spirit was seen. It was He who came. He awakened, drew, comforted, filled, and sanctified. Yet all this was the secret, hidden manna, the white stone, the life hid with Christ in God, the living water within. None of this was visible.

What, then, is meant? That the effects of this work were visible, just as the growth is seen round the mouth of a well, though you see not the secret spring from which the water proceeds, and just as you see the flowers appearing, though not the dew which brings forth their fragrance.

ii. Visible Marks of the Grace of God.

a. *Delight in the Lord Jesus Christ.*

Just as the jailor rejoiced, believing in God, so here they gladly received the Word. Before their delight was in other things. It was in sensual things: eating, drinking, diverse lusts; in intellectual things: books, persons of taste, novels, genius, poetry; in happy things: dress, dancing, parties, banquetings, revellings, cards. But now it is in Christ. The merchant man has found the pearl . 'What things were gain to me, these I counted loss for Christ.'

This was what Barnabas saw! It is a sure mark of the grace of God. If men are brought to a high esteem of Jesus, of His Person, offices, work, and character, this is a sure sign.

Nature could not lead them to this. Naturally men stumble at Christ. 'This is the stone set at nought of you builders.' Satan would not lead you to this either. He is the great enemy of Christ. He tries to beguile from Christ. If you see the minds of men delighting in Christ, then you may be sure there is a work of the grace of God. In heaven, all will delight in the Lord Jesus Christ. He is the Sun and Centre. All the redeemed will sing, 'Worthy is the Lamb', and cast their crowns at His feet and pour out their golden vials before Him, and play their harps to His praise. If you are on the road to heaven you will have this mark.

b. *Longing after holiness.*

Before their heart was toward sin, the world, and the things of the world, especially toward some besetting sin. They greatly hated those that reproved them or spoke against their favourite sins. This is the case very much where the grace of God is not. But now there was a universal hatred of sin, and especially of the sins wherein they had lived. Barnabas could not speak too ill of sin. This is a sure mark of a work of grace. Nature could not do this. The natural heart loves sin. Satan will not do this. If Satan cast out Satan, how shall his kingdom stand? His kingdom is one of darkness. Heaven is a place of universal holiness. Nothing that is unclean can enter. This is the great mark of a work of the Holy Spirit. Ah, would we had more of it in this place!

c. *Love.*

Before, they did not love God nor one another. Every man was selfish and sought his own things. But now, when united to Christ, there is evidently the oil of holy love poured into the heart. An amazing love to God, the heart drawn out to Him for what He is, toward Jesus, toward the saints, universal benevolence toward the world. 'Everyone that loveth is born of God. He that loveth not, knoweth not God, for God is love.' This is far above nature. A natural man may be kind, but he has no divine love, none of the love that was in the breast of Jesus. The moment a man is converted, this becomes evident in him. He partakes in the loving Spirit of the Lamb. It is far above Satan. Hatred and pride are the principles of his heart. He would not put it in to your heart if he could. This was what Barnabas saw! Oh, that we could see more of the same among yourselves, in every town, yea, in every land till the world were filled with the grace of God!

All God's works are beautiful – a daisy, a lily, is beautiful – but the work of grace in the heart is the most beautiful and amazing of all.

2. THE EFFECT ON THE MIND OF BARNABAS

When Barnabas saw these marks of the grace of God, he was glad.

i. He Was Not Angry.

If Barnabas had been an ungodly man, he would have been angry. Nothing makes an ungodly man so angry as seeing the grace of God. If he sees men slumbering under the gospel, neglecting Christ, living unconverted, like wine settled on its lees, this is rational religion, he is not angry. If he sees men living in profanity, swearing, drinking, playing cards, he is not angry. If he sees men without secret or family prayer, slipping thoughtlessly into eternity, he is not angry at this. But the moment he sees the grace of God, souls awakened to see their dreadful condition, Jesus sought after, sin put away, holy love directing the life, his heart rises against this.

i. Because it shows him the Bible is true.

ii. Because it shows that he must turn or die, that he is lost himself.

iii. Because it brings him into the presence of Jesus.

How often is it so here! Search and see: was it so with you during the late wonderful work of God?

ii. He Was Not Envious.

If Barnabas had had less grace he might have been envious. None of the Apostles had been engaged in this work. Barnabas had had no hand in it, though he was an experienced minister. Probably they were raw lads that had been so remarkably blessed. A man of small grace might have been envious. He might have said, 'I fear all is not right.' But no, Barnabas was glad!

iii. He Was Not Silent.

With less grace he might have been silent. He might have thought it prudent not to own the work. Probably there were many imprudences connected with the work. He might have been afraid of his character and gone away home without saying anything, without thanking God. Alas! I fear too many have done this in our day. Too many have been afraid of acknowledging God's work, and are like to blast their own ministries. So it may be with many of yourselves. Consider Barnabas' example!

iv. He Was Glad.

He saw the marks of the grace of God and was glad. He had no hand in the work; still he was glad. There might be many imprudences, false hearts, hypocrisies; still he was glad:

i. Because souls were saved. He could not but rejoice at that.

ii. Because Jesus was exalted.

iii. Because it was a mark that the Lord was still with him.

Try yourself dear friends, by the past. Or if the same occurred again, how would you feel? Would you be offended or glad? Barnabas was a good man, full of the Holy Ghost and faith. If you have the same, you will feel the same!

3. THE EXHORTATION OF BARNABAS.

He exhorted them to cleave to the Lord!

i. It Was Not Enough to Turn to the Lord.

Many of those young Christians of Antioch thought that all was done, that heaven was gained. They found such peace, joy, comfort, love, that they thought they would easily run to heaven. 'No,' said Barnabas, 'All is not done! You are only begun, cleave to the Lord!' Conversion or turning to Christ is but the beginning of the divine life. There will be many a temptation, affliction and enemy, and times of weakness will come. Cleave to the Lord! 'Abide in me', said Christ, 'If ye abide in my Word, ye are my disciples.' Many will seem to turn who will not cleave. The more that fall away, the more need there is for you to cleave. If another does not, cleave you to the Lord!

ii. The Main Business for a Christian Is to Cleave to the Lord.
Barnabas seems to have preached but one sermon and this was the sum of it. Probably they expected something very different from such an experienced minister: Counsel as to how they were now to live; fill up their time; what they were to do in time of temptation, persecution, death; how they were to behave towards unbelieving friends. All these were answered in this, 'Cleave to the Lord!'

a. *For righteousness.*
Keep your conscience clean, 'which some having put away converting faith have made shipwreck'. The more you cling to the perfect Immanuel as your Righteousness, the more peace and holiness you will have.

b. *For holiness.*
Cleave to the Lord: not to ministers, not to man, but to the Lord! Cling to His almighty arm. You little know how much comfort, life, grace, and strength are in Him! *Live* cleaving to the Lord. *Die* cleaving to the Lord. This is your main business. By this will all other questions, difficulties, and perplexities be answered.

11

Almost Persuaded[1]

Then Agrippa said unto Paul, Almost thou persuadest me to be a Christian (Acts 26:28).

PAUL WAS HERE PERMITTED TO PREACH before three persons of high rank. The first was Bernice, the sister of King Agrippa, a woman of great beauty, but living at that very time in open profligacy. The second was Festus, the Roman Governor, a soldier and a heathen man of great ignorance. The third was Agrippa, son of that Herod who was smitten of God for his pride and blasphemy. He, too, was a proud and wicked man, though well read in the law and the prophets. It is curious to see the different ways in which these three sat under the preaching of the Word from the lips of Paul.

Bernice, the lovely but wicked Bernice, sits silent. She has no interest in the Word. She may be thinking on some new scheme of pleasure or of sin. Her heart is like the hard footpath; the Word cannot enter in; the devil carries all away. Oh! how many hearing me this day are like Bernice! We may speak of heaven, or hell, it matters not; you have no ears to hear!

[1] Preached in St Peter's, Dundee, 3 September 1837.

Festus, the blinded heathen, listens with unbelieving wonder. He hears of Paul's strange conversion; he hears of the risen Saviour, and that all must turn to Him or perish. The proud Roman can hear no more. Festus said, with a loud voice, 'Paul, thou art beside thyself; much learning doth make thee mad!'

Oh, how many are like Festus in this! You hear us telling you of the need of conversion; that God alone can do it for you; that Christ hath sent us to open the blind eyes, that you may receive the forgiveness of sins. How many proud hearts would fain say, 'Thou art beside thyself; much learning doth make thee mad!' If we are at fault, it is in that we are so dead and cold in beseeching you to turn and have life.

It is you who are mad, walking about easy in mind without forgiveness, happy while the heirs of hell, prayerless, Christless, Godless – yet smiling, happy, and careless about your souls! It is you who display madness.

Agrippa, the proud and wicked Agrippa, was much moved by the discourse of Paul. Even the wicked may be moved by the preaching of the Word. The earnest manner of the preacher, stretching out his hand; the account of his conversion; his tender appeal to the conscience of Agrippa, 'Believest thou the prophets? I know that thou believest.'

All these things moved his heart. He felt, for the time, the misery of being lost, the need of being converted, the happiness of being forgiven, and he cried out, 'Almost thou persuadest me to be a Christian!'

Brethren, are there none among you who have been moved under the preaching of the Word? It is for your sakes, then, I have chosen these words this day, that I may show you, by the help of God, the utter folly of being only almost persuaded to be a Christian.

Almost Persuaded

1. THE PREACHING OF THE WORD ALMOST PERSUADES SOME TO BE CHRISTIANS.

So it was with Agrippa. He was sitting under God's chosen instrument for converting souls, the preaching of the Word, and his inmost soul was moved under it. So it is with many. When they hear the conversion of others described; when they hear the need they have of being converted; when they hear of Christ being a risen Saviour, willing to save all that come to Him; when they see the earnestness of the minister when He presses it home to their own conscience, they feel 'almost persuaded'.

'Surely it is true', they say, 'that I must be converted, or perish!' 'Surely it is true', they say, 'that they are happy who are brought into the forgiveness of sins! I wish it were my case. Nevertheless, it would be rash to yield just now; I would not like to leave all my pleasures and my companions in sin. Besides, another day may do as well. Almost thou persuadest me to be a Christian!' So it was with Agrippa; so it is with thousands. Is this your case? Oh, how utterly foolish you are!

Consider that you may never hear another sermon, you may die tonight! This night thy soul may be required of thee! If you are moved to flee from wrath, flee now. If you are melted by the thought of Christ, flee to Him now.

You never may have another offer of salvation through His blood and righteousness. And if you do hear the Word again, it is likely you will be less moved then. When iron is often heated, it becomes harder every time. When a surgeon sees many wounds and sores, he is much moved at first, but he soon becomes used to it. So you may be much moved at first, by hearing of Christ and His love, but you will soon turn hard if He does not make you, not almost, but altogether a Christian.

2. SOME ARE MOVED IN A TIME OF AFFLICTION TO BE ALMOST CHRISTIANS.

Affliction is one of God's strongest means for bringing sinners to feel their need of Christ. He comes into godless families like a lion. He tears and carries away, and all that many souls may say is, 'Come and let us return unto the Lord.' Times of affliction are times for seeking the Lord. Oh, it is a hard, hard heart that is unmoved in a time of domestic affliction! 'Why should ye be stricken any more? Ye will revolt more and more.'

Some unconverted persons are much moved in a time of distress. The long-neglected Bible is sought out; the knee that hardly knows how to bend begins to kneel; the minister is listened to; the mind is filled with solemn thoughts about death, and hell, and judgment!

It appears for the moment good to be a Christian. But the sun breaks through the clouds, the tears are dried off the face, prosperity comes back to the dwelling; and where is its Christianity now? Alas! it is fled. Christ speaks to those in affliction. God is pleading with you face to face. Remember, to be brought into the bonds of the covenant is no easy matter. Do not be contented to be made serious and gloomy for a day or two. That is not conversion. Be altogether, and not almost a Christian.

Christ speaks to those who have come out of affliction and sorrow. See what utter folly it is to be only almost a Christian. Your affliction has lost its beneficent end. It was sent to bring you to Christ. It almost brought you; that was all. If you have already resisted God's mightiest instruments, affliction and the Word, there is little hope that you will ever be a Christian indeed. God must do one of two things with you. Either He must persevere with you, send deeper waters of affliction; greater losses, sorer pains, more heart-rending bereavements to drive you to Christ, or He may let you alone!

'Ephraim is joined to his idols, let him alone.' He may give you your heart's desire, and send leanness into your soul!

3. SOME ARE MOVED IN A TIME OF AWAKENING TO BE ALMOST CHRISTIANS.

There are times of awakening in congregations and in families, and in such times there are always some who are almost, but not altogether, persuaded to be Christians. When one of a godless family is brought to the Saviour, there are many who will chide, and scoff, and mock. What need of all this work about the soul? They will say: what need of all this searching of the Bible, and continuing in prayer? They little know, poor souls, what is going on within the awakened bosom.

But if many chide and scoff, there are often some who are touched in the heart. Often a brother, a sister, a companion is moved to cling to them, saying like Ruth, 'Where thou goest I will go.' Oh, it is happy when companions lead companions to Christ. But how often they drop away before coming to Christ.

Some of you who have been truly converted may remember some who once wept with you, and prayed with you, and spoke of Christ and salvation with you, who have gone back to the world. They were almost, but not altogether, persuaded to be Christians. Some of you know that this is the case with your own souls. See then the folly of being almost Christians. Your companions are in Christ; you are out of Christ. If it was reasonable in you to flee with them, it was still more reasonable to persevere till you were in Christ.

How will you feel in the day of Christ, when you see them crowned with glory at the right hand of Christ, and you standing with devils on the left! You will say, I went so far with them; I was almost one of them, but I went back. Oh, the saddest place in hell will be for the almost Christian.

4. SOME ARE MOVED TO FLEE FROM HELL, YET STILL ARE ONLY ALMOST CHRISTIANS.

Some persons are really awakened by the Spirit of God to 'flee from the wrath to come'. They forsake their old 'pleasures of sin', their old companions, their old ways; they live in anxiety and dread. Still they will not come to Jesus Christ, in order to have life. They are almost, but not altogether, persuaded to be Christians. This arises from many things.

Sometimes it arises from pride. They are afraid of hell, but they think they shall escape by some way of their own; by tears, or prayers, or reformation. They hew out cisterns for themselves; they kindle a fire for themselves, and walk in the light of their fire, and in the sparks that they have kindled (Isa. 50:11). They will not come to Jesus Christ, and let Him be their light and salvation. Oh, how sad to be so near being saved, and yet to be lost! How sad to be almost Christians, and to be kept from being altogether Christians by soul-ruining pride!

Sometimes it arises from enmity to God. Christ is the Saviour whom God has provided. The way to honour God is to flee to Jesus Christ; but some awakened souls have so much enmity to God that they will not honour Him by believing on Jesus Christ. Oh, how mad it is to fight against God and your own soul! How mad to be almost Christians.

Sometimes it arises from mistaken views of God. Some anxious souls are suspicious of God. They dare not believe that He has such an infinite depth of pity as to provide a Saviour for them. 'No, it cannot be for me. It may be for other sinners, but it cannot be for me!' And so they will not come to Jesus Christ. Oh, how mad not to believe what God has said of Himself and of his Son!

Such are almost Christians. See here the folly of being almost a Christian. All your anxiety to flee from hell will do you no good if you be only almost a Christian. You have trembled much, and wept much, and prayed much, for your poor soul. Still, if you are not brought to Jesus Christ, it is all in vain. If you were swimming for your life, if you had breasted many a dashing wave, and were now close to the shore, just within reach of the rock; still, if you do not stretch out your hand to clasp the rock, you will be drowned; all your former pains and labours will be vain. A man may drown within reach of the rock just as well as a thousand miles at sea.

So, after all your anxiety, hearing, praying, and tears, you may perish where you are, just as surely as those who are out of sight of God. It is quite vain to flee toward the Ark, if you do not flee into it. A man might drown clinging to the Ark. Be 'shut in' to it! It was vain for Lot's wife that she fled out of Sodom, for she never reached Zoar. Just so vain is it to be almost, but not altogether, a Christian.

Your sin is far greater than that of other men. Agrippa's sin was far greater than that of Festus or of Bernice. He was moved to flee to Christ, yet did not flee. They saw no beauty in Him, that they should desire Him. So it is with you and the world. If a man were not in search of pearls, and he passed by the pearl of great price, it needed not to be wondered at; his eyes were busy with other things. But if a man be really seeking goodly pearls, going from place to place, night and day in search of them, and the pearl of great price is offered him, he looks at it, turns it round and round; he is told its value, worth all that he has, he lays it down, and proceeds on his anxious search.

Ah, that is the man who despises the pearl most of all. So you are they who despise Christ most of all. Other people tread Him under their feet, because they do not know Him, nor desire Him; but you, as it were, take Him into your hands, and examine His value, and yet you lightly esteem Him.

Oh, your sin is far greater, in thus lightly esteeming Christ, than all that you ever committed before. For Judas, despising mercy through the Lamb of God and hanging himself was a greater sin than betraying the Saviour. So your turning away from Christ is a greater sin than betraying Him at His table – than all that ever you did against Him. Oh, may God open your eyes, that you may not be almost a Christian, but a Christian indeed!

The deepest place in hell will be for almost Christians. In strict justice it will be so. The more sin the greater guilt and the deeper hell. And who has so much sin as the soul that comes nearest to Christ, yet is not ravished with His beauty, and attracted to Him by his loveliness. In the nature of things, the hell of the 'almost Christian' will be more severe than that of others. To be almost saved, and yet to be lost; to be not far from the kingdom of God, and yet to fall into the kingdom of wrath – Oh, that will be an awful thought to all eternity!

'I was once very near being in Christ', many a one will say in that day. 'I was made anxious for my soul; I wept and prayed, and searched the Scriptures. I listened with anxiety to the preached Word. I felt it was the power of God. I felt myself condemned by the law. I was quite different from my worldly friends; they did not understand my sorrow, they could only laugh me to scorn. I fled from them. I fled from my old sins. I was not far from the kingdom. I almost stretched out my hands to accept of Christ. I was almost persuaded to be a Christian; and oh, where am I now?'

The higher you cast a stone into the air, the deeper it will fall into the sea; so the nearer you are to Christ and heaven, the deeper you will fall into hell. If you come just up to the gate of heaven, and see the streets of shining gold, and the happy faces of the glorious ones who walk there; if you hear their songs of glory, loud as the voice of many waters, sweet as the harpers harping on their harps; and yet, if the gate be shut against you, and Christ say, 'I know you not, depart from me', what words of man can tell the agony with which you will go away to lie down in sorrow, to lie down in hell! If there be one wailing cry from that sad abode more dismal, more heart-rending than another, it will be the bitter wailing of him who was almost, but not altogether, a Christian.

Oh, be not content with half-work! Oh, be not sluggish in seeking converting grace! There is hope for every one of you. I would to God that not you only, but all who are hearing me this day, were both *almost* and *altogether* such as Paul was, except his bonds.

12

The Work of the Spirit in the Heart[1]

And hope maketh not ashamed; because the love of God is shed abroad in our hearts by the Holy Ghost which is given unto us (Rom. 5:5).

IN A PREVIOUS LECTURE, we saw that there are two kinds of hope mentioned in the Bible. There is *the hope of believing*, which rises in the heart the moment a man really believes, and *the hope of experience*, which does not arise in the heart until a man has evidence in his heart and life to satisfy him on Scripture warrants, that he is a believer.

The one hope we saw exemplified in the converted jailor of Philippi, who rejoiced, believing, in the very same night that he drew his sword and would have killed himself. The other hope we saw exemplified in John who says, 'We know that we have passed from death to life. We know that we know him.'

Now of this second hope, the hope of experience, it is said in the words before me, that it maketh not ashamed, it is an anchor of the soul which never gives way, it is a hope which does not deceive.

[1] Preached in Dunipace, 10 April 1836; Larbert, 17 April 1836; and in St Peter's, Dundee, 18 December, 1836.

The Work of the Spirit in the Heart

And the reason why it is so secure a hope is given: because the love of God, that is God's love to us, is shed abroad in our hearts by the Holy Ghost which is given unto us. A peculiar work of the Spirit, then, is here pointed to as that which gives sureness and stability to the hope of the sanctified believer. That work of the Spirit is here called 'shedding abroad God's love in the heart'. It is elsewhere called, 'sealing the soul unto the day of redemption', and again, 'the witness of the Spirit with our spirits that we are the children of God'. All these four names are given to this one blessed work of the Spirit. But, as the Spirit is the great Worker in our hearts from the beginning, it may be as well for clearness' sake to take the whole work of the Spirit in the human soul.

1. THE FIRST WORK OF THE SPIRIT IN THE HEART IS TO CONVINCE OF SIN.

You must all have observed how the great mass of mankind are living in perfect security. Whether men live in open sin or in outward decency, they are alike at ease in their consciences, they are without God and therefore without hope in the world. But it is not so in the day when the Spirit begins His work: when He reveals to the soul the breadth and length of the law of God; when He shows the sinner that God must cease to be God in the hour when one command of that law is broken with impunity; when He reveals to the soul the gospel message which he has so long been despising; when He points to the stretched-out hands of Jesus which the sinner has so often thrust away; when He speaks in the voice of awful tenderness, poor sinner, thou hast first trampled on the holiness of God by breaking His Law. And then thou hast trampled on the mercy of God by refusing His gospel. The curse of a broken law and the curse of a rejected gospel are both nesting over thy head. Canst thou still be happy with thy friends? Canst thou still cry, Peace,

peace, where there is no peace? Ah! my friends, when it is the Spirit of God and not a poor worm like ourselves that speaks this word to the same sinner's heart, then is the work of awakening begun in good earnest. Instead of peace of conscience, he has now nothing but war. He has no peace at his work and no peace at his meals and no rest in his bed. It has happened in many cases that, in his very dreams, he feels he is falling into the hands of the living God. He goes alone from the merry crew whose society he so much loved, and yet he fears to be alone. He would fain cry aloud to God, but he feels that he has no right to pray. He repeats over and over the words of David, 'The sorrows of death compassed me and the pains of hell got hold on me. I found trouble and sorrow.'

Ah! my friends, if you have never experienced any such awakening as this is, in any degree of it, then the Spirit has never so much as begun His saving work upon your soul. Yes, you are living unimpressed and unawakened and it is quite possible that you may live on in this way for years to come, nay, it is quite possible that you may pass through the awful scenery of the death-bed in this way, but I will tell you one thing which is impossible, you cannot enter on the world to come unawakened. You will be convinced of sin then, but oh! it will not be by the Spirit of God, but by the scorching breath of hell. And who can tell the agony of spirit that shall come on thee, secure sinner, in that awful hour when the sinners in Zion are afraid, and fearfulness surprises the hypocrites (*Isa.* 33:14).

2. THE SECOND WORK OF THE SPIRIT IN THE HEART IS TO CONVINCE OF RIGHTEOUSNESS.

When a man is seized upon by a violent and dangerous illness and the fear of dying really gets hold upon him, it is singular to notice

The Work of the Spirit in the Heart

with how much eagerness he obeys the directions of the physician and swallows down medicines which at other times he would have abhorred. Just so it is when a man is dangerously sick in his soul and has been really awakened to know the greatness of his danger. He is eager and willing to accept all remedies for his soul. Indeed the great danger is that just as a sick man sometimes follows the advice of mere pretenders in medicine and swallow what is hurtful, so the sick soul is apt to take up with the first remedy that offers itself.

Ah! how many refuges of lies are open to receive the wounded soul, who is crying, 'What shall I do to be saved?' Like the wounded deer which flies to the nearest cover, so the awakened soul seeks peace wherever it can be found. Happy that soul to which the Spirit reveals Jesus, the true covert from the storm, the only hiding place from wrath, the only rock to give a lasting shadow in this weary land. Happy the soul to whom He reveals the fulness, the suitableness, the freeness of Jesus as a righteousness! Thou art afraid of the wrath to come. Thou mournest over the stains of sin on thy conscience. Behold, here, a fountain filled with blood, opened on purpose to wash away sin and uncleanness. The soul believes and is at peace. Justified by faith he has peace with God.

Ah! my friends, have you never experienced such a change as this, a change from death unto life, from darkness into marvellous light, a change from the pains of an inward hell to the joyful hope of heaven? Alas then, you are a stranger to the saving work of the Spirit. Ah! how sad a thing it is to see our congregation Sabbath after Sabbath, listening to the setting forth of Jesus the Lamb of God that taketh away the sins of the world, and yet never giving any tokens of their heartily embracing Jesus. There was once a whole congregation who were moved as the heart of one man, to believe in a crucified Jesus and were found glad in His righteousness. And that same day there were added to the church about three thousand souls. Ah! when shall we see such days among us? Never, till we see the same anxiety among us which was among them! They were pricked in their hearts and cried, 'Men and brethren, what must we do?' If only we could get your hearts stirred up by the Spirit of God to the same degrees of anxiety, if it would but please the Lord once more to be glorious unto us, to send us days of awakening from this slumber that is on all eyes, then would a preached Jesus seem precious in your eyes, the chief among ten thousand, and altogether lovely.

Oh! what a depth of meaning there is in the command of the prophet, 'Break up your fallow ground, and sow not among thorns' (*Jer.* 4:3). What would you think of the farmer who, preparing land which had lain fallow time out of mind, should, without turning it up with the plough, begin at once to cast away his precious seed among the thorns and briers with which it was overrun? Yet this is our sad employment, as long as you bring to the preaching of the Word hearts overgrown with the cares of this life and unconvinced of sin, unawakened to seek the Saviour. Break up your fallow ground, then, and let us no longer sow among thorns!

3. THE THIRD WORK OF THE SPIRIT IN THE HEART IS TO SANCTIFY.

When a man is justified by believing, then it is that the Holy Ghost is given unto him. Indeed the Spirit had all along been working in his heart. In the hour that a branch is grafted into the true vine, in that hour does it receive the enriching juices of the vine. It may have been the degenerate plant of a strange vine, yet now, since it has become a branch of the true vine, its whole kind and character is changed, and it brings forth no more wild grapes but good

The Work of the Spirit in the Heart

grapes. I desire you to mark several things with regard to the sanctifying of the Spirit.

i. It Is Sure to All Believers.

The word of Christ is, 'He that believeth on me, as the Scripture hath said, out of his belly shall flow rivers of living water' (*John* 7:38). And it is one of the arguments by which Christ in Proverbs persuades sinners to come to God, 'I will pour out my spirit unto you' (*Prov.* 1:23). If any man then thinks that he has believed on Jesus, and yet has never received these rivers of living water, this gift of the Spirit, let him know that he is deceiving himself, for 'if any man have not the Spirit of Christ, he is none of his' (*Rom.* 8:9).

ii. He Dwells in the Believer as His Settled Home.

'Ye are the temple of the living God; as God hath said, I will dwell in them, and walk in them; and I will be their God, and they shall be my people' (*2 Cor.* 6:16). If the Spirit dwelt in the believer only at certain seasons, then He would only have seasons of holiness, and would be like the worst worldling who has his fits of religion. But the believer has God as an abiding guest, whether he is at rest or walks by the wayside. God dwells in him and walks in him. So the Spirit is not like a well of water to which the believer may go to draw the refreshing water of life, but the Spirit is in him, a well of water, springing up.

iii. He Sanctifies Secretly and Silently.

He says, 'I will be as the dew unto Israel' (*Hos.* 14:5). The dew descends secretly and silently in the twilight of a summer's evening, when the sky is scarcely blue, and no man can see whence it cometh or whither it goeth. As the dew yet comes and refreshes all the thirsty ground, bathing every leaf with its gentle moisture, calling forth the fragrant odours of every lily of the valley, and every flower of the mountain, so doth the Spirit descend secretly and silently into the heart of the believer, refreshing and renewing every thirsty soul, and calling forth the fragrant affections and praises and good works of all the saints, whether dwelling in the palaces of princes or in the cottage of clay.

iv. He Sanctifies by the Word.

It is written, 'Sanctify them through thy truth: thy word is truth' (*John* 17:17). It is never without the Word, but always through the Word, that the Spirit reaches the heart of man. It is in learning, in reading, in remembering, in meditating on the Word of God that the Spirit works in us to will and do of God's good pleasure. And here we find that man after God's own heart saying, 'Thy word have I hid in mine heart, that I might not sin against thee' (*Psa.* 119:11).

Oh! believing brethren, if you wish to know why you do not grow in holiness I answer fearlessly, it is because you do not read your Bible as you ought to do. If you would meditate therein day and night, then you would grow.

4. THE FOURTH WORK OF THE SPIRIT IS THAT HE SEALS BELIEVERS UNTO THE DAY OF REDEMPTION.

This is the work that is spoken of in the words before us in Romans, chapter 5. And just as from the last work we were considering He is called the Sanctifier, so it is from this work that He is called the Comforter, because He hereby gives strong consolation to the sanctified believer, stirring up in him a hope that maketh not ashamed, an anchor of the soul, sure and steadfast. I shall briefly explain the several names which the Bible gives to this work of the Spirit.

The Work of the Spirit in the Heart

i. It Is Called the Sealing of the Spirit.

'God... hath also sealed us' (*2 Cor.* 1:22–22). Again, 'After that ye believed, ye were sealed with that holy Spirit of promise' (*Eph.* 1:14). Again, 'Grieve not the holy Spirit of God, whereby ye are sealed' (*Eph.* 4:30). It was the custom in ancient times, instead of signing a document with the hand, to append a seal to it, which was therefore a mark of the document being completed. Now, believers are said to be epistles of Christ, written not with ink but with the Spirit of the living God, not in letters of stone but in fleshy tables of the heart (*2 Cor.* 3:3).

But when the Spirit comes to apply the seal, is it not plain that the document is finished, that He hath transcribed the whole character of Christ into the heart, and that by means of the seal He is acknowledging it to be His work? Such is the comforting work of the Spirit. Look in upon this fleshy tablet of thine heart, He is saying. Have I not written the whole law of God therein? Have I not made all the commandments delightful to thee? Have I not made universal holiness the aim of thy whole soul? Behold then, thou art sealed by Me unto the day of redemption!

ii. It Is Called Giving the Earnest of Our Inheritance.

He has 'given the earnest of the Spirit in our hearts' (*2 Cor.* 1:22), that Holy Spirit of promise which is the earnest of our inheritance until the redemption of the purchased possession. An *earnest* is part of the money paid in hand, as a token that the whole will be forthcoming in due time. A master, when he hires a servant, gives her an earnest of her promised wages. Now the promised inheritance which Christ hath purchased for His people in the world to come is just a full measure of the Spirit of God to dwell in them for ever. I doubt not that the blessed saints shall wander by the pure water of the river of life clear as crystal, and shall sit under the shade of the tree of life and taste its twelve blessed fruits. I doubt not that the Lamb which is in the midst of the throne shall feed them and lead them to living fountains of water, and God shall wipe away all tears from their eyes. And though I can easily imagine that the God who made this world of sin so beautiful, with its heaven of blue and green-carpeted earth, its snowy mountains and shady valleys, its lawns and trees and flowers – He who gave such beauty to a daisy that was to be trodden under the heel of some ungodly wretch – can give a surpassing loveliness which our earthly minds cannot comment on to the world that is to be trodden only by the pure feet that have known no stain of sin; yet, after all, the great blessedness of heaven is that the Spirit of God will fully dwell in us there. The holy thoughts which He keeps burning in our minds, the heavenly imaginings, the holy affections flaming toward God and the Lamb which He sends into the bosom, the exalting joy which the Bible says is joy in the Holy Ghost, these are the chiefest, the surpassing glories of the kingdom which is 'not meat and drink, but righteousness, and peace, and joy in the Holy Ghost'.

Accordingly, when God gives the believers an earnest of the coming glory, it is not a foretaste of the tree of life, nor a sight of the palms and the golden crown which he shall wear, but it is a partial indwelling of the Spirit in his heart now, as a foretaste or earnest of the full indwelling which shall be hereafter.

Hast thou indeed the first fruits of the Spirit in thy heart now? Believer, has the Spirit at length wrought His work so plainly in thine understanding, in thine affections, in thy life, that thou canst no longer doubt but thou hast been led by the Spirit? Rejoice, then, inasmuch as this work of the Spirit in thine heart is the earnest of thine inheritance, it is a part in hand of the full work of glorifying which shall yet be wrought in thee when Christ shall be glorified in His saints.

iii. It Is Called the Witness of the Spirit.

The Spirit Himself beareth witness with our spirit (*Rom.* 8:16). And here we must take heed lest we fall into the error of imagining that this witness of the Spirit is any sort of whispering by the Spirit to our spirits, that it is any secret words spoken, or any miraculous, supernatural light assuring us that we are God's children. The Bible tells us of no such witness to our salvation. It is the work of the Spirit in our hearts that bears witness to the self-examining eye of our spirits when we look within.

When holy tempers and habits are wrought in us, when we have lost the temper and bearing of the children of this world, when the whole bent of our soul is to cry, 'Abba, Father', then may we bless God and say, Here the Spirit has been at work indeed! He has transformed my wolfish heart into that of a lamb. He has changed my swearing and profanity and my worldly talk into the sweet breathings of affectionate prayer. Here, then, is the witness of the Spirit, or the testimony of the Spirit, of which my own spirit is the eyewitness that I am a new creature, that I am a child of God.

iv. The Love of God Shed Abroad in Our Hearts.

The fourth and last description of the work of the Spirit is that in our text, which I would not have departed from, except for the sake of gaining greater clarity and simplicity in our views of it. God's love to the believer is here said to be shed abroad in his heart by the Holy Ghost which is given unto him.

When a man comes to know that he is a justified believer by possessing the seal, the earnest, the witness of the Spirit in his heart, it is then that he feels himself a partaker in the everlasting love of God. That love is shed abroad in his heart. It descends like a precious dew, moistening, refreshing and gladdening the whole soul. This is not that compassionate love of God which is showered on the whole world and which does not ensure the salvation of all who come under it. God so loved the world, the whole wicked world, in this way. But this is the love of God to His justified ones. It is this which the soul now feels shining in like the beams of a midday sun, and he takes up the blessed argument which follows and says, If, when I was an enemy, God gave His Son to die for me, much more now shall I saved by His life!

Ah! if there be one blessed soul before me, who has this seal, this earnest, this witness in his heart that he is a child of God, he is a partaker in the electing, everlasting love of God. What unbounded room is there here, then, for your joy and consolation. You know that you are in Christ, for you have the soul of a believer in Jesus. Rejoice, then, in the Lord always. For when shall God cast out Jesus from His presence? When shall the Father refuse all glory and blessing to His well-beloved Son? Then, but not till then, can He forget thee!

You know that you are an heir of glory for you have the earnest of the inheritance in your heart. Grace within you is glory begun. A gallant ship that has weathered storms on a thousand seas, but is now safely moored on her native shore, rides securely at anchorage, whatever gales may blow, and cares not for the breakers that dash upon her prow. Just so, you may smile upon all the billows and all the breakers of this world's calamities. Though the sky frown and the gales rise, the anchor of your hope is sure and steadfast and it is fixed within the veil.

And even when death comes, you know that you are in the love of God, for the love of God is shed abroad in your heart. Keep yourself, then, in the love of God, and thus you will have the hope that makes not ashamed, the anchor of the soul, sure and steadfast, that enters within the veil, that is riveted on the golden shore of a blissful eternity.

13

Baptized into Christ

> *Know ye not, that so many of us as were baptized into Jesus Christ were baptized into his death? Therefore we are buried with him by baptism into death: that like as Christ was raised up from the dead by the glory of the Father, even so we also should walk in newness of life* (Rom. 6:3–4).

I LATELY OPENED UP TO YOU the first two verses of this chapter. I showed you that Satan may often tempt those who have come to Christ to continue in sin. He whispers to the soul, 'Continue in sin, that grace may abound.' He says, 'You know the fountain. You can easily go back and wash your fresh sins away. It is so simple and so easy to have another for your righteousness. What matter though you should bring a few more stains upon your garment?'

He says, 'You can never perish. "He that heareth my word, and believeth on him that sent me, hath everlasting life, and shall not come into condemnation; but is passed from death unto life" (*John* 5:24). Continue in sin, then, it will make no difference; you will be saved for all that.'

He says, 'The more sin, the more grace. The more guilty you are, the more will the blood of Christ get glory in cleansing you from all sin. Never was Christ more glorified than in washing out the sin of

Mary Magdalene and the dying thief. Continue in sin, that grace may abound.'

This is Satan's fiery dart. Consider the answer, 'How shall we, that are dead to sin, live any longer therein?' (*Rom.* 6:2).

Note: 1. *This does not mean that believers are insensible to sin.*

Joseph would not consent to be in the same room with his master's wife. David prayed, 'Turn away mine eyes from beholding vanity.' Paul says, 'When I would do good, evil is present with me.' Every believer feels that his heart is like tinder, ready to catch fire at every spark of temptation.

2. *But it does mean that we are dead to the curse of sin.*

In Christ, our Head and Surety, we have already borne the curse of sin, so that we are now brought into the love of God, and He will not let us live in sin any more. 'How shall we, that are dead to sin, live any longer therein?' Let us now consider this argument more fully in the words that follow in verses 3 and 4, 'Know ye not, that so many of us as were baptized into Jesus Christ were baptized into his death? Therefore we are buried with him by baptism into death: that like as Christ was raised up from the dead by the glory of the Father, even so we also should walk in newness of life.'

1. A FALSE INTERPRETATION.

Let me guard against a false interpretation of these words. They have been understood as favouring the idea that baptism is, to every person, believer or unbeliever, always accompanied with regeneration. They have been understood in this way, 'Everyone that is baptized is thereby united to Christ.' The falseness of this interpretation appears plainly in two ways:

Baptized into Christ

i From the Words Themselves.

It is not said, 'So many of us as were baptized *into water* were baptized into Christ', but 'so many of us as were baptized *into Jesus Christ* were baptized into His death'. That is, he is speaking of those whose baptism was not merely external washing, but real and internal, signifying and sealing our union with Christ. In most, I fear their baptism is baptism into water and not into Christ, just as, when an unbeliever eats the bread and wine, it does not mean that he feeds upon the Lord Jesus.

ii. From the Argument.

He argues that everyone that is baptized into Christ will be raised up to walk in newness of life. But this is not the case with those unconverted persons who are baptized and remain unconverted. If baptism were union with Christ, they would be made new creatures; but they are not new creatures, therefore their baptism was not union with Christ. It was only a solemn ordinance of Christ profaned, as in the case of Simon Magus, who was plainly not a renewed creature.

I now hasten to the true and simple interpretation of the words. (O Lord, send out thy light and thy truth: let them lead me; let them bring me unto thy holy hill!)

2. WHAT IS BAPTISM INTO CHRIST?

i. It Is from Christ.

It is not from the hand of any minister but from the hand that was pierced. 'I indeed baptize you with water; but one mightier than I cometh, the latches of whose shoes I am not worthy to unloose: he shall baptize you with the Holy Ghost and with fire' (*Luke* 3:16). Proud, presumptuous men have dared to say that their baptism would regenerate the soul, robbing Christ of His own most free, most gracious and most absolute sovereignty in the gift of the Spirit.

ii. THE SPIRIT IS THE AGENT.

It is not water that can unite the soul to Christ. 'John truly baptized with water; but ye shall be baptized with the Holy Ghost not many days hence' (*Acts* 1:5). 'For by one Spirit are we all baptized into one body' (*1 Cor.* 12:13).

It is the Holy Spirit's baptism, then, that is here spoken of. Poor blind men like well an easy religion. Many like well to think that the water of baptism can regenerate the soul, and thus they rob the Holy Spirit of His own most free, most absolute power in regenerating the dead soul.

iii. IT IS INTO CHRIST.

Baptism with water, however, often leaves the soul disunited to Christ. How many infants are baptized with water, who show plainly by their after lives that they have not been united to Christ? How many grown persons who have been baptized in ripe years are like Simon Magus, whose heart was not right with God? The baptism here spoken of is the internal work of the Spirit, awakening, enlightening, comforting and saving.

Far would I be from speaking lightly of the holy sacrament of baptism, any more than I would of the holy sacrament of the Lord's Supper. Both of them I believe to be signs and seals of saving grace to all worthy receivers. But may God ever keep me from the God-dishonouring error of confounding the work of the Holy Spirit on the heart with the sacrament of water.

Have you been baptized into Christ? You have been baptized into water in His name, but has the dew of the Holy Spirit fallen upon your soul, leading you to cleave to Jesus Christ? Without this brethren, your sacraments are but a lie. Without faith it is impossible to please God (*Heb.* 11:6).

3. ALL TRULY UNITED TO CHRIST ARE UNITED TO HIM IN HIS DEATH AND BURIAL.

To understand this aright, you must look on Christ and all that cleave to Him as one great body of which He is the head and we the members. This is the very way in which God speaks of us in the Bible. 'For as the body is one, and hath many members, and all the members of that one body, being many, are one body, so also is Christ' (*1 Cor.* 12:12). 'Now ye are the body of Christ, and members in particular' (verse 27). Again, God 'gave him to be head over all things to the church, which is his body, the fulness of him that filleth all in all' (*Eph.* 1:22). And Paul speaks of 'the Head, from which all the body by joints and bands having nourishment ministered, and knit together, increaseth with the increase of God' (*Col.* 2:19).

Just as it pleased God to unite us to Adam as members of one body, so that when he sinned we sinned, when he fell we fell, so it has pleased God to unite those who believe to Christ, so that when He obeyed we obeyed, when he died we died, when He was buried we were buried with Him. The moment a poor guilty sinner cleaves to Christ, he is reckoned by Jehovah a member of Christ's body; so that when Christ was nailed to the tree, we were nailed; when the cup of God's wrath was poured out to Him it was poured out to us; when His blood streamed from His wounds it covered us, for we were His members.

This explains the true meaning of Galatians 2:20, 'I am crucified with Christ'; and Colossians 2:20, 'Wherefore if ye be dead with Christ . . .'; and Colossians 3:3, 'Ye are dead.' When paleness spread over the dying frame of Immanuel, it spread over us. When the last drops of blood were oozing from His wounded hands and feet, that was our life blood. When He bowed His head in agony, crying, 'It is finished', that was our head that bowed. It was the curse due to our sins that was finished in that awful hour. And further still, when they laid Him in the rocky sepulchre, pale, cold, motionless, where He continued under the power of death for a time, we were buried with Him.

Let us learn from this how completely believers are freed from the curse of sin. 'He that is dead is freed from sin.' When a malefactor suffers the last punishment of the law, when his dead body is cut down from the gibbet and hurried to the malefactor's grave, the law has no more vengeance to pour out upon him. The law has poured out its whole cup of vengeance. So it was when Christ died. On the cross He was in the hands of justice. But when He rose from the grave the curse was all gone. He left sin behind Him like the grave clothes, or the napkin that was about His head! So free are you from the guilt of sin, believer in Jesus! You have left all your sins in the rocky sepulchre. Sin and you are quits. 'Ye are crucified', 'ye are dead to the law by the body of Christ'.

4. WE ARE RAISED TO WALK IN NEWNESS OF LIFE.

One great object of our being united to Christ in his death is that we should be raised up with Him: 'That like as Christ was raised up from the dead by the glory of the Father, even so we also should walk in newness of life' (*Rom.* 6:4).

How was Christ raised up from the dead?

i. It Was by the Father.

It is true that the resurrection is sometimes described as being in His own power: 'Destroy this temple, and in three days I will raise it up . . . But he spake of the temple of his body' (*John* 2:19–21). 'I have power to lay it down, and I have power to take it again' (*John* 10:18). He was one with the Father, and whatever the Father did the Son did also. But in general the Father is represented as providing the atonement and raising up Jesus. Christ was 'by the right hand of God exalted' (*Acts* 2:33). 'Him hath God exalted with his right hand to be a Prince and a Saviour' (*Acts* 5:31). He raised Him from the dead.

ii. It Was by the Glory of the Father.

This is commonly understood of the glorious power of the Father, but I think the meaning is deeper, and better. God had covenanted with Christ to raise Him up from the grave and, now that the work was accomplished, the truth, justice and love of God were all engaged to raise Him up. Had God not done it He would have dishonoured Himself. His glory was involved in the fulfillment of His Word in raising up Jesus.

iii. God Raises up All That Are United to Jesus.

They are raised to walk in newness of life. To this very end we are baptized into Christ's death and buried with Him, that the very same power which raised up Jesus from the grave may raise us up to walk in newness of life.

Here is sweet, sweet comfort to those who are struggling with lusts. Those of you who are God's children know that your lust is a sleeping hell. Ah, what depths are there. If all the hateful crimes that are now flowing over this earth, making it ripe for the burning, were displayed in a moment, you can say, I have the fountain of all in my own bosom. If all the fiendish lusts and raging passions that tear and ravage the bosoms of the lost spirits in hell were laid naked before you, you know that the same is in your own bosom. How can they be subdued? How can these hungry, hissing serpents be hushed in your bosom? Often you despair of ever reaching a sinless world. Ah, there is one blessed way.

If you are united to Christ, then God engages to make you walk in newness of life. He has pledged His glory that He will do it. His truth and covenant faithfulness, His honour and justice, His holiness and love are all pledged that He will raise you up by the almighty power of His Holy Spirit, that you may walk in newness of life! Greater is He that is for you than all that can be against you. He engages His Word and glory to give a new heart, a new mind, a new life. Be not afraid, only believe.

5. UNBELIEVERS ARE STILL IN THEIR OLD SINS.

Ah! my friends, most of you do not know what newness of life means. You have lived in the same way ever since you were born. You have experienced no saving change. To those who are in Christ, the Bible becomes a new book. It has not become that to you. The Sabbath becomes a new day, but it is not so with you. God's people have a new beauty about them unfelt before, but it is not so with you. They are not of the world, they look beyond it, live above it, hate its sins, despise its pleasures, but it is not so with you. Then hear the explanation – you have never been baptized with the Holy Ghost. You have never been born again, never united to Christ.

Some of you have had a change in your views and opinions, but not a change in your life. You have come to greater knowledge of divine things and of the Bible. You sometimes relish an entertaining sermon. You have come to great head knowledge, great talk, great professions, and yet you are not quite honest, or you sometimes tell a lie, or you sometimes swear, or you are not quite sober, or not quite chaste. You live in the same old sin still. Ah, hear the explanation

– you have never been baptized into the death of Christ! You may have a name to live, but you are dead. You may have a lamp and a wick and a flame, but you have none of the oil of grace. You are going to hell with your Bible in your hand, and the name of Christ upon your tongue. No one on earth may know that you are a hypocrite. Beloved, respected, listened to by men, you may be fast hastening to the regions of the damned, to the place of hypocrites, the lowest place in everlasting hell!

14

Dead to the Law by Christ

Wherefore, my brethren, ye also are become dead to the law by the body of Christ; that ye should be married to another, even to him who is raised from the dead, that we should bring forth fruit unto God (Rom. 7:4).

THIS IS ONE OF THE MOST WONDERFUL PASSAGES in the Word of God. It opens to us the way of pardon and of holiness in a remarkable manner. May it be blessed to the conversion of many of you!

1. SINNERS ARE BY NATURE MARRIED TO THE LAW.

The is implied by the pasage. It is the state in which we are born. In this state we remain as long as we are strangers to Christ. Just as a wife is under certain obligations to her husband – bound to her husband as long as he liveth – so a sinner is under certain obligations to the law of God. Every man is born under the law in two ways:

i. UNDER ITS DEMANDS.

The law of God is written on the conscience and written in the Bible. Every man may read its demands there.

Dead to the Law by Christ

ii. Under Its Curses.

Every man is born a sinner, under the guilt of Adam's sin, and with the seeds of all depravity lodged in his bosom. He is therefore under the curse of the law. And every day he is more and more brought under these curses.

Every unconverted man is, in this way, under a yoke of bondage. He cannot loose himself from it. Many a sinner would like to shake off the yoke of the law, but he cannot do it. The woman is bound to her husband so long as he liveth, and the sinner is bound to the law as long as it liveth.

Many sinners try to forget the law under which they lie. They forget its demands. They spend their substance in riotous living, as if there were no law upon them. They break the Sabbath as if God had never said, 'Remember the Sabbath day.'

They forget its curses too, and so they are happy and smiling and joyful in their sins. But for all that they have not divorced the law. A wife that has a bad husband may try and forget that she has a husband and, while he is away from home, may entertain herself with fancies of her happy state. But when her husband comes home, her dream vanishes. And so sinners may forget that they are under the law. But when the law comes home they will soon feel that all its demands and all its curses are lying upon them.

So there is a day coming when the law will come upon you, and you will discover that you are a lost soul. 'For I was alive without the law once: but when the commandment came, sin revived, and I died' (*Rom.* 7:9).

2. THE MARRIAGE TO THE LAW CAN BE DISSOLVED.

Marriage in ordinary cases is dissolved only by the death of either party. If the husband die, or the wife die, the marriage is dissolved

(*Rom.* 7:2–3). When husband and wife join hands in marriage, they promise to have and to hold, for better or worse, for richer for poorer, till death do them part. Here it is implied that only death should dissolve their marriage. So it is with a sinner and the law of God. Nothing but the death of the law or the death of the sinner can dissolve the union. The law lays hold of the sinner, and will not let him go till death part them.

If the law of God would die, then the sinner might go free. But the law cannot die. It is from everlasting to everlasting. It cannot die unless the living God can die. It was graven from all eternity on the heart of God, and there it shines through all the eternity that is to come. The law cannot die.

Or if the sinner were to die, then he would go free. But ah, the death the law demands of the sinner, is death eternal, not the death of the body only, but of the soul also, a death which he will be always dying. When the law takes hold of a sinner it kills and kills for ever.

Only one remedy remains. One must die for us! 'God so loved the world, that he gave his only begotten Son.' The Son of God took on him our nature: 'God sent forth his Son, made of a woman, made under the law, to redeem them that were under the law' (*Gal.* 4:4–5). Of His own free will He came into our place. He obeyed all the demands of the law with a divine perfectness. He suffered all the infinite curses of the law till infinite justice said, 'It is enough!' And now all that believe are 'dead to the law by the body of Christ'.

Ah, brethren, has the Spirit of God been poured out upon you, uniting you to a crucified Immanuel? Have you consented that the only begotten Son of God be your Surety? Then you are 'dead to the law by the body of Christ'. You can say, 'I am crucified with Christ.' The law has no more any hold upon you to condemn you. If the law lays its demands upon you saying, 'Obey this, in order to be just with God', you can answer, 'Christ is to me the end of the law for righteousness. It was said that He would magnify the law and make it honourable (Isa. 42:21), and God is well pleased with me for His righteousness' sake.'

If the law hurls its curses at you saying, 'Cursed art thou for not continuing in all things that are written in the law', you can answer, 'Christ hath redeemed me from the curse of the law, being made a curse for me. I was once exposed to its fiery darts but now through the body of Christ I am dead to the law.' This is the peace and liberty of the gospel. 'Stand fast therefore, in that liberty wherewith Christ hath made us free' (Gal. 5:1).

3. THE SECOND MARRIAGE OF THE SOUL IS TO A RISEN SAVIOUR.

A second marriage is lawful only after the death of the first husband (Rom. 7:3). So it is with the soul and Christ. As long as a sinner is under the curse of the law, he cannot be united to the living Saviour, he can bear no fruit to God. An unjustified soul is evermore an unholy soul. But whenever the soul is brought by the Spirit to cleave to Christ crucified, and so is parted from the law by the death of Christ, then the soul is united to the Lord Jesus, the risen Saviour.

Here is one of the most amazing declarations in the whole Bible, that a worm of the dust should be united to Him who was raised from the dead and who sits at the right hand of God. It is sweet to be united to a glorified Jesus, to Christ on the cross, and Christ on the throne. This is the promise made, 'For thy Maker is thine husband; the LORD of hosts is his name' (Isa. 54:5). Now His yoke is easy, and His burden is light.

i. THE AMAZING SOVEREIGNTY IMPLIED IN THIS RELATION.

The husband chooses whom he will. So it is in this lofty union. The Son of God chose His own bride before the world was. But whom did He choose? Not the holy angels, although they were His own creatures, without any stain, in some measure worthy to be loved. Neither did He choose devils, fallen angels, whom He might justly have redeemed and united to Himself to all eternity. Neither did He choose all men, though all were lost, all under His curse; but some, a little flock, many of them the chief of sinners. Ah! here is the wonder of angels and of the redeemed through all eternity, why He ever came to us. 'There are threescore queens, and fourscore concubines, and virgins without number. My dove, my undefiled is but one' (*Song of Sol.* 6:8). 'As the lily among thorns, so is my love among the daughters' (*Song of Sol.* 2:2).

Ah, poor sinners that do not come to be the bride of Jesus, how little you know the amazing happiness of being loved for no good in us, but only to be made monuments of what God can do in saving a wretched sinner!

ii. The Love That Is in This Relationship.

Marriage implies love, and such a marriage as this implies strong, heavenly love. This love began in eternity; or rather, it had no beginning.

Through all the sin and misery of the Fall, through all the original and actual depravity of men, the only begotten Son of God foresaw His own and loved them, not for any beauty He could see in them, or any beauty that was to be wrought in them, but only out of sheer free grace!

15

I Am Persuaded

For I am persuaded, that neither death, nor life, nor angels, nor principalities, nor powers, nor things present, nor things to come, nor height, nor depth, nor any other creature, shall be able to separate us from the love of God, which is in Christ Jesus our Lord (Rom. 8:38–39).

THE COMFORTING AND INVIGORATING DOCTRINE of this precious passage is that a soul in Christ cannot be separated from the love of God. But we must observe:

1. ALL CHRISTLESS PERSONS ARE BY NATURE OUTSIDE OF THE LOVE OF GOD SPOKEN OF.

God has no love of complacency towards unconverted souls. He sees nothing amiable in them, He sees nothing for which He can love them. 'What is man that he should be clean, and he that is born of a woman that he should be righteous? Behold he putteth no trust in his saints; yea, the heavens are not clean in his sight! How much more abominable and filthy is man who drinketh iniquity like water?' 'The righteous God loveth righteousness.' It is His very nature to do so; He cannot but love it wherever He sees it. But there is no righteousness in Christless persons; there is not so much as one clean white spot in all their garments. By nature, we are all 'as an unclean thing', and 'all our righteousnesses are as filthy rags'.

Therefore, it is impossible God can love the unconverted with the love of complacency. He must change His nature and become another God before He can cherish the least spark of esteem for an unconverted soul. But it may be objected, Did not God so love the world that He gave His only begotten Son, and did not Christ show great tenderness to sinners when he was on earth? Yes! we readily admit it, for it is quite true that God loves Christless persons with a love of infinite pity. If you saw a man lying wounded, bleeding and dying, your heart would flow out with compassion all at once. The benevolence of your nature being appealed to, you would love him with the love of pity. But if you found out that he was a wicked, abandoned man, you could not esteem him; your love of pity would continue; yea, it would be greater than before, but you could not have any love of esteem for him.

Just so is it with God. He saw the whole world lying in wickedness, and every imagination of man's heart only evil continually; and His gracious heart flowed out in pity towards the children of men: 'For God so loved the world that He gave His only begotten Son.' 'He is not willing that any should perish.' God 'will have all men to be saved, and to come unto the knowledge of the truth.' 'I have no pleasure', says He, 'in the death of the wicked, but that the wicked turn from his way and live.' Ah!, see what a large heart of pity God had! It embraced 'all men'. It embraced 'the whole world', and therefore He provided an infinite and all-sufficient ransom to which all are invited, to which all may come. Jesus, as the expounder of the Father's heart, says, 'Come unto Me all ye that labour and are heavy laden, and I will give you rest.'

But does God *esteem* Christless souls? Ah, no! God would require to change His essential nature, and become wicked before He could

I Am Persuaded

love unconverted, Christless men with a love of esteem. If He were a wicked God, then He could love wicked men. But so long as He is 'of purer eyes than to behold evil' (*Hab*. 1:13), He cannot have a spark of esteem for sinners, however much they may esteem themselves, or be esteemed by their fellow-sinners in the world.

God not only does not see anything to love, but He sees much to hate in Christless persons. In the seventh Psalm it is written, 'God is angry with the wicked every day.' And again, in the eleventh Psalm, it is written, 'The wicked, and him that loveth violence, his soul hateth.' And again, in Psalm 34, 'The face of the LORD is against them that do evil.' 'He that believeth not the Son shall not see life; but the wrath of God abideth on him.' 'Cursed is every one that continueth not in all things which are written in the book of the law to do them.' 'Because of these things cometh the wrath of God upon the children of disobedience.'

It is a part of the nature of God to love holiness, and to hate wickedness wherever He sees it. In whatever heart He discovers it, He cannot but hate it. God must cease to be God, before He ceases to hate the wickedness of the wicked.

But an objector may say, 'If God hates Christless persons on account of their sins, then He can have no pity for them.' But why not? He is infinitely just, but He is infinite in compassion too. He must cease to be God before He can cease to be compassionate. 'He delighteth in mercy.' Yea, the more He is angry with a soul, the more does He pity that soul, for its case is all the more deplorable in that it has rendered itself obnoxious to His holy displeasure. When Christ was on earth it is said, 'He looked round with anger' on some sinners, 'being grieved at the hardness of their hearts'. Here is the very thing the objector says cannot be. Here is *anger* and *pity* in the same breast. The lightning of just anger, and the tear of compassion were in His eye at the same moment.

This is the very 'image of the invisible God'. Again, when He came near and beheld the city (Jerusalem), He wept over it, and yet said that the things which belonged to her peace were hid from her eyes. Here the Saviour gave it over to perdition with tears in His eyes and the words of regret upon His lips. This was infinite compassion, and yet infinite indignation. Christ here is 'the express image of God's person'. 'In Him dwelleth all the fullness of the Godhead bodily.' God in human nature weeps at the very time He pronounces the holy sentence of wrath.

Let me here speak affectionately and faithfully to all Christless persons. I would implore you from this to learn exactly where you stand with regard to God. Let it sink deep into your ears and hearts that He has no love of esteem for you. He never had, and He never will have, until He sees you in Christ. You see many things in yourselves that you admire, and you foolishly think that God will also admire them.

Perhaps you pray a little in secret, and read the Word. Perhaps you feel some glowing of affection in hearing the preaching of the gospel, and you think all the time that God will look on that and approve it, and, as a necessary consequence, esteem you on account of it. But learn here that God sees nothing good in it, nothing worthy of his love. If you are out of Christ, you are all loathsome in the sight of the holy God, and even your very 'righteousnesses are as filthy rags'.

Perhaps you are amiable, good-natured, kind, hospitable. Your friends love and admire you, and you think God must also admire you. But learn plainly that God sees nothing to admire in you. He knows you are, 'wretched, and miserable, and poor, and blind, and naked'. You do none of all your fancied meritorious deeds out of regard for Him, and nothing will be regarded by Him with complacency, unless done with an eye to His glory. And, being out

I Am Persuaded

of His love, you are under His wrath. There is no other alternative. If you are out of His love, you must be under His wrath. You are the creature of His hand, and, as a moral agent, God cannot be indifferent to you or to your actions. God is angry with you every day.

The wrath of God abides upon you at all times! If you go on a journey, the wrath of God hangs over you all the way! If you go out to work, the wrath of God is hanging round your neck. If you sit down to your daily meals, the wrath of God is close by you! If you sleep, it rests over you all the night long! At any moment it may crush you into hell.

The time is uncertain, but the thing is sure! Whenever God cuts the thread of life, the wrath that is upon you will do its office. Oh! dear souls, how can you remain in this fearful and perilous condition? Be persuaded now to believe in Jesus, and thereby escape the 'wrath to come'. Your case is a very melancholy one, but it is not hopeless. God has infinite pity for you. His pity is as infinite as his wrath. He has no pleasure in your dying. He would rather that you would turn and live. He has provided blood enough in Christ to blot out all your sins; and raiment enough to cover your nakedness.

The more He is angry with you on account of your sinfulness, the more does He pity you. Christ strives most after the salvation of *Jerusalem sinners*. The more you have provoked Him, the more ready He is to cover you under His wings. Turn, sinner, turn! God will not always wait. He has said, 'My Spirit shall not always strive with man.' Give glory to the Lord your God, before He cause darkness, and before your feet stumble upon the dark mountains, and when ye look for light he turn it into the shadow of death, and make it gross darkness.

Then let us learn, secondly:

2. ALL WHO ARE IN CHRIST ARE IN THE LOVE OF GOD.

When any sinner is made willing to close with Jesus Christ as a Surety, then it is a righteous thing with God to love that soul with the love of esteem. He sees nothing now to hate in that soul. 'He hath not beheld iniquity in Jacob, neither hath he seen perverseness in Israel' (*Num.* 23:21). When any sinner is persuaded to embrace the Lord Jesus as his Surety, the sufferings of Christ are counted his, and so in Him he has suffered for all his sins already.

When the sinner stood before God in himself, God could not but loathe him; but when the sinner stands before God, not in himself, but in Christ, the Son of God, then God sees no iniquity in him; his sins have been carried away into 'a land of forgetfulness', and 'cast into the depths of the sea'. They were once 'like scarlet', they are now, 'white as snow'; and the sinner begins to sing, 'O LORD, I will praise thee: though thou wast angry with me, thine anger is turned away and thou comfortedst me' (*Isa.* 12:1). 'As far as the east is from the west, so far hath he removed our transgressions from us' (*Psa.* 103:12).

Anxious sinner, close quickly with Christ. Come out of darkness into 'marvellous light'. God is angry with you every day, so long as you remain out of Christ; but His anger will be all turned away the moment you consent to be found in the Lord Jesus. God sees something to love in the soul that is in Christ.

When a sinner accepts of Christ as his Surety, he accepts not only of His sufferings but of His obedience too, His infinitely pure and lovely obedience. This is all put upon the believing sinner. This is the 'clothing of wrought gold', this is, 'the raiment of needle-work.' Where God sees that upon the soul of the sinner, He cannot but love him with a love of infinite esteem and divine complacency. 'This is my Beloved Son,' He says, 'in whom I am well pleased.' Just as the sweet-smelling garments of Esau, when put upon Jacob, drew out all the affection of the heart of Isaac, and he said, 'The smell of my son's garments is like the smell of a field which the LORD hath blessed'; so do the sweet-smelling garments of Christ – for 'all his garments smell of myrrh, and aloes, and cassia' – draw out the infinite affection of the heart of God toward the sinner who is 'accepted in the Beloved'.

Then comes to pass the saying which is written, 'He will rest in his love, he will joy over thee with singing' (*Zeph.* 3:17); and again, 'The Father himself loveth you' (*John* 16:27). Anxious sinner, close with the Lord Jesus and thou shalt be in the love of God. There is nothing happier for the soul than to be loved. To be loved even by an affectionate dog is pleasant. To be loved by a little child is sweeter. To be loved by wise and good men, that is sweeter still. But oh! to be loved with the infinite heart of God, that is best of all. Oh, to feel that 'God is love'! Sinner, you have seen the midday sun pouring its rays into the bosom of a calm sea, an unceasing shower of golden rays, till the sea becomes a sheet of living gold, till its darkest caves are illumined, and every gem sparkling with heaven's light. Such is the love of God to the soul of a sinner in Christ, an unceasing, infinite shower of love! Oh! taste and see that the Lord is gracious. Only close with Christ and you will cry out, 'God is love!'

3. GOD IS LOVE, AND NOTHING CAN SEPARATE THE SOUL IN CHRIST FROM THE LOVE OF GOD.

As we say, 'Once Christ's, aye Christ's'. Whom He loves, He loves unto the end. None can ever be separated from the love of God who once come into it. There is no quality more precious than permanence. Most of the joys in this world do not last. The flowering of the apple tree is pleasant and lovely when, in early summer, it comes out with its ten thousand blushing promises; but its blossoms soon fade, are separated, and fall off the tree. The gourd of Jonah was pleasant while it lasted, but he was soon separated from it. It came up in a night, and perished in a night.

The sweetest friends are united only to be separated. One may almost see the shroud beneath the wedding garment. The love of the creature is not, 'an enduring substance'. Sometimes the kindest change and cease to love us, or, at the longest, they die and we are separated. But oh, how different is the love of God! It is all enduring good. It is a flame that is never extinguished, the 'good part' that cannot be taken away. 'For I am persuaded that neither death, nor life, nor angels, nor principalities, nor powers, nor things present, nor things to come, nor height, nor depth, nor any other creature shall be able to separate us from the love of God, which is in Christ Jesus our Lord' (*Rom.* 8:38–39). This sublime chapter, having opened with a strong declaration of 'no condemnation' *in* Christ Jesus, it is meet that it should close with a declaration equally strong of 'no separation' *from* Christ Jesus. It is a delightful and animating theme with which the chapter terminates. The last object it presents to the eye is JESUS. The last accents that linger on the ear concern the love of JESUS.

It is of great moment that we have a clear apprehension of the apostle's leading idea in these concluding verses. He refers to a love from which there is no separation. Of whose love does he speak? The believer's love to Christ? On the contrary, it is Christ's love to the believer. And this view makes all the difference in its influence upon our minds. What true satisfaction and real consolation, or, at least, how small its measure, can the believer derive from a contemplation of his love to Christ. It is Christ's love to him that is the source of his comfort.

To whom did Paul originally address this letter? To the saints of the early and suffering age of the Christian church. And this truth, Christ's love to his people, would be just the truth calculated to

I Am Persuaded

comfort, and strengthen, and animate them. Let the apostle allure their minds from a contemplation of their love to Christ to a contemplation of Christ's love to them, assuring them upon the strongest grounds that whatever sufferings they should endure, or by whatever temptations they should be assailed, nothing should prevail to sever them from their interest in the reality, sympathy and constancy of that love, and he has at once brought them to the most perfect repose. The affection, then, of which the apostle speaks, is the love of God which is in Christ Jesus.

The love of Christ! Such is our precious theme! Can we ever be weary of it? Its greatness, can we ever know? Its plenitude, can we fully contain? Never. Its depths cannot be fathomed, its dimensions cannot be measured. It passeth knowledge. All that Jesus did for His church was but the unfolding and expression of His love. Travelling to Bethlehem I see love incarnate. Tracking His steps as He went about doing good, I see love labouring. Visiting the house of Bethany, I see love sympathizing. Standing by the grave of Lazarus, I see love weeping. Entering the gloomy precincts of Gethsemane, I see love sorrowing. Passing on to Calvary, I see love suffering, and bleeding, and expiring. The whole scene of His life is but an unfolding of the deep, and awful, and precious mystery of redeeming love.

The love of the Father! Such, too, is our theme and it is proper that with this truth the chapter should close. 'The love of God which is in Christ Jesus our Lord.' The love of the Father is seen in giving us Christ, in choosing us in Christ, and in blessing us in Him with all spiritual blessings. Indeed, the love of the Father is the fountain of all covenant- and redemption-mercy to the Church. It is that 'river, the streams whereof shall make glad the city of God'.

How anxious Jesus was to vindicate the love of the Father from all the suspicions and fears of His disciples! 'I say not unto you that

I will pray the Father for you, for the Father himself loveth you.' 'God so loved the world that He gave His only-begotten Son.' To this love we must trace all the blessings which flow to us through the channel of the cross. It is the love of God, exhibited, manifested, and seen in Christ Jesus. Christ is not the originator but the gift of this love; not the cause, but the exponent of it. If we could only see a perfect equality between the Father's love and the Son's love! Then we should be led to trace all His sweet mercies, and all His providential dealings, however trying, painful, and mysterious, to the heart of God; thus resolving all into that from whence all alike flow, everlasting and unchangeable love.

Now it is from this love that there is *no separation*. 'Who shall separate us from the love of Christ?' The apostle had challenged accusation from every foe, and condemnation from every quarter; but no accuser rose, and no condemnation was pronounced. Standing on the broad basis of Christ's finished work, and of God's full justification, his head was now lifted up in triumph above all his enemies round about. But it is possible that though in the believer's heart there is no fear of *impeachment*, there yet may exist the latent one of *separation*. The aggregate dealings of God with His church, and His individual dealings with his saints, may at times present the appearance of alienated affection, or a lessened sympathy.

The age in which this epistle was penned, was fruitful of suffering to the church of God. And if any period, or any circumstances of her history threatened a severance of the bond which united her to Christ, that was the period, and those were the circumstances. But, with a confidence based upon the glorious truth on which he had been descanting, the security of the church of God in Christ, and with a persuasion inspired by the closer realization of the glory about to burst upon her view, and with the most dauntless courage,

I Am Persuaded

he exclaims, 'I am persuaded that neither death, nor life, nor angels, nor principalities, nor powers, nor things present, nor things to come, nor height, nor death, nor any other creature, shall be able to separate us from the love of God, which is in Christ Jesus our Lord.' Let us briefly glance at each of these things which may threaten, but which cannot succeed in separating us from the love of God, and from our union with Christ.

Death cannot. Death separates 'very friends'. Death separates husband and wife, soul and body. Death separates those who, for a lifetime, have shared one another's thoughts and cares. It takes us away from their love; we do not feel that the dead love us; we do not meet with their smile. But death cannot separate us from the love of God; it only brings us to the full enjoyment of it. Are you in Christ? Do not fear to die, for death will only bring you into the presence of your God, and you shall be a pillar in the house of your God, and go no more out. Death cannot separate us from the love of God!

Life cannot. I remember reading of one of Brainerd's converts, who, when brought to a full sense of the love of God, cried out, 'Oh, blessed Lord, take me away; do let me die, and go to Jesus Christ. I am afraid if I live I shall sin again.' She feared that *life* would separate her from the love of God. But no, life cannot, 'neither death, nor life'. The hope of life is meant. The apostle wrote, as we have remarked, in a peculiarly suffering era of the church, an age of fiery persecution for the gospel's sake. Under these circumstances, life was not infrequently offered on condition of renouncing the gospel and denying the Saviour. This was a strong temptation to apostasy.

When, in suffering times, in full view of the rack, the cross or the stake, life, precious life, with all its sweet attraction and fond ties, was offered, and when a simple renunciation of the cross, and a single embrace of the crucifix, would purchase it back – to some who were weak in faith, such a temptation might be well-nigh irresistible. But it shall not succeed in separating the suffering Christian from the love of Christ.

Nor shall anything connected with life, its trials, its vicissitudes, or its temptations, sever us from God's affection. Thus both life and death shall but confirm us in the assurance of our inalienable interest in the love of God, 'For whether we live, we live unto the Lord; and whether we die, we die unto the Lord: whether we live therefore, or die, we are the Lord's.' Are you in Christ? Do not fear to live. The love of God will still be poured into your heart, and the Spirit of God will be given you. 'I pray not that thou shouldest take them out of the world, but that thou shouldest keep them from the evil.' Neither death, nor life, can separate us from the love of God.

Angels cannot. Good angels cannot, even if they would. But they are all for us. When a soul is joined to Christ, 'there is joy in heaven among the angels of God'; they rejoice that another poor sinner is brought into the love of God, and they would not have us separated. But even if they were against us, our righteousness is above their reach, for the Lord of angels is 'the Lord our Righteousness'. Evil angels cannot. The devil has great power, but he cannot separate a branch of Christ from the love of God. You remember how he tried to separate Peter, and Job, and failed. Christ has overcome. If he could cast Christ down from the right hand of God, then he would separate us from the love of God; but as long as Christ is there we are safe. Are you in Christ? 'Resist the devil and he will flee from you.' He and all his legions cannot separate you from 'the love of God, which is in Christ Jesus our Lord'.

Principalities and powers cannot. Evil spirits are here meant; but also included are, not demons merely, but all evil agencies, men of the world, human governments, civil power, all that is hostile to the spiritual interests of Christ's truth and kingdom. Such are often

I Am Persuaded

found either powerful engines of spiritual persecutions themselves, or else, by indifference or connivance, sympathizing with and abetting the high-handed persecutor. But no human or superhuman power shall prevail to impair the interest of God's saints in his love. Have they in a single instance done so? Has God ever forsaken his people when the Evil Spirit has stirred up ungodly men and despotic governments to rob them of their rights, to fetter their consciences, to imprison or to slay their persons? No, never!

Often such powers have torn the believer from the love of father, and mother, and kindred (*Matt.* 10:21–22), but they cannot separate us from God, and from his love to us in Christ Jesus. Dear friend, are you in Christ? Oh, make sure, for there may be suffering days yet wherein you will be tried. Be rooted and grounded in Him, and the blasts of persecution will only make the roots of your faith take firmer hold. God will love us 'in the fires'. I believe the love of God has often taken away the pains of martyrdom.

Things present cannot. Of things present to the Christians of the apostolic age, some were good and some were evil; some joyous, others sorrowful; just as it is now among ourselves. And both prosperity and adversity are calculated to draw away the soul from God, but they shall never succeed. Riches, cares, business, houses, lands, cannot separate us from the love of God. Ah, these are more dangerous than even persecutions! But are you united to Christ? They shall not prevail, they cannot come between you and God, so as to separate you from His love. Only abide in Christ, and the love of God shall abide in your soul. These things cannot separate you. Indwelling sin, temporary trials, occasional temptations, the momentary suspensions of God's realized love, none of these, or any other thing present, shall separate us from Christ.

Things to come cannot. What lies before us? Who can tell what is 'to come'? Shakings among the nations and in the church, sickness, bereavement, temptation, the valley of the shadow of death, all these are things to come. But in Christ we are safe for ever. None of these things shall ever be able to separate those in Christ from the love of God.

No, 'nor height, nor depth, nor any other creature, shall be able to separate us from the love of God, which is in Christ Jesus our Lord'. Amen.

16

On Not Loving Christ[1]

If any man love not the Lord Jesus Christ, let him be Anathema Maranatha (1 Cor. 16:22).

THAT WAS A SWEET COMMAND of the Saviour, 'Bless them that curse you, do good to them that hate you, and pray for them which despitefully use you, and persecute you' (*Matt.* 5:44). And it is sweetly repeated by the Apostle Paul, 'Bless them which persecute you: bless and curse not' (*Rom.* 12:14).

It is not the part, then, of any Christian man or any Christian minister to curse. Ah no! We are, or should be, of a different spirit. How, then, does Paul here declare such a dreadful curse?

The answer is that these are the words of God and not of Paul, declaring soberly what the end will be of them that obey not the gospel. 'If any man love not the Lord Jesus Christ, let him be Anathema Maranatha.'

The doctrine which is to be found in these words, therefore, is this: All that love not the Lord Jesus Christ shall be cursed by the Lord at His coming.

---

[1] Preached in St Peter's, Dundee, 4 March 1838.

I wish to speak first of the marks of those who love not the Lord Jesus; then to show the greatness of their sin; and thirdly to show the dreadful nature of their punishment.

1. WHO ARE THOSE THAT LOVE NOT THE LORD JESUS CHRIST?

i. Those Who Feel No Need of a Saviour.

There are many in the world who say, 'Peace, peace', when there is no peace. Many who say, 'I am rich, and increased in goods, and in need of nothing', but they know not that they are wretched and miserable and poor and blind and naked. This is a sure mark that they love not the Lord Jesus Christ. A rich man has no love for alms; a whole man has no love for medicine; and an unawakened soul has no love for Christ. Oh! it is sad to see how those who have most need of Christ yet care least for Him.

The people in this Parish that need Christ most are those who never come to the house of God to hear His Name. The people in this congregation that need Him most are those of you who never attend to what we preach, who care for none of these things. Do you feel no need of the Saviour whom we preach? Are you saying in your heart, 'I thank God I am not the wicked person he takes me for'? Ah, then, this is a sure mark you care not for the Lord Jesus.

ii. Those Who Do Not Keep Christ's Sayings.

If you love any person, you will keep their sayings. 'If a man love me, he will keep my sayings.' Now there are many in the world who do not keep the sayings of Christ. They are not like David, 'I have hid thy Word in my heart.' They are not like Mary, 'Mary laid up all these sayings in her heart.' Many people have no memory for the words of Christ, they do not lock them up in their inmost heart.

On Not Loving Christ

This is a sure mark that they love not the Lord Jesus. How is it with you? Do you treasure up the sayings of great wits and storytellers, and the sayings of travellers and romancers, and yet have you no storehouse in your heart for the sayings of Christ? Then this is a sure mark you love not the Lord Jesus.

iii. THOSE WHO DO NOT LOVE TO GROW IN KNOWLEDGE OF HIM.

If you love anything, you love to know more of it, and to possess more of it. If a man loved the pearls at the bottom of the sea, he would always be diving for more, seeking for richer and goodlier pearls. If a man loved the gold of Peru, he would always be digging to bring up more of it. If a man love Christ, he will be always diving into the ocean of His love and digging into the mine of His heavenly gold. How many do not seek to grow in the knowledge of Christ? They are not anxious for more, they do not come to the house of God to gain more. They come to the wells, but not to draw water. This is a sure mark that they love not the Lord Jesus. Test yourself by this, if you are contented with what you know of Christ, then you have never seen Him, neither known Him. If you are not seeking, praying, pressing for more of Christ, then you are one of those who love not the Lord Jesus.

iv. THOSE WHO DO NOT MOURN HIM ABSENT.

Many do not care whether they hear of Christ or no. Many can be happy all the day long, though they have had no sight of the Saviour, no word of love from Him. This is a sure mark that they love not the Lord Jesus. How different it was with her in the Song of Solomon, 'I will rise now, and go about the city in the streets, and in the broad ways I will seek him whom my soul loveth: I sought him, but I found him not.' 'I charge you, O daughters of Jerusalem, if ye find my beloved, that ye tell him, that I am sick of love.' So it was with Mary. She stood at the sepulchre weeping, and said, 'They have taken away my Lord, and I know not where they have laid him.' Dear children of God, if you mourn an absent Christ, do not be cast down, this is a sure mark that you love Him. You would not mourn if you did not love. But ah! How many are there of you to whom this language of mourning is all Greek and Hebrew. You know it not: though Christ be away, you care not. Ah! how plain that you love not the Lord Jesus Christ!

v. Those Who Do Not Keep His Commandments.

'If ye love me, keep my commandments.' Wherever there is love there will be obedience. A child that loves its parents obeys them. Christ loved His Father with an infinite love; therefore said He, 'I do always those things that please him; my meat is to do the will of him that sent me, and to finish His work.' But men do not obey Christ, this is the surest of all marks that they do not love Him.

What a sweet, lovely paradise this place would be if all in it did strive together to obey Christ's commandments! It would be like a pleasant garden by the waterside, filled with the fragrant flowers wafting sweet odours and filled with fruit bearing trees, laden with golden fruit. The smell of it would be like a field which the Lord had blessed.

But oh! what mean these oaths and curses that pollute so many dwellings, when Christ says, Swear not at all! What mean these horrid excesses in drinking which keep so many families in beggary and away from the house of God, when Christ says, 'Take heed lest at any time your hearts be over charged with drunkenness'? What mean these outbreaks of hideous wantonness from which the sun might hide his face, when Christ forbids the look of lust? What mean these long prayers and outward show of religion, when there is nothing within but dead men's bones and all uncleanness? Ah!

Christ is not obeyed. Christ is not loved. Search your heart. If you obey Him not, you love Him not!

vi. THOSE WHO DO NOT LOVE HIS APPEARING.

'Henceforth there is laid up for me a crown of righteousness.' If you love a person who is on a far journey, you long for their return. Christ is on a far journey. All that love Him, love His appearing. How many of you would hate His appearing? How many of you would grow pale? Your knees would knock together if the cry was made, 'Behold! The Bridegroom cometh!' This is a sure mark that you love not the Lord Jesus Christ.

2. THE GREATNESS OF THIS SIN.

i. IT IS SELF-MURDER.

In one sense, every sin may be regarded as self-murder, because the end of these things is death, 'The wages of sin is death.' And Christ speaks in the prophet, 'O Israel, thou hast destroyed thyself; but in me is thine help.' Every sin that a man commits it is just bringing another drop of eternal death upon his head. It is just preparing another dagger to stab his soul throughout eternity.

But ah! much more is the sin of refusing Christ's self-murder, because it is casting away the only hope of salvation. 'How shall we escape if we neglect so great salvation?' If a man be dying of hunger and bread be set down beside him, but he refuses to eat and dies, you say that man has murdered himself. If a man be drowning and a rope be thrown him, but he throws it from him and sinks, you say, The man has destroyed himself. Ah! just so it is with those of you who love not the Lord Jesus. He is the bread of life to perishing sinners. He is the rope of salvation to drowning souls. But if you will not cleave to Him and love Him, your blood be upon your own head. You are the murderer of your own soul. But oh! if it be a dreadful crime to draw the life blood from your own veins, to take away the life that God gave; if it be a crime so great that nature shrinks back from it, that most are afraid to name it, and the body of suicide is in some countries denied Christian burial, ah! what words can utter the dark and dreadful crime of being the murderer of your own soul. Stand forth, thou that lovest not the Lord Jesus, for thou art the man!

ii. It Is the Basest Ingratitude.

When you read of Jesus saying to the Jews, 'O Jerusalem, Jerusalem . . .'; or when you see Him standing on the Mount of Olives and beholding the city and weeping over it, and not over it only, but over the unbelief of the Jews up to this day (for His eye looked on Jerusalem for ages to come), you cannot but feel that it was the basest ingratitude in them not to receive and love such a Saviour. Did He love them so tenderly, did He so often wish to gather them? Did He pour out His divine tears over them? Ah! surely there was a devilish hardness in hearts that would not be melted by the tears of the Son of God.

I come then to ask how is it with you? 'What things were written aforetime, were written for our learning.' Jesus is the same yesterday, today, and for ever. He does not weep in heaven, but He has the same heart. He would often have gathered every one of you. He is grieved that you do not own the day of your visitation. The same ocean of compassion rises in His bosom toward you. The same infinite longings after your salvation are breathed from His lips. Oh! that 'you would hearken to my commandments, for then would your peace be like a river', and do you still refuse Him? Still prefer your vile lusts to the pardon and holiness He brings? Ah! then here is the same black ingratitude. You are the same as Jerusalem, 'You will

On Not Loving Christ

not come to me that you might have life.' You love not the Lord Jesus.

iii. It Is the Highest Enmity against God.

The natural state of every mind is hatred of God. No unconverted man believes it, but the Bible declares it, 'The carnal mind is enmity against God.' In nothing more is this enmity seen than in hatred to Christ. 'Have I been so long time with you and hast thou not known me Philip? He that hath seen me hath seen the Father.' And soon after He adds, 'He that hateth me hateth my Father also.' Unawakened persons among you hate to hear of Christ because He is the gift of God, He is God manifest in the flesh.

You say, Tell us of heaven or of hell, of angels and of devils, but do not tell us of Christ. Awakened persons among you hate to yield to Christ. You will go naturally to every other refuge, the refuges of lies. You go naturally to every cistern, but never to the Fountain. You go from mountain to hill, seeking rest, and finding none. Nothing but the work of grace on your heart will persuade you to flee to Christ. Why is this? It is because you hate God. You do not like to give God all the glory. Ah! proud souls, you know not the blackness of this sin of not loving Christ. It is making God a liar. It is trying to cast God down from His throne. It is the highest sin of which any soul can be capable.

A word to you who are decent moral men: You say, 'I thank God I am not as other men are.' Now this may be all true, but Jesus says, 'Lovest thou me?' Hast thou any heart-drawings after Christ and relish for His name? Any sense of His fitness to thy case? Any hungering and thirsting after Christ? Any mourning for His absence? Any burning joy in His presence? Any delight in obeying Him? Any love for His brethren? Ah! if you have no love for Christ, you are but a blind Pharisee. Not to love Christ, that is a far worse sin than murder, theft, adultery. It is the murder of thine own soul. It is crucifying the Son of God afresh. It is trampling God under thy feet. For all your goodness, you shall be cursed of the Lord at His coming.

3. THE GREATNESS OF THE PUNISHMENT.

'Let him be Anathema Maranatha.' The literal meaning is, 'Let him be a curse; the Lord comes.' Or, 'Let him be accursed at the coming of the Lord.' Alas, this is a most solemn text.

i. It Will Be a Curse from the Lips of the Saviour.

It is not the curse of men that will light upon the soul in that day. If it was, you might say, 'Let man curse, but bless thou.' Ah! who would care for the cursers of all the sons of Adam, worms of the dust? If only Christ stood up to bless us. His blessing would outweigh all their cursing. But He will not.

ii. It Is Not the Curse of Devils.

If it were only that, they could not much hurt us. The furious spirits of hell have often raged against Christ's people, but they never can prevail. If devils were against us, but Christ for us, we would not need to care much. Greater is He that is for us than all that can be against us. But it is not so.

iii. It Is Anathema Maranatha.

For 'the Lord Jesus shall be revealed from heaven . . . in flaming fire, taking vengeance on them that know not God, and obey not the gospel of our Lord Jesus Christ' (2 *Thess.* 1:7–8). He will say to all that loved Him not, 'Depart from me, ye cursed.'

Dear souls, Jesus does nothing but invite you today. Oh! come while He says, 'Come!' For in that day He will say, 'Depart from me.' Not one invitation more, nothing but a bitter curse. Anathema Maranatha.

iv. IT WILL BE A CURSE WHEN OTHERS ARE REJOICING.

Heaven and earth will ring for jubilee on that day. It is the Marriage Day of the King's Son, and the Lamb's wife will have made herself ready. Christ will be glad in that day. He will see of the travail of His soul and be satisfied. It is the day He longs for. He will put on His crown, His many crowns, and come forth like the sun. 'Go forth, O ye daughters of Zion, and behold King Solomon with the crown wherewith his mother crowned him in the day of his espousals, and in the day of the gladness of his heart' (*Song of Sol.* 3:11).

Believers, you will be glad in that day, for Christ will be glorified in His saints and admired in all them that believe in that day. You will then be presented to Christ, a glorious church, not having spot or wrinkle or any such thing but holy and without blemish. Your vile bodies will be made like His glorious body. You will be like Him in holiness, for you shall see Him as He is. You will be smiled on by the Saviour. You will stand at His right hand in gold of Ophir. The righteous Judge will give you a crown of glory that fadeth not away. He will wipe off every tear, except tears of joy. You will receive a harp of pure gold. You will hymn celestial praises to the Lamb. The angels will be glad in that day for they rejoice over one sinner that repenteth, more than over all that need no repentance. God the Father will rejoice. It was meet that we should make merry and be glad, 'for this my son was dead and is alive again, was lost and is found'.

Will any be sad? Ah yes! those that love not the Lord Jesus. They will be cursed with a curse in that day and oh! it will be a bitter curse, when all around is joy. The very contrast will heighten your misery. When anything black is cast upon the white, drifted snow, it looks blacker because of the contrast. So will it be with your black curse in that day of jubilee, as it is written, 'Behold, my servants shall eat, but ye shall be hungry: behold, my servants shall drink, but ye shall be thirsty: behold, my servants shall rejoice, but ye shall be ashamed: behold my servants shall sing for joy of heart, but ye shall cry for sorrow of heart, and shall howl for vexation of spirit' (*Isa.* 65:13–14). Ah! dear souls, flee now from the wrath to come!

v. It Will Be All Curse.

'Let him *be* a curse', not, 'Let a curse light upon him', but, 'Let him be a curse, body, soul and spirit – all a curse.' Just as Christ says literally in Psalm 109:4, 'For my love they are my adversaries: *but I prayer*', as if He were nothing but prayer; just as John the Baptist said, 'I am the voice', nothing but a voice; so ye that love not the Lord Jesus, ye shall be Anathema, all curse, when the Lord shall come. Ye shall be a curse to yourselves and to all around you, a curse within and without, a curse in the judgment, a curse for eternity.

Ah, dear souls, flee from the wrath to come! While it is called, Today, harden not your hearts!

17

The Gospel Ministry[1]

Therefore seeing we have this ministry, as we have received mercy, we faint not; but have renounced the hidden things of dishonesty, not walking in craftiness, nor handling the word of God deceitfully; but by manifestation of the truth commending ourselves to every man's conscience in the sight of God. But if our gospel be hid, it is hid to them that are lost: In whom the god of this world hath blinded the minds of them which believe not, lest the light of the glorious gospel of Christ, who is the image of God, should shine unto them. For we preach not ourselves, but Christ Jesus the Lord; and ourselves your servants for Jesus' sake. For God, who commanded the light to shine out of darkness, hath shined in our hearts, to give the light of the knowledge of the glory of God in the face of Jesus Christ (2 Cor. 4:1–6).

THIS ANNIVERSARY IS A SOLEMN DAY. It is so because many who were here when I first came among you are gone. Many faces that we knew are wanting: they have gone to give account. Many, perhaps I myself, will never see another such anniversary. Many in the time I have been here have undergone hardening, and not conversion.

---

[1] Preached in St Peter's, Dundee, 28 November 1841, on the fifth anniversary of the commencement of his ministry.

It is five years this day, since I first began among you the work of the gospel ministry. It will be good for us both to pause this day and look back. It will be good for me to compare my ministry with the unerring standard of God's Word, and it will be good for you to enquire what benefit you have received from it.

1. FAITHFUL MINISTERS PREACH CHRIST.

'For we preach not ourselves, but Christ Jesus the Lord; and ourselves your servants for Jesus' sake' (verse 5).

i. We Do Not Preach Our Own Fancies.

Many teachers in this world teach their own fancies and opinions. All the philosophers of Greece and Rome taught their own fancies. But when the Apostles rose, they preached 'not themselves but Christ Jesus the Lord'. John the Baptist came, and he cried, 'Behold the Lamb of God.' Of the Apostles it is said, 'Daily in the temple, and in every house, they ceased not to teach and preach Jesus Christ.' Philip went down to Samaria and preached Christ unto them, and when he came to the Ethiopian, 'He preached unto him Jesus' (*Acts* 8:5). So it is 'that which we have seen and heard' that the apostles 'declare unto you' (*1 John* 1:3). This also has been my endeavour, though but feebly and sinfully. Why?

    a. Because it is the most awakening truth, the most comforting and the most sanctifying in the world.

    b. Because we are sent to preach the gospel, and nothing else.

ii. We Do Not Have Ourselves as an End.

Most men seek their own. They seek their own wealth, ease or credit. Ministers are specially tempted to this. It is a brave thing to have the world gaping after us. But it is not so with the faithful minister. He seeks that Christ may have a large crown of saved souls; that men may know Christ, may love Christ, may be like Christ. It has been said that we are to 'Feed the people, not with gay tulips and useless daffodils, but with the bread of life and medicinal plants, springing from the margin of the fountain of salvation'. King James compared these useless adornments to 'the red and blue flowers that pester the corn'.

2. FAITHFUL MINISTERS PREACH FROM PERSONAL EXPERIENCE.

'For God, who commandeth the light to shine out of darkness, hath shined in our hearts, to give the light of the knowledge of the glory of God in the face of Jesus Christ' (verse 6).

i. MANY MINISTERS TEACH IGNORANTLY.

They know not what they are saying. They are blind leaders of the blind. Many speak from head-knowledge. Or, like Balaam, they speak of a Saviour whose love they have never felt. Like Caiaphas, they may speak of one dying for the people, although that blood has never come on them. But it is not so with faithful pastors. They can say, 'God hath shined into my heart. I speak because I believe.' 'We cannot but speak the things which we have seen and heard' (*Acts* 4:20).

ii. OBSERVE WHAT MINISTERS HAVE.

a. *Not a sight of Christ's face with the bodily eye.* It is the light of knowledge, the knowledge of the glory of God.

b. *Not an imagination of a pale face with a thorny crown.* No, it is the pure light of knowledge. It is a discovery to the soul of the wisdom, love, grace and power of God, manifested in the face of a dying Redeemer. This is a spiritual, realizing gaze. Oh! it is then that a minister speaks with power, holy admiration and urgency.

iii. OBSERVE WHENCE MINISTERS RECEIVE IT.

God 'hath shined'. The world was a mass of darkness. Earth, sea and sky were all mingled in one dark, confused heap. Death and darkness reigned; death without any life, darkness without any light. Then a still small voice came saying, 'Let there be light', when suddenly the rosy blush of dawn appeared. Such is the conversion of the soul. It is God's sovereign work.

Oh! wait on Him for the work of conversion. Give Him all the glory.

Pray that ministers may thus speak to you, with the taste of the manna in their mouth; with the living water springing up in the hearts; with the light shining sweetly into their own bosoms.

3. THE MANNER IN WHICH FAITHFUL MINISTERS PREACH.

i. WITHOUT FAINTING.

'We faint not' (verse 1), though many things tend to make ministers faint in their work.

a. *Reproaches.*

We are called troublers of Israel; those that turn the world upside down. They laugh us to scorn. A faithful minister might as well think to go to heaven without dying as without reproach. We must bear about us the marks of the Lord Jesus, and reproach was one.

b. *Men turning away.*

Many went back and walked no more with Jesus. They were offended because of His sayings, and it is so with many still. Ah!

The Gospel Ministry

it is a heart-breaking sight to see men turn away because they cannot bear the light.

c. *Many remaining, but hardened under sin.*

It is a sore sight to see men going to hell under our ministry, eyes and ears stopped. It is like seeing a ship wrecked while we are standing on the shore, powerless to do anything about it.

d. *Some are like the stony ground.*

Some seem to be receiving the Word with joy, but then we see them falling back into sin.

Still, by God's help 'we faint not'. The work is so sweet. It feeds our own soul at the time we are feeding you. Our own eyes rest on Jesus, whether you will be saved by Him or no. And there are these encouragements:

a. *Some will be saved.*

The elect will be saved, while the rest are blinded. Yes, brethren, you may reject this ministry, but some will receive it, and be saved.

b. *Christ will get glory, though Israel be not gathered.*

Though you will not add your voice to the chorus of those that sing, 'Worthy is the Lamb', Christ will be glorified, even in your cry of misery. You may not join the company of the redeemed that shall wave their eternal palms and cast their crowns at Jesus' feet. Still Christ will be glorified in your righteous condemnation and therefore, 'Having this ministry, we faint not.'

ii. HOLILY.

We 'have renounced the hidden things of dishonesty' (verse 2). It is common for the world to accuse ministers of being outwardly sanctimonious in appearance, and secretly living lives of sin and shame. And so it is no doubt with many. And when one such case is discovered, the world looks wise and says, 'So is it with them all. The black coat covers a blacker heart.' It was not so with Paul, 'We have renounced . . .' 'Ye are witnesses, and God also, how holily and justly and unblameably we behaved ourselves among you that believe' (1 Thess. 2:10).

I would not have you think that ministers are of a different nature from other men. We are 'men of like passions'. We could not preach to you as we do if we had not a hell in our own bosom. But we can say, 'We have renounced the hidden things of dishonesty.' We have fled to Jesus to pardon the past and to sanctify us for the future. Pray for holy-living ministers.

iii. NOT DECEITFULLY.

'Not walking in craftiness, nor handling the word of God deceitfully' (verse 2). Too many teachers handle the Word of God deceitfully.

They do not show the danger in which unconverted souls are lying. Ah! I often marvel that God's thunder stops, when one whose work it should be to pluck brands out of the fire, speaks smooth things to the people, stroking their consciences with feathers dipped in oil, instead of piercing them with the sword of the Spirit. Ah! you will not thank us in eternity for rocking your cradle and lulling you asleep over the pit of hell.

They do not point to Jesus.

If you were beside a dying man and knew that in half an hour he would be in eternity, what would you say to him? Would you not tell him of the Person and love of Jesus? Many handle the Word deceitfully as to this. Ah! pray that honestly, simply and fully, I may show your danger and tell you of the remedy, and, 'the Lord watch between thee and me'.

4. MANY WILL REJECT A FAITHFUL MINISTRY.

Paul reckoned upon it, that his gospel would be hid from some. At Iconium, 'the city was divided: and part held with the Jews, and part with the Apostles' (Acts 14:4). At Ephesus, many believed but diverse were hardened and believed not. At Rome, some believed and some believed not (Acts 28:24). So Jesus warned us it would be. 'Think not that I am come to send peace on earth. I am not come to send peace, but a sword.' And so it is among you. I believe in my heart that there are some of you into whose hearts the glorious gospel has shone. But ah, how many are there to whom our gospel is hid!

i. How Is This?

The god of this world, Satan, blinds your eyes by means of the world. He brings the dazzling things of this world between you and the Sun of Righteousness. Oh! brethren if you perish it is not because the gospel is not shining on you, but because Satan blinds your mind. This is the condemnation.

ii. What Will the End Be?

You will be lost. Ah! what an awful word is that. Lost! Not found! Not one of those who are carried back to the fold in the arms of the Shepherd. Lost! Cast away for ever as one of the irrecoverable souls. Lost to your believing friends that loved you on earth. They will look round in heaven and miss you. You will be lost! Lost to God! God will part with you for ever, saying, 'This is not mine, it is lost!'

Is this to be the case with souls sitting here, that have sat here for years, whom I know well? Are you to be lost for eternity? Lost because you chose your sins rather than Christ? Lost because you despised our gospel? May it not be!

18

A New Creature in Understanding[1]

Therefore if any man be in Christ, he is a new creature: old things are passed away; behold, all things are become new (2 Cor. 5:17).

IT WAS ONCE SAID OF JESUS by some who heard his heavenly discourse concerning the kingdom, 'Never man spake like this man.' And just in like manner may it be said of the Bible, Never book spake like this Book. It is true, the unconverted man will hurry over its pages without once being arrested by the view of its unsearchable riches, just as the superficial traveller will cast his careless eye over a country without one thought of the hidden riches of its mines and coal-pits. But the child of God is like the possessor of the soil who, though not blind to the beauties of the surface, yet takes a far greater interest in the riches that are beneath. The gospel is to him a treasure hid in a field, and it is the labour and the delight of his existence to dig out more and more of those riches which eye hath not seen, nor ear heard, neither have they entered into the heart of man to conceive.

[1] Preached 6 March 1836 in Larbert; 13 March 1836 in Dunipace; and during Spring 1837 in St Peter's, Dundee.

A New Creature in Understanding

There are two expressions in the words before us which suggested these thoughts, and they are being 'in Christ', and being 'a new creature'. These two expressions, brief and intelligible as they may appear to many, are yet those that may be called the shafts or inlets into two inexhaustible mines of divine wisdom, by means of which the children of God descend to fetch up treasures for the soul, eternal treasures, compared with which the diamond loses its brilliancy and gold loses its preciousness.

Before attempting thus to make use of these divine words, let me first explain their simple meaning. To be 'in Christ', or 'in the Lord', is a phrase of constant occurrence in the Bible. Indeed I am quite sure that those of you who will take the trouble to mark every passage where it occurs will be most surprised. Isaiah says, 'In the LORD have I righteousness and strength' (*Isa.* 45:24). And again, 'In the LORD shall all the seed of Israel be justified, and shall glory' (*Isa.* 45:25), (that is, they, being in the Lord, will be justified). Our Lord Himself says, 'Abide in me . . . As the branch cannot bear fruit of itself, except it abide in the vine; no more can ye, except ye abide in me' (*John* 15:4). And again, Paul says, 'There is therefore now no condemnation to them which are in Christ Jesus' (*Rom.* 8:1). The simple meaning of this phrase is to be so united to Jesus that we are looked upon by God as one with Him, as if we were actually *within* Him. It may help us if we consider these illustrations:

1. *Jacob may be said to have been* in Esau *when he came in dressed in his sweet-smelling garments.* Isaac looked upon him as if he were Esau. He laid his hands on the hands of Esau. He counted all the good qualities of Esau to Jacob, and blessed him with the blessing due to Esau. So when we believe in Jesus we are said to be *in Jesus*, we are dressed in His sufferings and His obedience as one sweet-smelling garment. God looks upon us as if we were Jesus. He counts

all the good qualities of Jesus to us, and blesses us with the blessing due to Christ.

2. *Adam and Eve.* When our first parents sinned they made themselves aprons. But God clothed them with skins of beasts slain in sacrifice, and therefore typical of the Lamb of God. Being clothed in these, they were in the Lamb. God counted as theirs the death and innocence of the Lamb.

3. *The marriage union.* In Ezekiel 16 and Ephesians 2 this union to Christ is spoken of under the figure of the marriage union, in which two become one flesh, and in which the husband becomes liable for all the debts of the wife, in which he clothes her with raiment and with costly ornaments.

4. *Grafting into a tree.* This union to Christ is represented to us both by Paul and by our Lord Himself as a grafting of a branch into a tree, by means of which the branch becomes one with the tree. This, then, is to be *in Christ,* to have His sufferings and obedience counted ours, to be looked upon in His place. This blessing is freely offered to the chiefest sinner in the midst of you.

Now of every one who is in Christ it is true that he becomes *a new creature.* This is the second expression which I have to explain. It is also a phrase of common occurrence in the Bible. In Ephesians 2:10 believers are said to be 'created in Christ Jesus unto good works', and again in Ephesians 4:24, the new man is said to be, after God, 'created in righteousness and true holiness'. The meaning is that a complete and radical change is brought about in the soul of every one that is in Christ Jesus, a change as great as if the soul were created over again. There are several reasons why the work of regeneration is called a new creation.

A New Creature in Understanding

a. *It is so called to show that God is the Author of it.* In the beginning God created the heaven and the earth. No one can wield a creative arm but God. A man may mould and fashion that which is created, but he cannot 'call the things that are not as though they were'. He cannot make out of nothing. He is not God. No man can create his own soul.

b. *It is so called because the work of God upon the soul is parallel to the bringing in of new heavens and a new earth.* This work is yet to be wrought upon the earth which was created for man's sake. As it is written in Isaiah 65:17, 'Behold, I create new heavens and a new earth: and the former shall not be remembered, nor come into mind.' And Peter tells us plainly that, after these heavens and this earth have been burned up, we look for 'new heavens and a new earth, wherein dwelleth righteousness' (2 Pet. 3:13).

How great shall the change be when these skies that are now so often obscured by threatening clouds, swept along by the hurricane, that are so often rent by the crashing of the thunder, shall, when purified by fire, give place to new skies of a far more heavenly blue, skies unblotted by the thunder cloud and unruffled by the storm. How great shall the change be when this earth that is now cursed with heaviness, abounding in swamps and fens and sandy, wild desert, that is overgrown with thorns and weeds, that is visited with plagues and diseases, and, above all, that groans under the servitude of wicked men, shall, when purified by fire, all smile with an eternal spring – when the wilderness shall rejoice and blossom as the rose, when the inhabitants shall say that they are rich, and all shall be righteous.

Just such is the change in regeneration, the *new creation* which is taking place every day in the hearts of those who embrace Jesus, those who are *in Christ*.

Each such person is a new creature in his understanding. He is a new creature in his affections. He is a new creature in his walk and conversation.

In this discourse I shall only have time to take up the first of these and show:

1. IF ANY BE IN CHRIST, HE IS A NEW CREATURE, IN RESPECT OF HIS UNDERSTANDING.

This may seem a bold assertion to many of you and yet when the text says that 'old things are passed away; behold, all things are become new', it is obvious that so important a part of man as the understanding cannot be omitted. There are several ways in which this truth may be proved:

1. In taking a survey of the history of the world, it cannot be denied that *Christianity has entirely changed the intelligence of the human race,* and that, on whatever nation the light of Christianity has arisen most clearly, that nation has shone the most conspicuously, both in general intelligence and in particular examples of men of genius and understanding.

2. *The converted heathen.* We might visit some savage island in the South Seas and find there only men who delight in nothing but war and bloodshed. But we might also visit an island to whose shore it has pleased God to send those whose feet are beautiful upon the mountains because they bring good tidings and publish peace (*Isa.* 52:7). We shall find that the change upon the understanding of the converted natives is quite remarkable. They are new creatures indeed. They are not the men they were, and their superiority to their unconverted brethren in point of common understanding has been remarkably manifested.

A New Creature in Understanding

3. *Christians at home.* To come nearer home, if we visit a family in our own country of which, it may be, only one member has been induced to trust in the Lord Jesus and to become a child of God, the difference in point of intelligence, when other things are equal, is often most remarkable. Though it may be in the poorest regions of society, in a mere hovel that scarcely admits the light of day, yet the light of the Sun of Righteousness has penetrated into the bosom and shed such an illumination over the whole soul that the accurate but worldly observer has oftentimes looked on amazed at the dignity of mind wherewith it pleases God to invest His children; and he has been forced to say, 'This is indeed a new creature. This is indeed one taught of God.'

4. *The causes of the change.* Fourthly, we shall be still more convinced of this truth if we examine the causes of this change upon the understanding. The chief causes are three in number:

i. *When a man becomes a believer, a new field is opened up for the understanding to penetrate into.*

As long as a soul is not at peace with God, so long is everything connected with God, His being, His attributes, His government, a forbidden field of contemplation; that is, a field in which the mind has no pleasure or desire to occupy itself. The unconverted mind may and does occupy itself intensely about the things which are outside this field. But within this field it does not dare to penetrate. The earth, the water, the heavens, it may and does explore but the heaven of heavens, the machinery of providence and of grace, the movements of the hand that guides the stars, these form a world unknown, a field forbidden.

It is true that unconverted men have made dives into the character of God, His government and redemption, and some unconverted men have been preachers of Christ. But no unconverted man ever gazed upon these things with the love of one interested in them, and therefore he could not truly see them at all. God must be loved in order to be known.

Now, suppose that the Queen of Sheba, when she came to Judea, had come, not to see and hear King Solomon, but only to examine the land over which he reigned, to inquire into the state of cultivation, the rocks, the minerals, the fruits, and had gone back to her country to tell only of these fascinating objects of her admiration; would you not say that, however accurate and intelligent her observations might be, yet the chiefest of all the objects of inquiry had been, with amazing stupidity, neglected by her: the king upon the throne; the man gifted with wisdom above all the children of men.

Just so is it with unconverted men. Their minds are sharp and intelligent upon all objects but one, and that one the greatest of all. They are clever and acute when you ask them about ploughing and sowing and reaping. They are most judicious and sagacious upon the politics of this little island. But when you come to ploughing and sowing and reaping in the work of grace, or the politics of the universe, and the high administration of Him who has no man for His counsellor, then your intelligent man of earth, is utterly dull and stupid and ignorant. He has not a heart to know God. He does not like to retain God in his knowledge.

But reconcile that man to God, bring him nigh by the blood of Jesus, and, behold, a new creation! It is like the return of the Israelites from the captivity in Babylon. They were like men that dreamed, not believing their deliverance to be a reality, till the beloved mountains of their native land burst upon their view. Then their mouth was filled with laughter and their tongues with singing. Just so with the converted man. The face of God was manifest in

A New Creature in Understanding

clouds and frowns before. But Christ in reconciling has torn away the clouds, and now that face has burst out upon him, more brilliant than the Sun. The intelligence now springs forward to this, the greatest, the grandest of all objects of thought, the only object that can fill and satisfy it, and he exclaims truly, 'This is life eternal, to know thee, and Jesus Christ whom thou hast sent.' Is it not plain then that a mind which has such a field of exercise as this must grow in intelligence with a power to which the unconverted are utter strangers?

ii. But the second cause, why the converted man is a new creature in intelligence is that *he now enters on every pursuit out of love to God.*

Those of you who have had any experience in the training of children will know how important a point it is to interest the affections of the child in that which he is learning. Do you not often feel that, if you could implant in the hearts of your children a principle which would give them a constant desire to learn, they would learn, with the will, ten times faster than they now do, against the will?

Just so it is, not with children only, but with grown men. Well then, suppose them reconciled to God, and the love of God put as a moving affection in their bosom, how eagerly will they acquire knowledge for God's service! How fully will they lay it up, that God may be honoured in them. But the unconverted is continually working under a load. The question of his forgiveness is unsettled, and the sentiment will often cross his mind, the sad foreboding, that he may be treasuring up all his knowledge for hell.

Once remove the load and the man's state is lightened; nay, he acquires a holy inquisitiveness and retentiveness which he never had before. And when he looks on the world as the property and handiwork of his God, he says with delight, 'My Father made them all.' The peasant who but yesterday gazed with brutish unconcern on the everlasting mountains and deep floods now stands to consider the lily of the field and whispers to his soul, 'If God has clothed the grass of this field which is to be cast into the oven, how much more will He clothe me?'

iii. The third cause why the believer becomes a new creature in intelligence is that *God becomes a dweller in his bosom and gives new energy to all his faculties.*

In God we live, and move, and have our very being. Separate a man from God and he would crumble to decay. This is true of man's body. God keeps all its wheels and processes in motion. The busy heart beats on from day to day because God's hand impels it. The capacious lungs swell and fall with regular motion because God keeps them. And this is true of the soul also. The judgment is clear and vivid because God holds the balance of the mind even. The imagination and the affections are lively because God keeps them in play. But the soul of a man estranged from God lacks His indwelling presence and power. Never till he becomes a habitation of God through the Spirit can God employ the powers of his soul in His service.

Where was it, do you think, that Joseph acquired that deep wisdom and discretion by which he administered the affairs of Egypt so skilfully? Where but from the favour which God had to him and the indwelling of His Spirit within him. Where was it that Bezaleel got all his skill, as we read in Exodus 31, to devise cunning works, and to work in gold and silver and brass and all manner of workmanship, for the tabernacle? Does not God say expressly that he had filled him with His Spirit to this end? And what shall I say more? For the time would fail me to tell of Gideon and of Barak and of Samson and of Jephthah, of David also, and Samuel and the prophets, who by faith were made children of God, were then led by the Spirit of God, and lived as much distinguished by their wisdom in the camp and on the throne as they were by their walking near to God, and delighting in his commandments.

2. PRACTICAL LESSONS

And now brethren, from this deeply interesting subject, I wish to draw two practical inferences:

i. *Let us learn that, as long as we are out of Christ, we are positively deformed and imperfect in the understanding.*

It is commonly thought that unbelief, a refusal to be persuaded of the truth of the gospel, shows a manliness of understanding and a depth of sagacity beyond the common; whereas it is plain as day that, till a man be in Christ, he has not yet begun to know anything as he ought to know.

Oh! if an angel were to visit our world and enter in among you in the field and the workshop, and hear who it is that you call a man of sense and intelligence, a being that is not reconciled to his God, who excludes from his every thought the God into whose very presence he is rushing. Ah! brethren, would not that holy angel say in the words of Paul, 'These men have the understanding darkened, being alienated from the life of God through the ignorance that is in them, because of the blindness of their hearts'?

ii. *Let us put our understanding to the test.*

The second lesson that I would have you learn, is to try your own minds whether you have been thus made a new creature. If not, you are not in Christ Jesus. Do you remember the time when God and the things of God were a forbidden field into which your mind could not bear to enter? Do you remember the time when the Bible, and those books and those friends who entered most deeply into the revealed mind of God, were nauseous and distasteful to you? You could bear them for a little, as a penance or a work of merit, but they were not your bosom friends, the men of your counsel.

And say plainly, is the case otherwise now? Do you love to think of God and the things of God? Does your understanding expand there, as in its true element? When you are led into the wonders of redeeming love, then you are a new creature in understanding. You are in Christ Jesus. You are safe for eternity. And as, here, even the saint knows only in part, look toward the day when you shall know even as you are known.

But, brethren, if you are utter strangers to this new creation, be quite sure you are strangers to Christ. 'For in Christ Jesus, neither circumcision availeth anything nor uncircumcision, but *a new creature*' (*Gal.* 6:15).

19

A New Creature in Affections[1]

Therefore if any man be in Christ, he is a new creature: old things are passed away; behold, all things are become new (2 Cor. 5:17).

IN A FORMER DISCOURSE, I attempted to show that 'if any man be in Christ', he becomes a new creature in his understanding; that the moment a man savingly believes the gospel and becomes reconciled to God, he comes under an influence which produces a change in the intelligence or thinking faculties of the soul.

This is a change as great as if the whole faculties had been taken down or annihilated and created all over again. So that the strange fancy which some men have entertained that unbelief, or a hardness to be persuaded of the truth of the gospel, evinces a certain manliness in the understanding, and a sagacity beyond that of ordinary men, is plainly nothing else than another of those flattering lies whereby Satan beguiles poor, infatuated sinners to their eternal perdition. On the contrary, it is as plain as day that, till a man becomes a child of God, enlightened and led by the Spirit of all

---

[1] Preached 20 March 1836 in Larbert; 27 March 1836 in Dunipace; and during Spring 1837 in St Peter's, Dundee.

wisdom and of all understanding, he is groping in darkness, given over to believe a lie. Does that illustrate great depths of intelligence? He knows nothing, positively nothing, yet as he ought to know.

But leaving the change produced upon the understanding, I come now to consider the equally extraordinary change which is produced upon the heart, or upon the affections, by conversion. The soul of man is endowed with two principal faculties which, in common speech, are distinguished by the names of *the head* and *the heart*. The head includes those faculties by which we discern, compare and judge. The heart includes those by which the soul likes or dislikes, approves or disapproves. Having already seen in what way the head or intellectual faculties of the believer are created anew, it is my present object to show that the heart of the believer is also made new.

1. THE AFFECTIONS IN MAN

The heart or affections in man seem to occupy the same position of power which the mainspring does in a watch. It is the never-ceasing, impelling force of the mainspring which communicates a regular motion to all the little wheels and other parts of the ingenious machine. So that if the mainspring be broken, every wheel ceases its motion: the hands no longer do their office; and though, by external application, you may force on its wheels for a little, yet the spring of internal motion is gone, never to be renewed.

Just so the affections operate with never-ceasing power in impelling forward the human mind toward the objects on which the heart is set. They form the mainspring of the living machine, urging forward every wheel of the inner man. Take away, therefore, the affections and the human mind would remain like a standing watch, a curious piece of mechanism indeed, but without life, use

A New Creature in Affections

or activity. Now it is in this part of the soul of man, the affections, that the new creation is most visible and most important. And therefore we find conversion often described under this one name, a *change of heart*. So David prays, 'Create in me a clean heart' (*Psa.* 51:10), and Ezekiel describes the new creation as a taking away of the heart of stone (*Ezek.* 11:19).

In this discourse, I hope to show that the heart of the believer is created anew in respect of four things: in love to God; love to the people of God; love to the day of God; and love to the Word of God.

1. IF ANY MAN BE IN CHRIST, HE IS A NEW CREATURE IN LOVE TO GOD.

As long as a man is not reconciled to God he cannot love God. Every attribute of God is hateful to the unpardoned sinner. His inflexible justice that will let heaven and earth pass away before one jot or tittle of the law pass away – this is hateful to him, for it condemns him to his face. His unstained purity is hateful to the sinner, for it is so opposite to what the sinner delights in. His very mercy is hateful to the sinner, for it is all centred in Christ Jesus, to believe in whom would crush all pride and self-righteousness. But does any unbelieving man ask me to prove that such is the state of his mind with regard to God? I would prove it by one undeniable fact.

i. *It is an undeniable fact that the unbelieving mind does not love to think much or often about God.*

When he awakes in the morning his thoughts do not flow sweetly toward God. He cannot say with David, 'When I awake I am still with thee.' Through the business and the bargains of the day, there is no recreation sought for the soul by sweet thoughts of God. There is no bounding of heart, no rising of spirit, when worldly work is past and the heart has leisure to seek and commune with the objects of its affections. When the day is done, and the tired man is quieting soul and body to repose, the profits and pleasures of the day that is past, the prospects and projects of the day that is to come, are the only subjects of meditation. God is not in all his thoughts. He does not like to retain God in his knowledge.

Now I would ask the question of every intelligent man, is this the way you do with an object that you love? When the affections are entwined around some earthly object, are they not constantly bending and drowning the mind with a sweet but powerful influence to think on the object loved? Think of an exile from his native land, severed by a thousand seas from his home and kindred, need you ask why he so often sits alone and meditates in the unbroken silence? Need you ask what it is that his thoughts so eagerly bound to, when the bustle and the business of the day are over? A child will tell you! His eyes are with his heart, and that is far away! He is thinking of his home and the tender objects of his love. How plain, then, is it from this one fact out of a thousand, that the natural mind, which has no pleasure in thinking of God, has no love to God!

ii. *But if any man be in Christ, he becomes a new creature in love to God.*

Before a natural man is brought into Christ, he has to pass through the deep waters of conviction of sin. The load of guilt lies heavy on him. The waves and billows of God's wrath threaten to overwhelm him. He says with the Psalmist, 'While I suffer thy terrors I am distracted' (*Psa.* 88:15).

But no sooner does the Spirit open his heart to understand the Word than he sees that these are the very words of Jesus, groaning under the weight of human guilt. He appropriates the work of Christ to himself. He is in Christ, and is at peace for time and for eternity.

A New Creature in Affections

'Though thou wast angry with me, thine anger is turned away, and thou comfortedst me' (*Isa.* 12:1), is now his language.

Then it is that the flame of love to God who hath so loved him is kindled into a blaze in the believing bosom. This is the first love of the believer. Like the woman in the gospels, forgiven much, he cannot but love much. Nor is this a fitful affection, a mere blaze of romantic attachment; it settles down into an ever-growing, ever-increasing affection. Indeed, if we were left to ourselves this grace would all vanish away; the flame so happily kindled would flicker and die as a lamp would. But God is faithful and has declared that when He begins a good work He will finish it! He reveals to us more and more of the love of Jesus, and this adds new fuel to the flame of our love to Him. The more we gaze the more we love. The more we look upon that Sun, the more our faces shine with the refulgence. Beholding as in a glass this love of his, which is indeed the glory of God, we are changed!

Does the unbeliever doubt of the truth of such an affection? He may, if he will, but every believer knows that his new heart toward God is a happy reality. And all of you who have undergone this new creation can tell me how plainly it evinced itself in you to be a real and lasting affection.

You did not like to think of God. Now you love to think of Him. Communion with God was a task or a penance before, now it is a delight. You made all things bend toward the getting of money, or the pampering of the flesh, for money was your God, or your belly was your God. Now you make all things bend toward the enjoyment of much of the presence of God with your souls.

You cared not that God was absent from your house and from your heart. Now, like the spouse in the Song of Solomon when God is absent, you cannot rest till you find him: 'I will rise now, and go about the city in the streets, and in the broad ways I will seek him whom my soul loveth' (*Song of Sol.* 3:2). Like the same affectionate spouse, when you have found Him you will hold Him fast and not let Him go. You will say, 'Set me as a seal upon thine heart, as a seal upon thine arm: for love is strong as death . . . Many waters cannot quench love . . . If a man would give all the substance of his house for love, it would utterly be contemned' (*Song of Sol.* 8:6–7). How plainly, then, are you a new creature! Old things have passed away.

2. IF ANY MAN BE IN CHRIST, HE IS A NEW CREATURE IN LOVE TO THE PEOPLE OF GOD.

While a man is out of Christ, he does not love the people of God. On the contrary, Christ plainly told His disciples that they should be hated by all men, that because they were not of the world, but had been chosen out of the world, the world hated them. There are many reasons why the world hate the godly:

i. *The presence of the godly is a living sermon, a monument of the power and grace of God.* This is hateful to the world. The presence of the godly rebukes all sin, by their continually breathing of the universal tidings of the gospel. This is hateful to the world.

ii. *The godly are anxious for redeeming every opportunity,* walking in wisdom toward them that are without (*Col.* 4:5). They are anxious to save them with fear, pulling them out of the fire, hating even the garment spotted by the flesh.

This 'meddling' is still more hateful to the world. But make a man a believer in Jesus, give him peace of conscience and love to God, and he will soon show that he is passed from death unto life by his loving the brethren. Instead of proving this truth to you, let me point to two men who were the most eminent examples of it ever seen.

A New Creature in Affections

a. *Saul of Tarsus.* You remember Saul the persecutor, how he tells us of himself that he thought he ought to do many things contrary to the name of Jesus of Nazareth, which thing he also did in Jerusalem, shutting up many of the saints in prison and when they were put to death giving his voice against them. 'And I punished them oft in every synagogue, and compelled them to blaspheme; and being exceedingly mad against them, I persecuted them even unto strange cities' (*Acts* 26:11).

And you remember Paul, the Apostle of the Gentiles, how the wolf was turned into a lamb. Did ever man shine with love to man as did this converted Jew? What are his words to those saints whom he had seen and watched over? 'We were gentle among you, even as a nurse cherisheth her children. So being affectionately desirous of you, we were willing to have imparted unto you, not the gospel of God only, but also our own souls, because ye were dear unto us' (*1 Thess.* 2:7). What are his words to those believers whom he had never seen? 'I would that ye knew what great conflict I have for you, and for them at Laodicea, and for as many as have seen my face in the flesh; that their hearts might be comforted, being knit together in love . . . For though I be absent in the flesh yet am I with you in the spirit' (*Col.* 2:1–2, 5).

In a word, as a godly minister has said, when you read the Acts you would think Paul was never off his feet; when you read the Epistles you would think he was never off his knees on behalf of his brethren in the Lord. Is it possible that the hardest-hearted sinner among you can shut his eyes to the fact that it was by being in Christ Paul became this new creature?

b. *The second example I would give you is the Apostle John.* Of his unconverted life we know nothing, but doubtless it was like the life of an ordinary man among you, spent in love with the world and the people of the world. But of the converted John we know the very secrets of the soul, and truly it would seem as if, by leaning on the Redeemer's bosom, he had caught the holy infection of love that burned within; for never was human heart more inflamed with love to the brethren. The whole argument of his Epistles may be comprised in these words, 'If God so loved us, we ought also to love one another.' And truly this was no passing affection, for of him the story is told that, when he was old and well stricken in years, and could no longer preach to his beloved Ephesians, he would cause himself to be carried in before the assembly, the last of the Apostles. And while his silver locks floated on his shoulders, he would lift his venerable hands and say, 'Little children, love one another.'

How plain it is, then, that by this all men shall know the disciples of the Lord Jesus, that they have love one to another. And if you seek outward proof of it you will find it:

1. In that believers make companions of each other. Others may be found in their company, but their bosom friends are the children of God.

2. That believers shrink from marriage with unbelievers according to the apostle's command, 'Be not unequally yoked together.'

3. That believers are peculiarly charitable to poor believers, as John says, 'Whoso hath this world's good, and seeth his brother have need, and shutteth up his bowels of compassion from him, how dwelleth the love of God in him?' (1 John 3:17).

4. That believers pray without ceasing and give thanks one for another, even for those they have never seen in the flesh.

A New Creature in Affections

I intended to have shown you that, if any man be in Christ, he becomes a new creature in love to the Word of God and in love to the Sabbath of God, in both of which the change from his life before conversion is equally important and remarkable and may well be called a new creation of the heart. But I hasten to draw brief partial instructions from this truth.

3. PRACTICAL LESSONS

i. *If the believer is created anew in his affections, a holy life must be pleasant to him.*

I am quite sure there is not an unconverted man before me who does not believe that a life of holiness is a life of uphill work, a going against the grain – that when a man becomes serious he must bid goodbye to pleasure, he must walk contrary to all his affections, and learn to do and speak what his heart detests. And so it would be if the heart were unchanged.

And those of you who begin religion at the wrong end, by trying to walk holily before you have got the new heart, and while your abominable, carnal heart remains in your bosom, you will find it uphill work indeed. But if a man begins at the right end by being in Christ, and becoming a new creature, then he is made new, his affections are changed. You will love holy people and therefore make bosom friends of them. You will call the Sabbath a delight, and therefore refrain your foot, your hand, and your tongue, from profaning it. You will love the Bible, and therefore meditate therein day and night.

Oh, then, my unconverted brethren, will you not open your eyes to see that you have quite mistaken the nature of true gospel holiness. It is heaven on earth. It is pleasantness and peace. The new heart acts as surely as the old heart. I know well that your unchanged heart finds pleasure in the lust of the flesh, the lust of the eye, and the pride of life. I never will deny that there are pleasures in sin. Why, then, should you deny that there are pleasures in holiness, that the new heart finds pleasure in thoughts of God, in the company of the saints, in prayer and praise.

Do not show a besotted understanding by joining the hue and cry of the drunken world who blaspheme the pleasures of holiness because they know them not. Sit down calmly and reckon up whether the pleasures of sin which I allow to be many, but which are for a season, and issue in the pains of an eternal hell, whether these are so good and so desirable as the pleasures of holiness from a new heart, pleasures which eye hath not seen, pleasures which begin on earth and never shall have an end in heaven.

ii. *If believers are created anew in their affections, how easily may most of us know whether we are believers.*

Have I experienced any change in my affections which can in any sense be called a new creation? This is the question which I would have every man put to his own soul.

There was once a time when you had no pleasure in thinking of God, no pleasure in pouring out your heart to God. Say honestly, is it otherwise with you now?

There was once a time, when you had no love for the people of God. You derided their strict and holy conversation. You would bear their society when they would talk only of earthly things, but you never loved them as your peculiar friends. On the contrary, all your chosen comrades were children of this world. Say honestly, is it otherwise now?

There was once a time, when the Sabbath was a weariness to you. You said, When will it be over? Perhaps a sense of decency kept you from openly profaning it, but you felt this a restraint and a grievous

A New Creature in Affections

bondage. Once you delighted in worldly conversations on the Sabbath. Say honestly, is it all otherwise now?

There was once a time when the Bible was a weariness, when you read it from habit or for form, but not for pleasure. You did not, as a newborn babe, desire the sincere milk of the Word. Say honestly, is it otherwise now?

I, your fellow-sinner, have put the question. I leave God to hear the reply!

20

Desiring to Depart and to Be with Christ[1]

I am in a strait betwixt two, having a desire to depart and to be with Christ; which is far better (Phil. 1:23).

IT IS A HAPPY THING TO LIVE. To breathe the fresh air of heaven, to move from place to place, to see, to hear, to speak – in a word, to live is happiness. But the Bible says that to be in Christ is better than life. 'In his favour is life' (*Psa*. 30:5); but 'thy lovingkindness is better than life' (*Psa*. 63:3). To be converted by the Spirit of God, to be convinced of sin, and then to be convinced of righteousness, to be led to a hearty and saving acceptance of Christ as my only and all-sufficient Saviour, that 'is better than life'.

And, indeed, I am quite sure that those of you who have been thus converted by God are feeling at this moment that this 'life of the soul' is better and pleasanter than even natural life, that the light of God's countenance is sweeter far than the light of the sun, that the saving health of His countenance gives more joy than does the joyous current of health and life that bounds through the youthful veins. Ah, yes, brethren, you never knew what life was till

[1] Preached in St Luke's, Tealing, Blairgowrie, and St Peter's, Dundee, 1837.

Desiring to Depart and to Be with Christ

you could say, 'Christ liveth in me'. But the words before me point us to greater things than these. 'For', says Paul, 'I am in a strait betwixt two, having a desire to depart and to be with Christ; which is far better.' To live is good and happy. To be in Christ is 'better than life'. But to be with Christ is far better than all.

The words of my text in the original are much more full and expressive than they are in our English translation. Indeed, they are so very full of meaning that it is impossible to translate them perfectly. The word here rendered, 'I am in a strait', is the same as Christ uses when He says, 'I have a baptism to be baptized with, and how am I *straitened* till it be accomplished!' (*Luke* 12:50). It implies great anxiety of mind; not a sudden overwhelming anxiety, but an abiding anxiety, ever pressing on the mind. The word rendered 'desire' is the same which Christ uses where He says, 'With *desire* have I desired to eat this passover with you' (*Luke* 22:15), and indicates an intense desire of the mind. The word rendered 'to depart' signifies to be unloosed, like a vessel set loose from its moorings. The words rendered, 'far better', if translated literally, would be, 'by much more better'.

The departure to be with Christ appeared so excellent to Paul, that he heaps up words more than our language can hold in order to express it. 'I am continually in a strait betwixt two, having an earnest desire to depart, to be unmoored from the shores of this world, and to be with Christ, which is much better, aye, far better.' The doctrine taught by the passage is this: To be WITH Christ is far better than to be IN Christ.

1. NO MORE DOUBT OF SALVATION

To be *with* Christ is far better than to be *in* Christ, because *then we shall never have any doubts of our salvation*. When God brings a man out of 'the horrible pit' and 'the miry clay' and 'sets his feet upon a rock' (*Psa.* 40:2), that man is safe for eternity. When a sinner, under a sense of the dreadfulness of his natural condition, closes with Christ as the Saviour of lost sinners, he becomes a member of Christ's body and is, therefore, as sure to be saved as if he were already sitting on the throne with Christ.

And not only is the sinner safe in the moment of believing, but he has a sweet sense of safety. He is not only, 'founded on a rock', but he feels that his feet are on a rock. He is not only a member, but he feels his union, and has a sense of acceptance in the Beloved. And this sense of safety is what is called the 'rest' or 'peace' of believing. It is a calm and tranquil feeling poured over the anxious breast, a sense that God's anger is all turned away; a feeling that all past sins are cast behind God's back; yea, buried in 'the depths of the sea'.

Now, though the safety of a believer never changes, yet his sense of safety very much changes. When he is once founded on Christ, the only foundation stone, he never can be shaken off; but still he may often lose all sense of being safe. When once a member of Christ's body, he can never be torn off again, yet he may, for a time, and through his own sin, lose all feeling of being a member. He may become so cold, or lukewarm, that he may altogether doubt whether he is, or ever was, a saved person. As long as we are in this world, there are many things to cloud and obscure the peace of believing.

i. *The believer falls into some open sin and, by so doing, brings guilt upon his conscience.* Again, he begins to hear the condemning voice of the law. A cloud seems to intercept his view of the Saviour. He falls into sin, and *should* fall from all sense of safety; for it would be a calamity to feel safe while he is in a backsliding condition.

ii. *He is betrayed into worldly company; and from the beginning to the end of the feast, he hears nothing but worldly conversation.* All around him people are taking thought what they shall eat, and what they shall drink.

The name of the Saviour is not once mentioned. To introduce it would be like bringing in a poisonous serpent, from which every one would shrink back with horror. The believer sits silent and is half ashamed of Christ. He is ashamed to show that he is a Christian. And when he comes home at night, what wonder if prayer and the Word be all distasteful to him, and he has lost all sense of safety.

iii. *The believer wearies in well-doing, and thus also he loses his sense of safety.* Once he 'put his hand to the plough', in 'every good work'. But now he draws back his hand. He grows weary of feeding the hungry, and clothing the naked, and visiting them that are sick and in prison. The work has turned burdensome to him, and he has wearied of it.

The poor have been ungrateful, his time is too much occupied; or, on some pretence or other, Christ's service is neglected, and darkness and insecurity are the consequence. He begins to doubt his safety, and well he may.

iv. *The approach of death often clouds the view of Christ.* The pains of dissolving nature are often very dreadful; the mind is often altogether taken up with looking at them; and so the eye is lifted away from Christ; and thus the dark valley becomes very dark. Clouds and darkness rest upon it. The believer, who rejoiced all his life long, has often a long night of darkness on his death-bed, much doubt and much perplexity, and though the everlasting arms are underneath him, yet he has no full sense of his safety.

But to depart and be with Christ is to be freed from all these doubts and obscurations of the Sun of Righteousness, and therefore, it is far better. When the soul of the believer has left its mortal body, it finds itself in the arms of the holy angels. These angels rejoiced when he was 'born again' into the world of grace, and how they rejoice far more when he is born a third time, into the world of glory; for at death 'the souls of believers... do immediately pass into glory' (*Shorter Catechism*, Q. 37). No sooner do they leave the body than they are with Christ, and there they are not only safe, for they were quite safe before – they are no safer than they were – but their sense of safety is now complete and everlasting. It shall never be clouded any more. Not another doubt shall ever darken their joy, not another fear disturb their 'perfect peace'.

No more shall that soul fall into sin to take away his sense of pardon and acceptance. No more shall he mix with worldly company, for nothing can enter in there that defileth. The name of the Saviour shall gladden every feast of love and joy. The praise of the Saviour shall be the only melody; no more shall worldly friends and worldly talk darken his sense of acceptance. No more shall he weary in well-doing, for they that are before the throne serve God day and night in His temple. No more shall sloth creep over the soul, no more shall vain excuses keep back the hands from deeds of love.

No more shall unchristian coldness take away the sense of safety. No more shall God take away the light of His countenance. He shall be 'with Christ', admitted to closest intercourse; always in sight of the Lamb that was slain, for 'the Lamb that is in the midst of the throne shall feed them, and lead them to living fountains of water'.

Often they wept on earth because Christ had withdrawn from them, but now God shall wipe all tears from their eyes. He is with

Christ. He shall not die any more; no more shall the pangs of a dissolving body take up his thoughts; no more shall clouds arise from the dark grave to obscure the face of the Saviour. He is with Christ, and his sense of safety is complete. He sees the hell from which he is delivered. He feels the heaven into which he is brought, and he is filled with an unvarying sense of safety. Like some spent swimmer to whom a rope is cast, he is safe as soon as he has tied the rope around him; and he may have a lively sense of safety even amid the waves; but it is only when he is safely brought ashore, and sits down upon the rock, and looks upon the deep gulf from which he has been saved, and feels the rock beneath him; it is only then that his sense of safety is complete.

Just so, brethren, when some poor sinner, spent with vain struggles to save himself, at length consents to be saved by Christ, he is safe, quite safe for eternity; and he may have a real sense of safety, even amid the billows of this world's trials and sorrows; but it is only when he is brought ashore, when he is brought to be 'with Christ'; when he looks upon the gulf of hell from which he has been saved, and feels himself casting his crown at the Redeemer's feet; it is only then that his sense of safety is complete for eternity. It shall never be shaken and never be darkened any more.

Oh, believer, the joys of *faith* are sweet beyond expression! 'Though now ye see him not, yet believing, ye rejoice with joy unspeakable, and full of glory.' But oh, what shall the joys of *sight* be, when we are, 'with Christ', and when we shall see Him as he is; and when we feel that the ocean is passed, when we feel that the shore is won; when we, 'see the King in His beauty', and we are put in possession of 'the land that is very far off'! Oh, it is 'far better' to be 'with Christ'!

Why then, cling to the world as if it were your all? Why tie yourselves to riches, and houses, and friends? Flee these things, O man of God! In the brightest sunshine of this world, when friends are dearest, and all things go smoothest, still, if you are taught of God, you will say, 'To be with Christ is far better.' And the more doubts you have, O feeble believer, so much the more let the thoughts of departing be sweet and pleasant unto you, for there are no doubts yonder.

2. WE SHALL BE LIKE HIM IN HOLINESS.

To depart and be with Christ is far better: it is far better to be with Christ, for *then we shall be like Him in holiness*. When a sinner flees to Christ he is 'born again', by the Holy Ghost. A new life is begun in his soul which shall never come to an end. A spark has been lighted that shall never be quenched. The 'leaven' is thrust in, and the whole shall yet be 'leavened'. The seed is sown, and there shall yet be a harvest. The Spirit has come to his soul, and will never wholly leave it. 'He which hath begun a good work in you will perform it until the day of Jesus Christ.' But as long as the believer is in this world, there are many things to retard the progress of this life of holiness.

i. *There is a body of sin and death.* The believer is quite different from the world. He hates all sin; strives against all sin; prays against all sin; and yet he has a body of sin and death. Sin does not reign in him as a king, and yet it dwells in him as a hated guest. Now, this of all things most keeps back the life of holiness. The world is full of temptation suited to his natural heart. He cannot go into any company but he will meet with some thing drawing him to sin. The believer often has wicked acquaintances who side with the evil part of his nature and, above all things, try to draw him into worldly compliances. Besides, his old habits return upon him again and again. Before he was a believer he followed in some path of sensuality, or covetousness, or passionateness, and now he will at times experience almost irresistible impulses to go back to his old courses.

ii. *Above all, Satan, the accuser of the brethren, tries to beguile him from the simplicity that is in Christ.* He knows that there is but one way in which a believer can walk holily, that is, by abiding in Christ, so that Christ may abide in him, and he may bear much fruit; and, therefore, against this Satan directs all his energies. In this way, most of all, does Satan try to keep down the life of holiness. But when we 'depart' and are 'with Christ' all these hindrances shall drop off; and therefore it is far better 'to depart'.

The believer at death is 'made perfect in holiness'. Nothing that defileth can enter into paradise; nothing that makes or loves a lie. The body of sin and death has been laid in the gloomy grave. No more does he cry out, 'O wretched man that I am! who shall deliver me?' The world with its busy hum, with its fascinating companies, and pleasures of sin, that world is left behind. The dead ear cannot hear its siren melody. The glazed eye cannot behold its vain show. And the spirit is safe 'with Christ'. The wicked companions, too, are all left behind. Their jests and their raillery are heard no more.

No more does the hand of friendship tempt to sin. There are no wicked companions with Christ. The old habits are now put off for ever. There is no fear now of returning to old courses of sin! The heart is now made perfect in holiness. He is led by the Lamb to living fountains of water. And, last of all, Satan his great enemy cannot reach him now. He is the prince of the power of the air. But to be with Christ is to be above the air, it is to be 'in Paradise'. Satan cannot enter into this Paradise. 'There shall in no wise enter into it any thing that defileth, neither whatsoever worketh abomination' (*Rev.* 21:27).

And not only shall the soul be freed from all that would draw it to sin, but every thing there shall incite it to holiness. In this world, almost everything we see, or hear, or handle, may lead the soul to sin. In that world everything shall lead the soul to holiness. We shall see Christ. We shall see God. 'Blessed are the pure in heart, for they shall see God.' 'We shall be like him, for we shall see him as he is.' And how can we see His loveliness without loving Him? How can we love Him without serving Him? And if we love Him, we will keep His commandments.

Oh, professed believer in Christ, do you love holiness? You are no believer if you do not. Do you long after it, and pray for it? Do you groan under sin, and are you wearied to be rid of it? 'To be with Christ' is to be rid of it for evermore! Oh, then, how plainly should it appear to you that it is better to depart and 'to be with Christ'!

Why, then, will any of you cling to this world, as if it were your all? Why will you labour to be rich, and pierce yourselves through 'with many sorrows'? And why are you so afraid of death? Why do you shudder at the very name of death? It is a dark avenue; but it opens into the world of holiness and never-ending life. 'To depart and to be with Christ is far better.'

3. NO MORE TRIBULATION

It is better to be with Christ, for there will be *no more tribulation*. When a sinner flees to Christ, he is pardoned, justified, has peace, rejoices in God his Saviour, and is enabled to 'glory in tribulations also'. The God of providence becomes his Father, and therefore he will not fear what man can do unto him. He has the ordinary troubles of other men; pains, and losses, and bereavements; but he

Desiring to Depart and to Be with Christ

feels that a Father's hand administers every cup of suffering, that a Father's hand gathers all his tears 'into his bottle'. He has troubles which other men have not, persecutions and hatred from the world; and yet he has joy here too, for he knows that God is able to shut the lions' mouths, and to shelter him from the 'world's dread laugh'. But still, this world is to the believer a world of sorrow. This is a fact which cannot be concealed. The Bridegroom is not here. But 'to be with Christ' is to be free from all tribulation, and, therefore, it is far better.

When Christ ascended to His Father and our Father, He bade farewell to sin and sorrow for evermore. No more will He bear the pangs of infancy in His hard cradle in the manger! No more will He bear the pains of hunger in the wilderness! No more sit down wearied by the well of Sychar! No more will He sleep for weariness in the fishermen's boat, rocked by the dashing waves! No more will He bear the pains of false friends! No more will He bear the kiss of the betrayer! No more will He feel the pains of His pierced hands and feet! No more will He feel the shame of the cross! No more will His tongue cleave to his jaws for thirst! No more will He say, My heart is melted like wax in the midst of my bowels! No more will He bow the head in dying agony! All His pains are past, and all His wounds are healed! The scar in His side is now whole. His body is now 'a glorious body'.

His raiment is white as the light, and His face is as the sun shining in its strength! Oh, brethren, if ye be members of Christ's body, ye, too, shall be free from tribulation, sin, and suffering when you die. You shall bid farewell to sin and sorrow for evermore. Now you may be often hungry and often thirsty, often faint and weary, toiling in the sun. But then you shall hunger no more, neither thirst any more, neither shall the sun light on you, nor any heat. In this world you may have 'much tribulation', but at death you shall come out of great tribulation, and serve Him day and night in His temple. Here the world may scorn you, and point the finger, and put out the lip; but with Christ you shall be free from all; you shall be out of hearing of 'the world's dread laugh'. Oh, is it not far better to depart and be 'with Christ'?

4. WE SHALL PRAISE MORE HEARTILY.

It is better to be with Christ, for *then we shall praise God and Christ more heartily.*

When a sinner is first brought to cleave to Christ, then, for the first time, does he praise God heartily. Unconverted men may join in singing 'psalms, and hymns and spiritual songs', but they never praise God from the heart. But often the first opening of the mouth of a poor sinner brought to Christ is in praises. 'Bless the LORD, O my soul: and all that is within me, bless his holy name.'

Nothing gives more joy to a true believer than to praise God. The singing of psalms of praise has always abounded most in the best times of the church; and hence it may clearly be seen how small the company of believers is in our day, when the singing of psalms in families is so little known, and so few join heartily in the praises of the sanctuary.

But the believer cannot always praise in this world. He is often afflicted, and, being afflicted, he prays; or, even if he be merry and sings psalms, yet, oh, how cold are his praises compared with the praises which he might be expected to give! How little proportioned to the glory of Him we praise!

Oh, how seldom does the believing heart glow with a flame of praise! But when we are 'with Christ' we shall always praise, and praise Him in the highest degree; therefore it is far better to be with Christ.

Desiring to Depart and to Be with Christ

i. We Shall Always Have a Vivid Sense of What We Are Saved From.

On earth, we have low and poor conceptions of the wrath of God, and these only at times; therefore we are little thankful for being brought to Christ. But in heaven we shall see the wrath of God poured out upon the Christless; we shall see their pale, dismal faces, we shall hear their sad cries and the gnashing of their teeth; we shall see the smoke of their torment ascending up before God for ever. Oh, how shall we praise God for His electing love that chose us to salvation! How all believers shall praise Christ for His redeeming love, for enduring such pains in our stead! There shall be no end to our praise, and it shall be rendered with all our heart.

ii. We Shall Always Have a Vivid Sense of What We Are Saved To.

On earth, we have low and poor conceptions of the blessedness of God's favour, and friendship, and love, therefore we are little thankful. But then we shall feel more fully the warmth of His love. We shall drink the rivers of his pleasures, our joy shall be full; we shall be like vessels filled to overflowing: 'In thy presence is fullness of joy; at thy right hand there are pleasures for evermore.' We shall feel all this, and feel that we have been redeemed that we may enjoy all this. Oh, how we shall praise Christ then for his obedience in our stead, and God the Father for His love in sending His Son to be our Substitute and Surety!

iii. We Shall Have a Constant Sight of the Beauty and Glory of God and of Christ.

On earth, we have very poor conceptions of the infinite loveliness of God. It is only now and then that a believer enters so fully through the rent veil as to 'behold the beauty of the Lord, and to enquire in his temple' (*Psa.* 27:4); but then we shall be like pillars in the temple of our God, and go no more out. It is only in the works of creation and providence, sometimes in the ordinances, in the Word, or broken bread, that we can see God. It is, at the best, but 'as in a glass darkly'; but then 'face to face'. We shall know even as we are known. No more 'in a glass', but in reality, we shall see God, and eternally gaze on His uncreated loveliness. Oh, what praises shall this draw from our burning hearts to all eternity! 'This God is our God for ever and ever.' Oh, then, brethren, is it not better to be 'with Christ', that we may love and praise God more?

Even on earth much of the believer's happiness consists in praise. The happiest Christians are always most engaged in praise. The more heavenly-minded you grow, the more you will abound in praise. The work of heaven is often described as praise. Every description of heaven given in the book of Revelation contains much of praises in it. The true happiness of a creature consists in giving praise to the God who made him. Oh, then, how much better to depart and be 'with Christ'! It is far, far better!

iii. This Should Reconcile Us to the Death of Believing Friends.

They are now with Christ, and that is far better; and shall we grudge them their happiness? When friends are removed to a distance in this world; when they go to the golden shores of India; when they make money, or settle well in the world, we do not grudge them their happiness. And why would you grudge believing friends to be with Christ, which is far better than thousands of gold and of silver?

iv. This Should Reconcile Us to Die.

If we are, indeed, believers, to die is to be with Christ, which is far better. Do you doubt if it be better to be with Christ than to be here? Then you are no believer. You say, I am a feeble believer. Then it is most of all good and blessed for you to be, 'with Christ'. The feeblest swimmer is the one that should long most for the shore. The ship that is tempest-tossed and most shattered should long most for the harbour. So you, if you are a feeble believer, should see more than others how desirable it is to be with Christ. If you have many doubts and fears, if you have much opposition to your holiness, if you cannot bear the world's scorn and raillery, if you have but seldom a full heart of praise, then you should, most of all, long 'to be with Christ': for to you, more than to others, it is 'far better' than to be here.

v. See Also How Sad It Is to Be Christless!

All this time I have been speaking to the children of God, the little flock. Oh, do not think that I have been speaking to you, poor Christless souls! It is not better for you to depart. Oh, it would be far worse for you. This world is your only heaven. Beyond it everywhere to you is hell. May God write this truth upon your hearts – If you be not 'in Christ' in time, you will never be 'with Christ' in eternity.

21

Peter the Apostle

Peter, an apostle of Jesus Christ, to the strangers scattered throughout Pontus, Galatia, Cappadocia, Asia, and Bithynia, elect according to the foreknowledge of God the Father, through sanctification of the Spirit, unto obedience and sprinkling of the blood of Jesus Christ: Grace unto you, and peace, be multiplied. Blessed be the God and Father of our Lord Jesus Christ, which according to his abundant mercy hath begotten us again unto a lively hope by the resurrection of Jesus Christ from the dead (1 Pet. 1:1–3).

1. THE WRITER OF THIS EPISTLE

NOTICE FIRST WHO WRITES. It is 'Peter, an apostle of Jesus Christ'. This is the man to whom Jesus, in full knowledge that he would deny him, said, 'Simon, Simon, behold, Satan hath desired to have you, that he may sift you as wheat: but I have prayed for thee, that thy faith fail not: and when thou art converted, strengthen thy brethren' (Luke 22:31–32).

God has not chosen angels but sinful men to bear His message. He has not chosen saints that never went back, but those who are like Peter; who have denied their Lord times and ways without number, that we may speak without pride, that we may speak more earnestly, as having felt the misery of falls and backslidings.

Peter the Apostle

He was an apostle of Jesus Christ, that is, he was sent by Christ, and sent to make Christ known. Ministers are sent of God. The word 'Apostles' means 'sent ones'.

When we preach from Scripture you should look upon our word not as the word of man but as it is in truth, the Word of Christ. This is one great reason for the lack of success of the preaching of the Word. Hearers say, 'I am of Paul, I of Apollos, and I of Cephas.' 'Will you go and hear such-and-such a minister today?', people say. You do not come to hear the Word of Christ, and so you have your reward. You get the word of the minister, but you lose the Word of Christ, which alone can pierce the heart.

2. THOSE TO WHOM HE WROTE

Those to whom Peter wrote are described in two ways:

i. AS TO THEIR TEMPORAL CONDITION

a. *They were strangers.*

They were Jews scattered in a foreign land, among a strange people, reproached, a proverb and a by-word among the nations, yet grace found them out. God often chooses the most unlikely: a stranger, an orphan. Oh! happy stranger if God has chosen you! How many He has left, the rich, the whole, the wise, the good. 'O, to grace how great a debtor daily I'm constrained to be!' Learn to feel strangers here. This is not your home.

b. *They were scattered.*

These Christians would fain have been all together in one flourishing colony, but God says, 'Let them be scattered.' All are one in Christ. One in affliction, one in life, one in glory, but on earth it is the will of God that they should be scattered, one in one house another in another. Why? For two reasons:

1. *That their faith may be tried.*

Faith grows best when it has something to try it. A young person is taught of God in a godless family. There is plenty to contend with there. Faith grows like the palm tree: the more it is held down, the more it grows.

2. *That they may be witnesses for God.*

When a king has a proclamation to make, he does not send his heralds in a body but scatters them. So it is with God. In lighting a town, you scatter the lamps. The same is true in lighting a house. In salting meat, you scatter the salt. So does God.

c. *Where they were scattered.*

Men from the countries mentioned heard Peter preach at Jerusalem, as recorded in Acts. Ministers love to feed their own children in the faith, and their children love to be fed by them. This is human nature. God does not forbid that it should be so.

ii. As to Their Spiritual Condition

Peter refers to the work of the Father, the Son and the Spirit in their salvation. They were strangers and scattered, yet not so in the eyes of God. Father, Son and Holy Ghost were all interested in their salvation. So is it with some among you. Some are strangers and scattered, little known among men, yet they are jewels in the sight of God. Father, Son and Spirit are all concerned about you. Angels are sent to minister to these heirs of salvation.

a. *They are 'elect according to the foreknowledge of God the Father'.*

'Blessed is the man whom thou choosest' (*Psa.* 65:4). The beginning of salvation lies in the choice of the Father.

This is so in natural things as well. In His providence, God chooses one to be blind, deaf, rich or poor, lame, born in this land or that, according to the good pleasure of His will. It is not for the goodness or badness of the people concerned, but for His own glory. He has power over the same clay to make vessels for different purposes. It is especially so in salvation. He chooses whose hearts shall be broken, who shall believe. So it comes to pass that as many as are ordained to eternal life believe, not for any goodness in one more than another. For all are lost by nature; none is good, none deserves to be chosen. Indeed, He sometimes chooses the worst, or the wickedest, like Paul, the chief of sinners, publicans and sinners, or Mary Magdalene.

OBJECTION:
Some will say that this is inconsistent with the freeness of the gospel. Christ died for all, and God is willing that all should be saved.

ANSWER:
a. I could not reconcile these, yet I would believe both, for I find both in the Bible, and I would wait patiently till the day declares it. Childlike Christians receive both, believe both.

b. I believe that the heart of God wishes every one to come to Christ and be saved. But still, His infinite wisdom as the ruler of ten thousand worlds, might determine otherwise. It might be more for His glory if some were made a monument of unsparing justice in hell, and therefore He has, according to His own free grace, chosen some to everlasting life, and left others to perish.

OBJECTION:
This will make men proud.

ANSWER:
Rather, it makes men lowly. Oh, Christian, it is this that sinks you in the dust. You are no better than the thousands among whom

you are scattered, yet God has chosen you. Love Him who has so singularly loved you.

b. *They are elect through sanctification of the Spirit.*

The word 'sanctification' is here taken in the same sense as in Hebrews, to describe the work of the Spirit. This is the work of awakening, comforting, and sanctifying; the whole work by which He severs a soul from the world. The Bible cannot do this; ministers cannot; but the Spirit can! Remember, you have no evidence that you are a child of God, if you have not the work of the Spirit in your heart.

c. *They are elect unto obedience and sprinkling of Christ's blood.*

1. *It is to the sprinkling of the blood.*

Whenever there is a true work of grace, it leads to a real sprinkling. No tears can blot out sin. Only blood can, the blood of the Son of God; not a bare knowledge of Christ, but real sprinkling. The veil is rent, and anyone *may* enter, but none are saved but those who *do* enter. The sacrifice is slain for the sins of the whole world, but none are saved but those who are sprinkled. Do not live without the sprinkling of His blood.

2. *It is to obedience.*

They that are sprinkled from dead works love to serve the living God. Test if you be forgiven in this way: do you long to obey God? Is this the language of your soul: 'O that my ways were directed to keep thy statutes! (*Psa.* 119:5)?

22

Blessed Be God!

Blessed be the God and Father of our Lord Jesus Christ, which according to his abundant mercy hath begotten us again unto a lively hope by the resurrection of Jesus Christ from the dead, to an inheritance incorruptible, and undefiled, and that fadeth not away, reserved in heaven for you (1 Pet. 1:3–4).

1. CHRISTIANS ARE ALL BORN AGAIN.

ADDRESSING THE SCATTERED CHRISTIANS, Peter says they have been begotten again. He says it all with the utmost freedom and without qualification, so it must be true of all Christians. No man is born a Christian. By nature we are all 'children of wrath' (*Eph.* 2:3). You will observe selfishness and passion in your youngest children, just as you will see fierceness in a wild beast before its teeth are grown. Every one needs a supernatural change.

Some wonder why we always preach about conversion. The reason is that you must *all* be born again, or you will perish. If we preach against drunkenness, it applies only to some. If we preach against swearing, it applies only to some. But when we preach, 'Ye must be born again', it applies to all, to the respectable, the amiable, the kind, as well as to abandoned prodigals.

i. THIS IS A SUPERNATURAL CHANGE.

It comes from God. Many changes come from man. Take a wild child, and put him to school; he will learn to be quiet and orderly, and this is the change of education. Take a person that never attended the church, and bring him to regular ordinances. He will learn to sing the Psalms, to stand up at prayer, to become outwardly decent and quiet. Take a person that was addicted to drinking and open brawling: if you can convince him that he is ruining his credit, he will become sober and quiet. These are all changes, but none of them is conversion.

Conversion is from God, the Father of Christ. It is a work of God on the soul. The means of it is the Word (*James* 1:18). Although in 1 Corinthians 4:15, and also in Galatians 4:19, ministers are said to be spiritual fathers to believers, yet it is altogether a divine hand that renews the soul, that gives life to the dead. A man can as soon bring himself into being as renew his soul. There is a danger of putting off this change from year to year. Are you born again? If not, you cannot see the kingdom of God. You may be decent and nice, but if not born again, you will perish. You cannot just do it any time.

ii. IT FLOWS FROM HIS ABUNDANT MERCY.

When I go into a house and persuade a man to be in earnest about his soul, and to convince him that he needs a new birth, he begins to try to do it for himself. When he fails here, he seeks to make himself worthy of it. He tries to recommend himself to God. But look at the text: God does it of His abundant mercy, not for any goodness in man. Struggles after self-salvation will end in failure. We must either submit to a divine work or, like the rich young man in the Gospels, we will have to go away sorrowful.

iii. God Should Be Praised.

'Blessed be the God and Father of our Lord Jesus Christ'! God has done everything for His glory. Sun, moon, and stars were created that they might show forth His praise. So was all of creation. So also is the new creation! A soul born again is a matter for great praise to God. Christians, be sure to praise Him for what He has done for your souls. 'Blessed be *God*', not ministers. Although we are to esteem them highly in love for their works' sake (*1 Thess.* 5:13), we are to bless God. You should praise Him for others, as well as yourselves. You should be interested in other Christians and praise God for them. Praise Him in your life, and then eternity shall be all praise.

2. ALL THOSE BORN AGAIN HAVE A LIVING HOPE OF AN INHERITANCE.

i. Before a Man Is Born Again He Has No Living Hope.

Unconverted men seldom really think of the eternal world. When they are forced to do so, they have a dead, dry hope that the Bible will prove false and that, though they have no work of grace in their hearts, yet they shall somehow get in.

ii. When a Man Is Brought to Christ He Receives Hope.

He believes in Christ as his Surety, risen from the dead. He feels that an inheritance has been purchased for him, yea, Christ has taken possession of it, and that he shall have his portion, therefore he cannot but hope.

iii. It Is a Living Hope.

This hope is undying. It cannot be quenched in the Christian's bosom. Despite suffering and bereavement, it still lives. Strip a

Christian of everything, you cannot strip him of this. Let him lose hope of health, of friends, of life, all these hopes may die. But this hope dies not. It is a living hope, as long as the eye is fixed on a living Christ, as long as the bosom is filled with a living hope of being with Him.

Oh, Christians, maintain this if you would be cheerful and happy! It is the grand secret of happiness. We are saved by hope. It is an anchor of the soul, sure and steadfast, entering within the veil. The anchor holds when all other things fail. The night may become dark, so that you cannot see the shore. The stormy waves may forbid all boats to come near – still the anchor holds.

3. THE INHERITANCE THE CHRISTIAN HOPES FOR

i. It Is Incorruptible.

It never degerates. A thing may never fade away, and yet be corruptible. But the inheritance is subject to no normal decay. Its joys do not become dry; they do not turn bitter. Everything here is corruptible. The finest garments become moth-eaten. Bread grows stale and sour. Even gold is 'corruptible' (*1 Pet.* 1:18). Everything there is incorruptible. It is like the garments of Israel which waxed not old during their journeyings in the wilderness.

ii. It Is Undefiled.

Nothing unclean can enter. The inheritance is without stain of sin. Everything here is defiled. The purest friendship is defiled. Even the holy assemblies of Christians show much defilement. But there, there is no defilement. Christians, in using the world, do abuse it. How seldom do they eat their meat without defiling themselves. In the feast above, everything is completely pure.

iii. It Is Unfading.

It used to be said of the *Amarantus*, or amaranth, that its flowers never faded.[1] Crowns were made of it to adorn the brows of victors. So is it with our inheritance. It never fades. Here the best things are fading. Some that took sweet counsel with us in the year that is past have faded away. Like a broken vessel, they are forgotten. Our sweetest, holiest joys here are fading. But one thing is unfading, the glory of Christ's inheritance, and our inheritance in Him; and this is reserved in heaven for all who believe.

---

[1] Pliny (1st century AD) wrote of the *amaranth*, a flower that never faded, and Clement of Alexandria (2nd century AD) said the amaranth was the symbol of immortality. Milton also referred to it in *Paradise Lost*.

23

Kept by God's Power

Who are kept by the power of God through faith unto salvation ready to be revealed in the last time (1 Pet. 1:5).

1. THERE IS AN INHERITANCE KEPT FOR BELIEVERS.

As we have seen in verse 4, there is an inheritance for believers, reserved for them in heaven.

i. It Is in Christ's Keeping.

It is in the keeping of Christ, their elder brother, for He is not ashamed to call them brethren (*Heb.* 2:11). He is keeping it for them, and is already in possession of it. He will take care that they receive it, and that it is not any the worse for being kept.

ii. It Is Kept in Heaven.

The inheritance of believers is kept in heaven where nothing can invade, there is no rust, no war, and none can break in and steal. Paul speaks of a crown of righteousness laid up for him (*2 Tim.* 4:8).

Being in heaven, it is therefore most precious. If I were to speak of a jewel kept in the cabinet of a Queen, you would say at once, It must be most precious. So it is in this case.

2. BELIEVERS ARE ALSO KEPT BY THE POWER OF GOD.

They are guarded around. They are like sheep, or lambs, kept by the Shepherd. However mighty their enemies may be, God is for them, and who then can be against them (*Rom.* 8:31)? The omnipotence of God guards them. They are held in the hand of God, and none can pluck them out of the Father's hand (*John* 10:29). They are like Daniel in the lions' den. God shuts the lions' mouths so that they do no hurt.

'I know whom I have believed', says Paul, 'and am persuaded that he is able to keep that which I have committed unto him against that day' (*2 Tim.* 1:12). So it may be said to them, 'Fear not, thou worm Jacob, and ye men of Israel; I will help thee, saith the LORD' (*Isa.* 41:14). They may seem to be only a few frail men, but God is their strength.

3. THEY ARE KEPT THROUGH FAITH.

i. GOD IS THE AUTHOR OF FAITH.

He first tears away the veil of prejudice, and enables us to believe. He grants us faith to look to Jesus and have peace, to believe the testimony of God concerning His Son. Faith may be very small, like a grain of mustard seed, only a small spark; but, if real, it is very precious.

ii. HE KEEPS UP FAITH IN THE HEART.

The power of God is required to maintain faith in the hearts of His people, just as it is required to keep the world in being. Some seem to be kept with a steady gaze on things invisible, others seem to go on by fits and starts. But God relights the lamp of faith if it should go out. He suffers it not to fail.

iii. In This Way the Soul Is Kept.

By the maintenance of faith, the soul is kept in peace and holiness, despite the opposition of the world, the devil, and the flesh.

4. HOW LONG ARE THEY KEPT?

They are 'kept . . . unto salvation, ready to be revealed in the last time' (verse 5).

We see from this verse:

i. that God will keep believers to the last, till the soul enters into glory.

ii. that salvation is ready and waiting for the believer.

iii. that we really know very little of it – so little that it has to be *revealed*, when the valley of death is past. What a revelation that will be!

24

Rejoicing in Affliction

Wherein ye greatly rejoice, though now for a season, if need be, ye are in heaviness through manifold temptations: that the trial of your faith, being much more precious than of gold that perisheth, though it be tried with fire, might be found unto praise and honour and glory at the appearing of Jesus Christ (1 Pet. 1:6–7).

1. THE BELIEVER REJOICES DESPITE TRIALS.

THE CHRISTIAN IS ENABLED to rejoice greatly, even when he is grieved by manifold trials. He rejoices and grieves at the same time. He is a mass of contradictions. He is weak, yet strong; has no righteousness, yet is divinely righteous; has no strength, yet is invincible; a worm, yet threshes mountains (*Isa.* 41:14–15); poor, yet making many rich; sorrowful, yet always rejoicing. Joy and grief fill his heart at the same time, so that it is possible that he may 'receive the word in much affliction, with joy of the Holy Ghost' (*1 Thess.* 1:6).

i. ALL MEN HAVE TROUBLES.

'Man is born unto trouble, as the sparks fly upward' (*Job* 5:7). There is a crook in every one's lot. Some men appear very happy when you look at them from a distance, but come near and you will see that they have their trials too. The poor think the rich have no pain. The rich think the contented poor must be happy. But if the truth were known, it would be found that all have their pains. Why? Because God is pleading with all, bringing them into the wilderness and pleading face to face.

ii. THE CHILDREN OF GOD HAVE TROUBLES.

Even his dear children are not free, but have manifold trials. A young believer thinks he is to go on a soft carpet or on moss all the way to glory. He soon comes on thorns, indeed, thorn upon thorn. We must 'through much tribulation enter into the kingdom of God'.

Things fall out contrary to their natural inclinations. There are sudden piercings and breakings into the serenity of their lives. The believer grieves, and is heavy. He feels every pang. Is he not a man like every other? The foot of a believer is as tender as that of any other to the piercing of a thorn. His affections are also as keen. He cannot but grieve. Our Saviour entered into this: 'Jesus wept' (*John* 11:35). Many are the afflictions of the righteous, and of many different kinds, and they are a matter of real grief.

iii. THEY REJOICE AT THE SAME TIME.

One part of the body may rejoice, and another be sick. A man may have a thorn in his foot, and yet taste something sweet at the same time, yea, the taste may be so excellent, as to drown the pain. So it is with the soul. Its source of joy is infinite. Believers are born again unto a living hope. They are kept by the power of God. What can affect this joy? The brightest gleams of sunshine are amid the storm and clouds.

As the rainbow is brighter the darker the cloud, so is this joy, very often. As the sea bird delights to ride upon the top of the angry billows, so does this joy of the Christian ride upon the wave top. Pain in one part does not hinder a great joy in another. The thirst of fever makes the draught more pleasant.

2. BELIEVERS' TRIALS ARE ONLY FOR A SEASON.

A believer's trials are only for a season. The very word 'trial' proves this. Gold is tried only for a season. Everything here is but for a season. *The pleasures of sin* are but for a season. *The world* is but for a season. These light afflictions are but for a moment. In childhood, every day seems an age, but when childhood is done, how short and dreamlike it seems; it is but a season. So when we come to the manhood of our being, what a little spark our dark days shall be! Our joy is truly endless joy, our grief for a season.

i. Often Only for a Season in This World.

When God's end in sending the rod is answered, he takes it away. He is a Father, and chastises only in measure. Jacob lamented for Joseph, but it was for a season. His sorrow was turned into joy. Job lamented for a season, but the clouds went past. So whenever God's end is accomplished, he lifts the trial away. The children of God should enquire as to God's intention in their affliction. Obey God's wish in it, and then He will lift it away.

ii. Certainly Only till They Come to Die.

Believers should learn not to be over-burdened with anything in this life. It is for a season only. It may be said, Surely the world has the same troubles and the same comforts as the believer. No, they differ. To say no more than this, their troubles are not for a season only. Unless they obtain the salvation of God, they will be eternally troubled.

3. THERE IS A NEED BE FOR THEM ALL.

i. A Need for the Unconverted's Troubles

a. *To convince them of sin*. His own wickedness shall reprove him. The troubles of Joseph's brethren were of this sort.

b. *To restrain them from an excess of wickedness.*

c. *To give them an aversion to sin and to allure them.*

ii. A Need for the Troubles of God's Children

a. *They try faith.* The trials of Job were all of this kind: to try the character of his faith. True faith is more precious than gold.

b. *They purify faith.* They are like the trial of gold. It purifies it. Our trials wean us from leaning on the world. If we have been bent on backsliding, we are driven to retrurn.

c. *They make faith grow.* Trials strengthen faith. They drive us to prayer.

4. THE OUTCOME OF AFFLICTIONS.

As a result of the trials of believers, faith is turned into praise. The Christian will hear the words, Well done, good and faithful servant! Trials are necessary to all God's children. Our best qualities are tried, purified and strengthened. Abraham was tried in his faith. Moses was tried in his meekness. Many things make affliction needful to every believer. And they have a glorious issue: faith tried will be found at length 'unto praise and honour and glory at the appearing of Jesus Christ' (verse 7).

25

The Trial of Faith

That the trial of your faith, being much more precious than of gold that perisheth, though it be tried with fire, might be found unto praise and honour and glory at the appearing of Jesus Christ (1 Pet. 1:7).

FAITH IS 'more precious than gold that perisheth'. This is why it is tried – it is worth more than gold. When a person is thoroughly awakened all the world will not cure their heart trouble. But let the person once have faith – that brings peace. Oh! it is more precious than gold. Faith lays hold of all that is in Christ. Gold cannot get at this. Gold can buy many things, but not this.

1. FAITH IS MORE PRECIOUS THAN GOLD.

   i. IN ITS ORIGIN

   It is the gift of God to His chosen. Gold He gives to many. He scatters it broadly, but what does He give his favourites, His chosen ones? He gives faith. Faith, then, must be much more precious than gold. Poor in this world are often rich in faith.

   ii. IN WHAT IT CAN DO

   It gives peace to a troubled conscience. Gold cannot do this. Again, it purifies the heart, gold cannot. There is no greater misery than to be the slave of sinful passion. Can gold purify the soul? No, Faith alone can. 'This is the victory that overcometh the world, even our faith.'

iii. IT WILL LAST THROUGH DEATH.

Gold will perish. Sometimes it is stolen, or takes wings and flies away. At best we are torn from it. You may grasp your money till you die. You may hide it beneath your dying pillow, and squeeze it in death, but you will be torn from it all. Your bonds and bills may hold good till you die, but at the end they will be vain for you. A vessel may be riding at anchor and, while the anchor holds strong, she drifts away. The anchors remain but the vessel is drifting in a stormy sea. So it may be with you. Your bonds and bills may hold fast, your houses may yield their rent, but you may be drifting in the rough sea of an undone eternity. But faith holds on to and is held by an unseen Saviour.

A word to those who seek money.

Do not make it the one thing needful. See, here is something much more precious! Not I, but God, says so. But the wicked cannot take God at His Word.

A word to the poor.

I would say to the poor, Be rich in God. Gain is not ungodliness, but godliness with contentment is great gain.

2. GOD WILL TRY FAITH.

Christ is a Refiner. The first thing that is done with gold when it is taken from the mine is to cast it into the fire. So when Christ comes to any soul, He comes as a Refiner. He sits by the furnace, yea, He walks in the furnace. Why must this be done?

i. To Make Manifest that It Is Faith

'Can this be gold?', the miner cries. 'It is all encrusted. It is something like gold. Put it in the furnace and we shall see.' So does your Refiner. 'Can this be a believer? He is something like one. Put him in the furnace and we shall see.' So it was with Job. If they cleave to Jesus in the furnace, then it is true faith. When a house is standing in a sunken garden, uninvaded by storms, you cannot tell if the foundation is on rock. But when a storm drives everything away, then it is seen that it is founded on rock. In fair weather, you do not know if a graft has taken effect. The wind will try it.

A word to those that are in trouble:

The Refiner is trying you. See that you come out as gold. Contending with the storm, you do not know whether you swim or no. Often poverty shows that men have no faith. Often they forsake God, abandon prayer, and look to the world to comfort them, though before they seemed religious.

ii. To Purify It

There is great mixture with gold. The goldsmith does not want to lose his gold, but he wants to take the dross away. So Christ does not want to lose anything of faith when He tries it. He wants to take the dross away. There is much dross in most believers.

iii. To Strengthen It.

Faith grows strong when contending with difficulties.

a. *In natural troubles*

The storm on the lake was to strengthen the disciples' faith. 'O ye of little faith!' 'Where is your faith?' When you are threatened with poverty, be assured that God will never let you want. As you feel old age creeping on, still believe God that you shall not lack any good thing.

The Trial of Faith

A knot is all the tighter, the more you pull on it. Iron is all the stronger, the more you beat it. In times when all is bright, it is hard to look beyond. In learning to swim, the thing which strengthens our stroke is the opposing billows. Swimming up the stream strengthens us most. In learning to wrestle, you do not sit still.

b. *In spiritual troubles*

The effect of these is the same, to strengthen faith. It is easy to believe when all goes well, when the face of God is toward you, and you have no temptations. But can you believe in trials and in temptations? Can you lean all the more on Christ? Can you say, 'Lord, if thou help me not, I am unhelped.' This strengthens faith. Be not angry if God try you. It is good for us, even here. He tries us always in our strongest part. He tried Abraham's faith, Job's patience, Moses' meekness, Peter's courage, John's love.

3. THE END IN VIEW.

Gold is always wanted for a great end: to be made up into a crown, or into coin, or for some great end. So God tries us for a great end.

i. *We shall come out of the furnace.* There is a world where faith is not tried any more, as there is a time when the gold is taken out. He will not always be trying it.

ii. *Tried faith shall be found in that day.* Just as none of the gold is lost, so no faith shall be lost. All that ever believed shall be found unto praise, honour and glory in that day, amid the ruins of the world.

iv. *It will be, above all, to the praise of Christ.* He gave us faith, preserved us, and upheld such worms as we are. To Him be all the endless glory!

26

Loving Christ Unseen

Whom having not seen, ye love; in whom, though now ye see him not, yet believing, ye rejoice with joy unspeakable and full of glory: receiving the end of your faith, even the salvation of your souls (1 Pet. 1:8–9).

1. THESE BELIEVERS HAD NEVER SEEN CHRIST.

MANY WHO SAW HIM in the days of His flesh were none the better, and many who shall see Him shall wail because of Him. From this we learn that faith is not seeing. When Jesus says, 'Look unto Me', He does not mean a look of the bodily eye, nor a sight of Him in a vision, nor fancying you see him with a smiling face. No, these people were quite happy, though they had never seen Christ. Many believe in Christ who have never seen Him.

i. Faith Is Not Seeing with the Bodily Eye.

Many saw Christ in Capernaum, preaching out of the boat, in the temple of Jerusalem, on the great day of the Feast, yet did not believe. Yea, many saw Him on the cross, His hands and side pierced, saw the darkness come over Him, saw His face of agony, His bowed head, and yet were none the better. Some wagged their heads, some smote on their breasts, yet none were converted thereby.

Many will see Christ in clouds of heaven when He comes a second time, and shall wail. John fell at His feet as dead. How much more His enemies when He comes to destroy them, no more a Saviour, but a Judge. Ah! it is no sight of Christ that shall give peace in that day. Men shall wish that they had not eyes to look, so terrible will His appearance be.

ii. Faith Is Not Seeing Christ in a Vision.

It is not seeing any beautiful form, or imagining you see a smiling countenance. Some enthusiastic persons have been led to think themselves pardoned because of their imagination, having a sight of Christ in their minds. I do not say this is impossible, but I say faith is quite another thing, and far more excellent.

2. THEY BELIEVED IN HIM UNSEEN.

Faith is a heart reception of God's Word concerning an unseen Saviour, and so does not depend on sight. They believed on Him unseen, and that gave joy.

When a soul is brought to feel itself lost and condemned, and brought to be wearied of that condition; when it is brought to find the emptiness of all human means of obtaining righteousness, then when the truth of God shines brightly upon it, like the sun upon snow, the soul joyfully says, 'It is true, it is true; He died for sinners. He died for me.'

Again, a person feels his emptiness, and feels his own sinful passions very strong. He is driven to see the vanity of all resolutions to help. He believes the record of the unseen Saviour: Christ as an Advocate, Christ an Intercessor, Christ giving the Spirit. This does not at all depend upon sight. Christ is coming again, we know not when. We see Him not yet, but believe in His appearing.

3. Faith in Christ Unseen Brings Joy.

If you saw a man with an open letter in his hand weeping tears of joy, his heart too full for utterance, you would say, He has had some good news from a far country. He believes something which he does not see. So is it with the Christian when God opens his heart to the message of the Bible: he sheds tears of joy.

i. Unconverted People Have Much Joy.

There is joy in living, the elation of health, the bracing air – these are real to everyone. They are the joys of nature which are felt by all. *There is joy in business*. You cannot look upon the active bustling air of your men of business, their active steps, their quick look of intelligence, their regularity like the hands of the clock, without feeling something of this. *There is joy in friends* – in home, the fire, the smiling faces there, the meeting in the morning, the parting at night. In the most godless families there are drops of daily joy from this which can scarcely be numbered. *There is joy in sin* – from the magic charms of the theatre and the fascinating delights of the low tavern, there is a troubled joy in sin. Stolen waters are sweet and bread eaten in secret is pleasant.

ii. When God Begins a Work of Grace, Joy Vanishes.

When God reveals his past life in the light of the law, or in the light of His countenance, or in the light of the cross, the sinner feels condemned already. The curses of the law shut his mouth when he looks to it for help. He also feels condemned when he looks to God. 'He that believeth not is condemned already' (*John* 3:18). He has no more joy in sin. The cup of pleasure has a bitterness in it. His flesh trembles lest he should be now taken to judgment. Oh! with what a heavy heart some live in sin. Joy in friends departs. Home no more wears a smile. There is no joy in business, for the business of the soul is not settled. Joy in living is almost extinguished. The sun cheers not for it is not the Sun of Righteousness.

iii. The Soul Is Wearied of This Condition.

No one loves pain, either of body or of mind. If a thorn pierces your hand, you do not bear the pain, you try to take it out. If a mote enter your eye, you do not sit quietly. Just so when the soul is convinced of sin, it does not sit still. It is wearied of this doleful condition.

iv. The Soul Resorts to Broken Cisterns.

'There is hope, there is hope', the newly awakened soul cries out. Where? 'Oh, I shall make my way into light. I shall pray and read the Word, and then we shall see.' Thus awakened persons set out cheerfully to remedy their case until they find that they are hewing out only broken cisterns.

v. Joy Comes from Believing in an Unseen Saviour.

God shines on the Bible and makes the Word concerning Jesus, the Son of His love, a Surety, shine brightly. God does not show Christ to the bodily eye, nor in a vision, God persuades the soul of the excellency of Christ as a Saviour, of His own love and Jesus' love, of the completeness of Christ. The soul rejoices in Him with a joy that is unspeakable and full of glory.

I appeal to you who have felt this. Do you remember a day when the Word concerning Jesus came with convincing efficacy to your soul? Can you tell the gush of joy that filled your bosom? That filled your eyes? Do you remember your first cry of thanksgiving? Oh! it is unspeakable! The words of man cannot tell this joy!

There is joy in believing on a risen Saviour. In the pain of a soul struggling with sin, and with broken resolutions, there is joy in the revealing of Christ within the veil, an Advocate, an Intercessor, the Giver of the Spirit.

There is joy in believing on a coming Saviour. When the wicked world gets the upper hand, when there is persecution, when men will not listen, when the young care not to hear of Christ, when some go back and walk no more with Christ, what gives joy? A look at an unseen but coming Saviour. He is behind the door. We cannot see through the door. If we could, we would see Jesus there. This gives joy. His kingdom shall come. We shall soon have our harp and crown, and shame shall cover them that now talk so proudly. Oh! it is unspeakable joy.

vi. THIS JOY IS UNSPEAKABLE.

Four things are said in Scripture to be 'unspeakable', the words which Paul heard when caught up into paradise (*2 Cor.* 12:4); the gift of God in giving grace to the soul (*2 Cor.* 9:15); the prayers of a Christian when the Spirit dwells in him (*Rom.* 8:26); and the joy of a believer looking at an unseen Saviour.

a. *To the world,* I would say, You have many joys, but they can all be spoken, and have no glory. They will soon come to an end. But this is unspeakable, and full of glory. Would that we might provoke you to jealousy, and to some sense of this unspeakable joy.

b. *To believers with little joy,* I would say, it is because you have little faith. Seek to believe more, look more into the glass of the Word. Oh! one look of Christ gives a joy that is unspeakable.

2. BELIEVING ON AN UNSEEN SAVIOUR GIVES LOVE.

i. *The unawakened have no love to Christ.* They do not love to hear His name. They do not think of Him. They do not pray to Him. They do not speak of Him.

ii. *The merely awakened have no love to Christ.* They are going about to establish their own righteousness. They cannot look on Christ with pleasure. They do not wish to give honour to God and Christ.

iii. *Only believing in an unseen Saviour gives love, not sight.* Many saw, and loved Him not. Many shall see, and cry for terror. It is believing the record given that produces love: believing that He left glory, believing that He suffered – this makes the soul cling to Him. It cannot but love. Like Mary, it falls at his feet saying, Rabboni; like the woman forgiven much; like forgiven Peter, 'Thou knowest all things, thou knowest that I love thee.'

Do you love Jesus? Do you love to hear His name? If you love Jesus, feed His lambs. Do you meditate upon all His doings? Do you keep His commandments? Do you seek Him when He is absent?

3. BELIEVING ON AN UNSEEN SAVIOUR GIVES HOPE.

This especially relates to His coming again. The unconverted have no hope of the appearing of Jesus Christ. There is no doctrine which excites more the enmity of the natural heart than the Second Coming. Scoffers abound. But faith in the unseen Saviour gives hope. My Saviour stands behind the curtains of this frail world. When the day comes He will draw the curtains aside and come. Oh! what support in the furnace this affords! The end of your faith is at hand. Believe to the end, and be saved.

27

Salvation Long Promised

Of which salvation the prophets have enquired and searched diligently, who prophesied of the grace that should come unto you: searching what, or what manner of time the Spirit of Christ which was in them did signify, when it testified beforehand the sufferings of Christ, and the glory that should follow. Unto whom it was revealed, that not unto themselves, but unto us they did minister the things, which are now reported unto you by them that have preached the gospel unto you with the Holy Ghost sent down from heaven; which things the angels desire to look into (1 Pet. 1:10–12).

THE SALVATION PREACHED UNTO US cannot be suspected of novelty, because the Spirit witnessed of it long ago in the prophets. Their anxious enquiries into these things related to their private desires, not to their public office.

This passage teaches us:

1. That the prophets who prophesied of the grace which Christ has exhibited to us by His coming were deeply anxious to know the time of His full revelation.

2. That the Spirit through them predicted the future state of Christ's kingdom, which we partly see and partly hope for; namely, that for Christ and for His whole body there is destined an advance to glory, through various sufferings.

3. That the Prophets ministered to us more richly than to their own age – and that this was revealed to them – because in Christ, at length, there is the full exhibition of those things of which God then gave only an obscure shadow.

4. That in the gospel is contained not only a clear confirmation of the teaching of the prophets – since He is the same Spirit who speaks in the gospel as spoke in the prophets – but a much fuller and more familiar exposition, because He now demonstrates openly and to our eyes the salvation which formerly He indicated by the prophets.

'Which things the angels desire to look into': How admirable, then, must be the glory of the salvation promised in the gospel, if even the angels who enjoy the face of God yet desire to look into it.

i. We learn here that it is not in vain that a glorious issue out of sufferings is promised. The sufferings of Christ were followed by His glory.

ii. And we learn that we are not afflicted by chance, but suffer according to the will of God.

28

Gird Up the Loins of Your Mind

Wherefore gird up the loins of your mind, be sober, and hope to the end for the grace that is to be brought unto you at the revelation of Jesus Christ (1 Pet. 1:13).

THE WORD, WHEREFORE, shows that this exhortation follows from what went before, that is, Since you have such an inheritance, or since your salvation is so great that prophets, apostles and angels are interested in it, 'gird up the loins of your mind'.

Girding up the loins was something servants did when serving at table (*Luke* 12:37; 17:8). So did Elijah and Gehazi when they ran (see *1 Kings* 18:46). In this way they ate the Passover, like travellers. The sense is that we are to be sober, either as to the body, as in Luke 21:34, or as to the soul, in the sense of being watchful, as in 2 Timothy 4:5.

1. CHRIST IS TO BE REVEALED.
   i. HE HAS BEEN REVEALED.

The Father opened His bosom and revealed His Son, the brightness of His glory. The Son took on Him a body, so that men saw and handled the Word of life (*1 John* 1:1). They beheld the Lamb of God. He was revealed as a suffering Son.

ii. He Is Also Revealed by the Spirit.

The Spirit takes of the things of Jesus and testifies of Him to the soul. This is an inward revelation of Christ, a gracious manifestation, needful for salvation: 'When it pleased God . . . to reveal His Son in me' (*Gal.* 1:15–16).

iii. There Is a Revelation Yet to Come.

'Behold, he cometh with clouds; and every eye shall see him' (*Rev.* 1:7). Nothing is more certain than that Christ will come again, a 'second time without sin unto salvation' (*Heb.* 9:28). He will come in His glorious body. All will see Him. But we do not know when.

2. GRACE IS TO BE BROUGHT TO CHRISTIANS THEN.

i. The Favour of God

They have much of it now. When first brought to Christ they came under His favour, out of the shade into the sunshine. In times of refreshing, there is much grace. But when Christ comes there will be such fulness of it that all that went before shall be counted nothing. Then shall Christians be openly acknowledged and acquitted.

ii. Holiness

'We shall be like him.' We have some holiness here; we strive after it and pant after it, but we shall have the full grace yonder.

3. CHRISTIANS SHOULD HOPE FOR THIS.

They are to be like travellers, like Israelites, like servants. They are to 'hope to the end', implying a perfect, full hope. They are to be girded and watching, not fashioning themselves according to the former lusts in their ignorance, being holy, in conformity with their holy calling.

29

Obedient Children

As obedient children, not fashioning yourselves according to the former lusts in your ignorance: but as he which hath called you is holy, so be ye holy in all manner of conversation (1 Pet. 1:14–15).

1. WHAT CHRISTIANS ONCE WERE.

EVERY CHRISTIAN had a time of ignorance. He was ignorant of his guilt and danger: 'I knew not my danger, I felt not my load.' He was ignorant of his bondage to lust and the devil. He did not know that he was a slave. 'We were never in bondage to any man', said the Jews (*John* 8:33).

They were in ignorance of Christ. They did not know the love of God in providing a Saviour; the love of Christ in coming, in lying down under the wrath of God; the love of Christ in seeking the lost.

I would speak to those in ignorance. Every one of you would flee to Christ if you knew the wrath to come. If you knew your true case, you would not be able to remain where you are. It is only ignorance that keeps you from fleeing.

I would speak to those who are anxious. If you knew Christ, you would flee to Him. It is only your ignorance that keeps you back.

I would speak to Christians. Remember the days of your ignorance. 'I raised thee up under the apple tree', says Christ (*Song of Sol.* 8:5). We must remember this to keep us lowly, to keep us loving, to inflame our love to Christ, to keep us from being bitter against others.

2. HOW THEY ONCE FASHIONED THEMSELVES.

As long as a man is in a state of nature, he fashions himself according to his lusts. Whatever lusts are most predominant, his habits, his mind, his life, his face – all take their stamp from them.

i. Many Lusts Reign.

There are two forces acting upon all the bodies that fly round the sun, one drawing them to fall into the sun, another driving them away. The course of each planet is shaped by these two forces. So it is with a natural man: love of money draws him one way, lusts of the flesh another, love of meat and drink a third, so that his course is shaped, his habits, the features of his face, according to his lusts, of which there are many. This is the picture of all who are unconverted. Christians, this was your picture also.

ii. Men Fashion Themselves.

The planets do not shape their own courses, but every unconverted man shapes his. You are willingly carried by lusts. You give your consent to every breath of passion. You say, It is sweet and pleasant, and you willingly go. You willingly go where you know you will be tempted, and you know you cannot stand temptation. You willingly shut your ears to the Word of God and the convictions of conscience. Woe is me, how sad that you fashion yourself to be a brand of hell. He that is filthy shall be filthy still. You are shaping what you are to be in eternity.

3. WHAT THEY BECOME WHEN GOD CALLS THEM.

i. Obedient Children

They become children. God makes the natural soul become a little child. It casts away its own wisdom, feels that it has been living in ignorance, and sits down at the feet of Jesus to learn of Him.

They become children of God. He brings their souls into His family. They are clothed with Jesus' robe of righteousness, fed with the children's bread, loved with the children's love.

They become children of obedience. Once they willingly obeyed diverse lusts and pleasures. Now they no more have a heart to fashion themselves. God is their Teacher, they sit at His feet. They are guided by His eye. They want to obey Him, and sin no longer. They say, 'Let not any iniquity have dominion over me' (*Psa.* 119:133).

ii. Holy

There was a time when you were ignorant of yourselves, of Christ and of grace. It is a time past. Then you lived under the power of lusts: not one, but many. But God has called you, has brought you into His family, has made you children of obedience instead of children of disobedience. Now, do not shape yourselves according to your old lusts. Do not let your words, thoughts and actions be guided by your old passions, but shape yourselves now after the holy God, your Father who called you; not in one thing only but in everything, publicly, privately, outwardly, inwardly. And this is the command of your Father, 'Be ye holy; for I am holy.' He will work in us, and therefore commands us to be holy. He will change our nature. We cannot dwell with Him without it. Without holiness, no man can see God. The more like Him you are, the happier you shall be.

30

Calling on the Father

And if ye call on the Father, who without respect of persons judgeth according to every man's work, pass the time of your sojourning here in fear (1 Pet. 1:17).

IN THESE WORDS God commands Christians to fear to sin. He persuades them by three arguments:

1. Because they pray to the Father.
2. Because God will judge all impartially by their works.
3. Because we are sojourners in a strange land, and for a time.

Consider these three arguments:

1. CHRISTIANS CALL ON THEIR FATHER.

This is a true mark of Christians. Many call on God, but not as children on a Father. All Christians have the Spirit and cry, 'Abba, Father.' God is their Father. They are children. It is the distinguishing mark of Christians that they pray.

Many call on God, but not as children. They ask God to damn them and to damn others, or else to help them. Alas, that is a common way of calling on God. Many do not pray, do not call on the Father. These are not the children of God. The Spirit cries,

'Abba, Father.' If you do not pray, you may set it down in your notebook, 'I am no child of God. I am not born again. I am an heir of hell.'

Christians, consider the command to you, Pass your time in fear. Be like little children who fear nothing so much as offending their father. If you pray to God as a Father, pass all your time fearing to sin against Him. Work out your salvation with fear and trembling. Consider what an awful mockery it would be in you, to pray that you may not sin and then go away and sin. Take one example, you pray, Lead me not into temptation. Oh! then flee temptation! Remember, you were on your knees before God. Is it fitting you should be thus in the company of the world? Remember you were within the veil. Is it fitting that you should sit down in the temple of pollution?

2. GOD WILL JUDGE ACCORDING TO WORKS.

The whole Bible tells us that God will judge the world according to their works. Tremble, therefore, hypocrites! It is not according to your words but your works you shall be judged.

They that have come to Christ have been washed, accepted and given the Spirit. They live a holy life and feed Christ's poor. These shall inherit everlasting life. But they that have lived in their natural state shall rise to the resurrection of damnation.

God will judge Christians according to their works. This is the true meaning of these words. They who have little occupied for Christ shall get little glory. They who have fled all sin and made great advances in holiness, shall have an exceeding weight of glory, an abundant embrace. One shall differ from another. This is the meaning of the parable of the talents. Fear to sin, then, for your weight of glory depends upon your holiness.

You have but a short while to live, a few days, a journey. Pass the time fearing to sin, working out your salvation with fear and trembling. Remember both that God is your Father, and that He is an impartial Judge.

3. THIS IS A TIME OF SOJOURNING.

Therefore, fear to sin. You are strangers in a strange land, like Israel in the wilderness. There are serpents and thorns in the way, so pass the time in fear. Keep tremblingly near to God. The time is short – a few years and all will be in the land where none hurts or destroys. Christians, fear to sin.

i. FLEE TEMPTATION.

To some Christians, I say, You are directly contradicting this. You are bold and without this fear. We desire you to consider if that way of mixing in all sorts of company can be consistent with this fear to sin. I do not wish you to be hermits, very far from it; but, 'I am a companion of all them that fear thee' (*Psa.* 119:63). Do you know a company where some meet who jest at holy things, where things are spoken of that should not be named, where late hours are kept? Child of God, I charge you not to go once more. Pass the time of your sojourning here in fear. And here I cannot but allude to an awful provocation of God which has grown, it is to be feared, to a great height. I mean, young persons after the holiest exercises, plunging at once into the unholiest companies; rejoicing in the house of God one hour, and enjoying very godless mirth and company the next hour.

I speak to those whose hearts are at all affected by the Word of God and charge you to leave off this practice. Spend the time of your sojourning here in fear. When the public exercise of worship is over, that is the time for keeping the Word in your heart. Flee the world, flee company at that time especially. The devil carries off all the seed in this way.

ii. F<small>LEE THE</small> B<small>EGINNINGS OF</small> S<small>IN</small>.

Eve looked, then took, then ate. So it is always. Do not dally with sin. If you are now dallying, leave it off. Flee beginnings. Do not become familiar with sin. It is in this way that the sin of drunkenness is commonly successful. The man says, I will take but one glass, and what harm can there be in that? Or if I should take two, still that is nothing to hurt me, and so on till he tarries long at the wine cup. Child of God, flee the beginnings of sin. It is in this way that the sin of impurity has come to such an alarming height among us. Flee the beginnings of sin. Child of God, do not put the cup to your lips.

iii. D<small>O</small> N<small>OT</small> J<small>EST ABOUT</small> S<small>IN</small>.

There is reason to think that, in some companies, sin is a matter of jest. The words of the Bible have become for some a matter of jest, so that even in the street you cannot pass some door but you may hear an impure or unholy jest sounding forth, and the rude laugh of many following after. Dear children of God, never laugh at sin! Have you been to the Cross? Have you been past the gates of hell and heard its wailings? Ah! There is no laughing at sin there. It is all serious work there. How can you laugh? Have you been to the cross? Ah! Will you laugh at that which crucified the Lord? You have but a short while. Pass the time in holy fear. A man who is afraid of a serpent will not jest about it.

31

Redeemed with Precious Blood

Forasmuch as ye know that ye were not redeemed with corruptible things, as silver and gold, from your vain conversation received by tradition from your fathers; But with the precious blood of Christ, as of a lamb without blemish and without spot (1 Pet. 1:18–19).

IN MY LAST SERMON, I showed that Peter brings three arguments to persuade Christians to fear to sin, not to be held in sin as they too often are. And indeed, I am sure that those of you who are children of God, if you have been considering the matter, will see how much need there is to forsake that boldness with which you have so often ventured within the precincts of sin. Instead, have 'fear and trembling'.

In these words, Peter brings another argument, still stronger than all, Ye know you have been redeemed with the blood of Christ, therefore fear to sin.

1. THE CONDITION IN WHICH CHRISTIANS WERE

This is shown to be 'vain conversation' and slavery. Christians lived in 'vain conversation', 'foolish behaviour'. Every unconverted person lives in a vain, foolish manner. The whole Bible shows that the unconverted man is a fool, that his conversation is vain and foolish. They generally think they are wise, and they smile contemptuously on the children of God, as if to say, 'Poor things!' But it is they who are poor and foolish. I will prove this.

If a man were to work a whole week and get no wages, would you not say he was a fool? Yet this is what the unconverted do, they work night and day at sin and get no wages at the end.

If you saw a man lying under a heap of stones, yet heaping on more, you would say, 'A fool!' Such are the unconverted, they are condemned, yet they heap more wrath over their souls.

If you saw a man clothed in rags and dying for warmth, and if he said he was rich and pointed to his rags and said they were fine raiment, you would say he was a fool. Such is the unconverted soul.

If you saw a man hewing our cisterns for himself, and every one turning out to be broken, but still persevering, although a fountain was there beside him, you would say, 'He is a fool.'

If you saw a man who rented a house, a tenant at will, laying out a deal of money and care upon improving this house, painting it inside and out, would not the worldly-wise among you shake the head and say, 'The man's a fool!' This is what the unconverted are doing. They are tenants at will. Whenever God says the word, the soul leaves its dwelling, and yet what care and money men lavish on their bodies, to ornament them. Surely men walk in a vain show!

If you saw a man at the top of a mast fast asleep, and an awful storm coming on, you would say, 'The fool!' Such are the unconverted. They are sleeping at the giddy mast head.

I would speak to the unconverted: Consider your ways. Consider if you are not walking in a dream from which you will wake to find yourself in hell. Remember what a dream the rich man lived in. Remember his waking too. You that are poor and live in known sins, what do you mean to gain by this way of living? The end of this way is death.

Christians, this was your case. 'What fruit had ye then in those things whereof ye are now ashamed?' Your way of life was vain, empty, not answering its end. It promised enjoyment and left empty sorrow behind.

This way is 'received by tradition from your fathers'.
It is inherited from father to son. Grace does not always pass down the generations like this, but nature always does. You were born with it; it came in the blood.

There are two ways in which children receive wickedness from their parents. Just as they inherit the pattern of the body, so do they inherit the features of the soul. The branch has the same sap as the tree.

And sin comes by example. It is amazing how soon children begin to copy what they see. Ah! parents, think what you are doing when you sin before the eyes of your children.

Consider, then, have you been brought out of the way of your fathers? The rest of your friends perhaps are walking down the broad way – have you been brought to turn against the stream? Happy are you if this is so!

2. CHRISTIANS HAVE BEEN REDEEMED.

All who are Christians have been brought out of this condition. A price has been paid for them. They are bought out of it, and now belong to another Master. What is the price that has been paid?

i. NOT SILVER OR GOLD

A natural person is under the just wrath of God. All the silver and gold in the world cannot pay the price of his redemption. 'The redemption of their soul is precious' (*Psa.* 49:8). No corruptible thing can redeem it. There is much ignorance on this point. Nothing we can offer will redeem us. 'Will the Lord be pleased with thousands of rams, or with ten thousands of rivers of oil?' (Mic. 6:7). How many have been redeemed and are this day in glory, yet not one by corruptible things, not one by any price of man's procuring. Some think to redeem their souls by giving money to the poor; ah no! Do not rely on self-contrivances to redeem your soul. Nothing will do. Lie down an insolvent debtor, at the foot of God.

ii. The Blood of Christ.

Precious blood! Nothing but blood can blot out sin. Without the shedding of blood, there is no remission. Ah! it is the blood-shedding of the Lamb of God that gives peace. His blood is precious in the sight of God, of angels, of awakened sinners. There are not many things called precious in the Bible. We read of precious faith (2 Pet. 1:1), precious promises (2 Pet. 1:4), and to those that believe Christ is precious (1 Pet. 2:7). Here, we find 'precious blood', precious because divine, the blood of the Son of God.

Suppose you were in debt, and a friend paid it by laying down some costly jewel, a thousand times more valuable than all the money you owed. This would be paying your debt with a precious thing. This is what Christ has done. His blood is a thousand times more precious in the sight of the Father than the blood of sinners. If he died for me, then I have been redeemed with precious blood.

It is the blood of a spotless Lamb. This made it precious. Had Christ been sinful, His sufferings would have been for Himself. For this reason He can suffer for another, that He was a spotless Lamb, without sin in His life, without sin in His death, so that every drop of His sufferings was for our sins.

That a price had to be paid shows that we were in a state of slavery. We have been bought back from it, not with silver or gold, not with corruptible things, not with things that rust and grow old. Rather, with the precious blood of Christ, the blood of a spotless Lamb.

3. CHRISTIANS KNOW THIS.

Christians should remember this, and fear to sin. 'Pass the time of your sojourning here in fear' Peter says, 'forasmuch as ye know' the price of your redemption. Oh! Christians, here is the grandest argument to persuade you to dread sin. Remember how you were redeemed. When tempted to sin, look to the cross.

Then say, 'These wounds were made by the wrath due to my sins. Shall I love sin any more, or trifle with it any more? Shall I love that which kindles the fires of hell, and crucified my Lord? I have been washed in His blood so that I might be made holy, and shall I go back to sin? Shall I not rather look to the cross, and keep from sin?'

32

Christ Foreordained and Manifest

Who verily was foreordained before the foundation of the world, but was manifest in these last times for you, who by him do believe in God, that raised him up from the dead, and gave him glory; that your faith and hope might be in God (1 Pet. 1:20–21).

1. CHRIST WAS FOREORDAINED TO BE A SAVIOUR.

BEFORE THE FOUNDATION OF THE WORLD, Christ was foreordained to be a Saviour. The Bible gives us glimpses of what was before the world. From John 17:5, we learn that Jesus had glory with the Father 'before the world was'.

What that glory was, who can tell? It was not the worship of ten thousand angels round the throne, for angels were not. It was the glory of being with God, and being God. I know not how to speak of it. The infinitely glorious Son in the bosom of the infinitely glorious Father! How can I speak of this? 'I have been only like a boy playing on the seashore,' said Sir Isaac Newton, 'diverting myself in now and then finding a smoother pebble or a prettier shell, whilst the great ocean of truth lay all undiscovered before me.' What can we say of Christ's glory? I stand, and wonder, and adore.

Christ Foreordained and Manifest

From John 17:24 we also learn, 'Thou lovedst me before the foundation of the world.' Again, 'I was daily his delight, rejoicing always before him' (*Prov.* 8:30).

On this let me speak with trembling. Who can tell what is going on in the cabinet of an earthly king, let alone in the cabinet of the King of kings! Yet in our text we see that He was marked out to be the Saviour before the world was made. Before men had fallen He was fixed upon to die in the stead of sinners, and to rise to be their Head for ever. He was ordained to undertake for sinners. The Father undertook to help Him and give Him for a covenant of the people, for a light of the Gentiles. The Son said, 'Lo, I come (in the volume of the book it is written of me,) to do thy will, O God' (*Heb.* 10:7). The same love was in the bosom of Father, Son and Spirit, infinite harmony and love. Their purpose was to save man, in compassion to provide a ransom for all who believe on His name. This is beyond our understanding, and our explaining.

Many stumble at this to their own misery. They will not become like little children. A man who walks with his eyes on the clouds and a stately step falls over a stone and injures himself. A little child with his eyes upon the ground passes easily over it and is safe. Believe His Word, and be happy. Let us learn confidence in the Saviour. It was no rash burst of pity that made God give His Son. Often a man, on a sudden, is overcome by compassion and gives away what he regrets after. But not so with God, for Christ was foreordained before man fell.

Learn too that it is more glorious to God that we should come to Jesus than if we had remained unfallen. He will lose nothing of His glory. Believers, by looking to Jesus, 'believe in God'. Christ was manifested that we might look to Him, raised and glorified, and so believe in God as our Friend and Father, and hope to receive every good thing at His hand (*1 Pet.* 1:21).

2. CHRIST WAS MANIFESTED.

He was manifested when He was born into the world. He came from God and was manifested among men. When it is said, 'God was manifest in the flesh' (*1 Tim.* 3:16), the same word is used.

Again, He is manifested in preaching. The apostles preached Him as dying for sinners, then raised from the dead and glorified. He is also manifested by the Spirit, when He is revealed to the soul.

3. WHY WAS HE MANIFESTED?

It was so that your faith and hope might be in God, that you might believe in God, and hope in God – that you might believe in God as reconciled, as loving us, not as filled with wrath; and also that you might believe in Him as to the working out of His providence on your behalf.

Believe that God is favourable to you! He has taken away your sin, and accepted you. The end of revealing Christ to the soul is that we might lean on God. Christ is the Way to the Father.

No one says, I will sit down here on the wayside and live here. No, hasten on to the home at the end! By Him we believe in God. Christ is the Door into the fold of God's love. No man says, I will stay in the doorway. No, enter in!

Christ is the Rent Veil. That veil was rent, not that we might remain outside, but that we might enter in. 'Then will I go unto the altar of God, unto God my exceeding joy' (*Psa.* 43:4). Let us draw near. Christ is the Ladder. 'He that hath seen me hath seen the Father' (*John* 14:9). We are to believe that God loves us, that He will keep us from evil, that He will be with us in death. Believing Christ makes us believe every word of God.

33

Obeying the Truth

Seeing ye have purified your souls in obeying the truth through the Spirit unto unfeigned love of the brethren, see that ye love one another with a pure heart fervently (1 Pet. 1:22).

THOSE TO WHOM PETER WROTE had made their souls holy by obeying the truth, through the Spirit, unto genuine brotherly love, out of a pure, clean heart. As such, they were to love one another earnestly, stretching forward in it. The Spirit brings the soul to obey the truth, to purify itself thereby, and to love the brethren fervently.

1. THE SPIRIT MUST WORK.

i. In Awakening

Just as the earth was without form and void till the Spirit moved on the face of the waters, so it is in the soul. There is nothing so dark and formless and empty as an unawakened soul. There is no movement till the sovereign Spirit comes. Death reigns till He comes. It is like the vision in Ezekiel 37. The soul is dead and dry, and, even if there are bones and sinews, it is still dead, till the Spirit breathes. Then there is life! The Spirit alone can make you obey the truth. He awakens the soul when He reveals the holy law, or the holiness of God, or the sufferings of Christ the Surety. If the soul is convinced that he is lost and condemned, he flees, crying, 'Lord help me!' If you are unawakened, living in sin and ease, you are disobeying the truth, you are living as if the Bible was not true, as if God were a liar. If you have had these things revealed to you, yet do not flee, you are not obeying the truth.

ii. In Bringing to Christ and Rest

The Spirit brings the soul to Christ. He convinces of righteousness. The veil is taken away by the Lord, the Spirit (2 *Cor.* 3:18). Ah! none but the Holy Spirit can persuade a weary soul to take refuge in Christ. The dove fluttered round the Ark till Noah put out his hand and took her in. A burdened soul sometimes wanders long in search of rest. It gropes like the blind, weary and dissatisfied. Yet we may be burdened from seeking our own ease, and not submitting to be led by the Spirit into God's peace. The Spirit shows Christ undertaking for sinners. He leads to Golgotha, and to the finished work there, accomplished once for all by the Surety for sinners.

iii. In Sanctifying

How is God to make Israel holy? 'I will put my Spirit within you, and cause you to walk in my statutes' (*Ezek.* 36:27). 'Walk in the Spirit, and ye shall not fulfil the lust of the flesh' (*Gal.* 5:16). The fruit of the Spirit is love.

In awakening, in giving rest, in making holy, the Spirit is the great Workman. Give Him all the glory, you who have come under His power. Wait for Him, He is a sovereign Spirit. Weary souls, it is the Spirit who must lead you into light and peace. It is not a man, nor a book. It is through the *truth* that He works. Do not say, It is useless to read the Bible and pray and attend ordinances. Obey the *truth*, through the *Spirit*!

2. THE INSTRUMENT IS THE TRUTH.

In awakening, in bringing to peace, in sanctifying, the truth is always the Spirit's instrument. That is why it is good to wait on ordinances, to come within reach of the hammer of the Word. True, the hammer will not break the rock of itself; but it is just as true that it cannot break it if you keep out of reach. Keep within range of the arrows. Keep within range also of the healing balm.

i. IN AWAKENING

The truth is always an instrument. Sometimes it is the holy law. Paul said, 'When the commandment came, sin revived and I died.' Sometimes it is the holiness of God, as in the case of God. Sometimes the truth of Christ. We are made to look on Him we have pierced and mourn because of Him (*Zech.* 12:10). We are convinced of sin, because we believe not on Christ. The view of a long-despised Saviour can break the heart. Oh, unawakened souls! Do not keep away from the Bible and the house of prayer. It is like keeping away from the hammer and the arrows of the Word.

ii. IN BRINGING TO REST

An awakened soul will never come to rest by brooding on itself, its sins and its miseries, but by looking to the truth. So it was with the Ethiopian eunuch (*Acts* 8:30–35). The Spirit leads us to the cross. Anxious souls ask, Why read the Bible any more? Why pray? Because thus you will be brought to peace, and in no other way.

iii. IN SANCTIFYING

'Sanctify them through thy truth', our Saviour prayed. It is as milk to a little child, and we will grow thereby. How shall a young man cleanse his way? By hiding God's Word in his heart (*Psa.* 119:9–11). There is so little holiness because there is so little feeding on the truth, so little babe-like desire for the milk of the Word.

3. THE COMMAND TO ALL WHO HAVE OBEYED

All who have obeyed the truth through the Spirit are commanded, 'Love one another with a pure heart fervently.' Through obeying the truth, their souls have been made pure. The Spirit has awakened them. He has brought them to rest. He has brought them to holiness.

If there has been any work of grace in your heart, it will be the business of your life to purify your soul. Every one that has this hope in Christ purifies himself, even as He is pure (*1 John* 3:3).

There is now no obstacle to their loving one another, not feignedly but fervently, not in word only, but in deed and in truth.

No heart other than a pure heart is capable of loving the brethren. Christians are stones built on same foundation, as a habitation of God through the Spirit. The same pure Spirit dwells in them. Oh! then, how they ought to love one another! 'Look not every man on his own things, but every man also on the things of others' (*Phil.* 2:4). In the world, all seek their own. But Christians are branches of the same vine, with the same sap. The fruit of the Spirit is love.

Christians are members one of another. In Ezekiel we read, 'I will give them one heart, and I will put a new spirit within you' (*Ezek.* 11:19). It is out of *one* pure heart that we are to love one another, not many hearts. So we are with one mind and one mouth to glorify God (*Rom.* 15:6).

And our love is to be fervent, increasing, and stretching itself out to embrace all who love our Lord Jesus Christ.

34

Born Again

> *Being born again, not of corruptible seed, but of incorruptible, by the word of God, which liveth and abideth for ever. For all flesh is as grass, and all the glory of man as the flower of grass. The grass withereth, and the flower thereof falleth away: But the word of the Lord endureth for ever. And this is the word which by the gospel is preached unto you* (1 Pet. 1:23–25).

IN THE PREVIOUS VERSE, the command was to love the brethren. Peter now comes to the grand reason: because we are brethren in one divine family. All Christians have been born again by the Word of God, the incorruptible seed, living and abiding, so different from their natural life, which is like grass. The Word has come to them in the preached Gospel.

You have been born again, he tells them. The beginning of this work of grace in you is to be traced to your new birth. I do not mean that you entered into your mother's womb and were born a second time. The second birth you have undergone is not of the flesh, which would be a corruptible second birth, as a poor, dying worm. But the birth of which I speak is of an incorruptible seed. It is a birth of the Spirit. The instrument in this birth is the Word of God which, brought home with power, has life in it, and also continuance. It lives in the heart, and always lives. For the Bible shows the difference between these two, between the frail, perishing life we are born to and the enduring Word, by which we are born again. This enduring Word is the word concerning Jesus!

1. ALL CHRISTIANS HAVE BEEN BORN AGAIN.

He had told them this before (verse 3). Here he tells it as the root of all good in them, their new birth. If they have purified their souls, if they love one another, it is because they have been born again. We should never weary in thinking of our new birth, and that all our change comes from it. This would keep us in blessing, and keep us humble, seeing that it is what has made all the difference. Those who think to purify their souls and love the brethren without being born again are foolish. Seek a new birth. Seek converting grace. This only strikes at the root of all sins. This only begins all graces in the heart.

All Christians agree in this. Christians differ in many things. In their first birth they are very different. One was born in a cottage, another in a palace, one in the crowded city, another in the wilderness. One was received into the tender arms of rejoicing parents, another homeless and friendless in infancy.

They differ in circumstances. One is rich, another poor, one clothed in humble raiment, though clean, another clothed in fine raiment, for it is possible with God that there may be a rich Christian. They differ in character. One has much faith, peace, joy, love; another little faith, much doubting, darkness, distress. But all are born again. The river of their peace has as its source the same fountain. It is at the cross and the grave of Jesus.

Have you been born again? Try yourself by this. You may lack many of the spots of God's children (*Deut.* 32:5). You may find it difficult to discern their faith, their love, their hope; but have you been born again? All Christians have. If you are not Christians it is

Being Born Again

the very thing you should hear. All unconverted persons must be born again or perish. You all need this. You are not all drunkards or swearers or liars, but you all need to be born again! Yea, the woman that is delicate among you, that would not adventure to set her foot on the ground, still needs to be born again. Lydia was a decent woman, yet she needed to be born again. Nicodemus was a ruler of the Jews, a man of integrity and good breeding, yet he must be born again. So must you! Lydias and Rulers, rich and poor, you must be born again!

If you are Christians so were they to whom Peter wrote. Yet see how he reminds them, 'Love one another, being born again.' It is the root of all the graces. It is vain to think of loving or being holy if you are not born again. Go and look at the fountain from whence you came, and it should encourage you in all holiness!

2. THIS NEW BIRTH IS INTO AN UNDYING LIFE.

It is 'not of corruptible seed, but incorruptible'. When a child is born, it is into a dying life. If you stretch the eye, you will see the winding sheet – we face the grave. How often a worm is at the root of the gourd. Earlier or later, it dies; but it is not so with the new birth. The first birth is 'of corruptible seed'. 'That which is born of the flesh is flesh.' But we are born of God into an undying life, of an incorruptible seed. A Christian may be often sickly, often ready to die, yet the word of Jesus is sure, He shall never perish! He is born for eternity.

Rejoice if you are born again. You shall never die. I can be 'confident of this very thing, that he which hath begun a good work in you will perform it until the day of Jesus Christ' (*Phil.* 1:6). Your new nature is not a frail, dying nature. It is divine. Oh, what a contrast! Within a frail, consumptive body, wasting away, the spirit may be mounting with wings like an eagle, soaring with untiring, immortal life.

All should rejoice over those who are born again. It is often made a matter of joy when a child is born into this dying world. Ah! How much more when one is born again. All heaven rings with Hallelujahs, as the Saviour stoops to lift the sheep upon His shoulder, and will you be silent? A star is rising that will never set, but will blaze throughout eternity.

3. THE MEANS IS THE WORD OF GOD.

The new birth is by the Word of God. It is a living Word, an abiding Word, a gospel Word.

i. A Living Word

In the hand of the Spirit, the Word is all life. The Word of God is *quick*, or alive (Heb. 4:12). A sword lying on the ground is a dead thing, it can do nothing. But let the warrior snatch it up and brandish it, it lives, it gleams. So it is with the Word. When we speak it, it touches no-one. But when the Spirit takes it in hand, it lives. It is the living Word. Nothing was so dead before; nothing is so living now! Oh, let us be determined to give ourselves more to prayer. We are too apt to prophesy more to the dry bones than to the Spirit (Ezek. 37:1–10). Often we have done so. Come, let us change our plan and engage in more secret prayer. Let us set apart days for prayer.

ii. An Abiding Word

Some roots take such fast hold of the ground that when they have taken possession, it is impossible to remove them. You may turn or hoe, still they remain. So is it with the engrafted Word, the Word made living by the Spirit. Affliction, prosperity, persecution, may hew and burn it, still it abides for ever. The natural man is like grass, but this Word endures. 'If a man keep my saying, he shall never see death' (*John* 8:51).

iii. A GOSPEL WORD

It is the Gospel Word that the Spirit blesses to the new birth. It is not the preaching of the law or of moral virtue, but gospel preaching. It is the preaching of the Word concerning Jesus and His cross, concerning the high priest within the veil, concerning the Son of God who is to come again, that the Spirit uses to bring about the new birth.

35

Tasting and Growing

Wherefore laying aside all malice, and all guile, and hypocrisies, and envies, and all evil speakings, as newborn babes, desire the sincere milk of the word, that ye may grow thereby: if so be ye have tasted that the Lord is gracious (1 Pet. 2:1–3).

1. ALL WHO ARE BORN AGAIN BY THE WORD HAVE TASTED THAT THE LORD IS GRACIOUS.

ALL THOSE that have been born again have tasted that Christ is gracious. As the psalmist says, 'O taste and see that the LORD is good: blessed is the man that trusteth in him' (*Psa.* 34:8). It is not that they have read it or heard it merely, but tasted. They have had an inward taste and sense of the excellency of Christ, and of the kindness and love of God. Faith is compared to all the senses:

i. SMELLING

Christ is typified in the burnt-offering, which is always called 'a savour of rest', a smell which satisfies God and is infinitely pleasing to Him. It is sweet and pleasing to the sinner also. 'The LORD smelled a sweet savour [savour of rest]; and the LORD said in His heart, I will not again curse the ground any more for man's sake' (*Gen.* 8:21).

[252]

Tasting and Growing

'We are unto God a sweet savour of Christ', says Paul (*2 Cor.* 2:15). Christ has given Himself 'an offering and a sacrifice to God for a sweet-smelling savour' (*Eph.* 5:2). Christ is a sweet smell to God, while the self-righteous are a smoke in his nose. Christ is also a sweet smell to the soul that cleaves to him: 'Thy name is as ointment'; 'A bundle of myrrh is my wellbeloved unto me . . . a cluster of camphire in the vineyards of En-gedi'; 'His cheeks are as a bed of spices, as sweet flowers: his lips like lilies, dropping sweet smelling myrrh' (*Song of Sol.* 1:3; 1:13–14; 5:13). Oh, have you smelled the sweet savour of Christ?

ii. SEEING

We look to Christ and are saved, as they looked to the brazen serpent Moses lifted up (*Num.* 21:8–9). 'They looked unto him, and were lightened' (*Psa.* 34:5). 'Sir, we would see Jesus', is our cry (*John* 12:21). 'They shall look upon me whom they have pierced' (*Zech.* 12:10). We are said to 'see the Son' (*John* 6:40), and to look unto Jesus (*Heb.* 12:2). Have you seen the Lord?

iii. HEARING

Blessed are those who 'know the joyful sound' (*Psa.* 89:15); who hear the trumpet announcing the jubilee. He that hath an ear is bidden to hear. 'Blessed are your ears', said Jesus. The good tidings are heard. 'Faith cometh by hearing' (*Rom.* 10:17).

iv. TOUCHING

'I held him, and would not let him go', says the bride in the Song of Solomon. The disciples held him by the feet (*Matt.* 28:9). If we may but touch the hem of his garment, we shall be whole. Wrestling Jacob said, 'I will not let thee go, except thou bless me' (*Gen.* 32:26). Like the church of Philadelphia, we are to hold fast what we have.

v. TASTING

His fruit is sweet to our taste, and His love better than wine (*Song of Sol.* 1:2; 2:3). He has prepared a feast of fat things for His people (*Isa.* 25:6). 'O taste and see that the Lord is good'! How great is his goodness! The manna in the wilderness and the Lord's Supper both represent to us partaking of Christ, under the figure of tasting and eating.

Let us learn from all this that the saving knowledge of Christ is different from all other knowledge.

The knowledge we get by our senses is quite different from the knowledge we get in all other ways. You may read about honey, and hear lectures about it, but one taste is better than all theoretical knowledge. So you may read about Christ, and hear about Him, and discourse about Him, but you must *taste*, if you would know Him savingly.

It is not an outward perception of Christ by the senses.

Some are looking for a sight of Christ with the eye. Oh no, it is far more excellent than that. It needs all the senses to express the fulness and excellency of believing on Christ. It is a sweet inward feeling of His suitableness to me as a Surety, a Saviour.

We cannot give it to one another.

When you have tasted you can tell another that it was sweet, but your neighbour must taste before he can feel this.

The remembrance of having tasted will not keep up the sweet feeling.

Some are for looking back to what they felt, treasuring up their feelings; no, this is like keeping the manna to taste again and again. God must give its sweetness afresh each day.

2. ALL WHO HAVE TASTED WILL PUT AWAY ALL INIQUITY.

The sweetness of this manna should make everything tasteless by comparison. Christians should lay aside all the sins they had a taste for before; all malice, all sins against the second table of the law. They should fulfil the law in loving one another.

i. THE WORLD FAILS IN IMPROVING MEN.

There is a great difference between the teaching of the world and that of Christ. The world tries to make men better. Christ makes men holy, as God is holy. The world says, Lay aside some malice, some guile, and so on. Christ says, Lay aside *all*. As long as you judge by your natural heart, you are like an unwise gardener who has a bad tree. He prunes and prunes it. When some fruit appears, he takes it away. The tree is as bad as ever. A graft or a change is needed. I appeal to you who have tried in yourself or in your children. You have tried the most approved methods of overcoming your temper, but have failed. Take one thing, *evil speaking*: you have tried to keep silence, but you have wholly failed. You found malice lurking beneath. Ah! the tree is corrupt.

ii. CHRIST'S WAY SUCCEEDS

a. *A taste of Christ helps us to put all sins away.*

Taste Christ! You came into God's family, pardoned, under God's smile. Even if nothing more, this does much for the temper. It is amazing how sweet-tempered you become when reconciled to God. You are so happy you cannot be envious. You have no wish to hide. You lay aside all hypocrisy. Everything there is so calm that you become calm. Even in nature, when an angry soul looks out on a calm evening, it has been known to tranquillize his soul. Music can have a similar power. How much more grace!

b. *When we taste of Christ, the Holy Spirit is given to us.*

The sweetest thing about this olive tree is that He pours the golden oil into our souls (*Zech.* 4:12), and that makes us put all malice and guile away.

QUESTION: Is a Christian perfect then?

ANSWER: No, but it is his own sin and shame that he is not. In Christ, all things needful for life and godliness are given to us. If it is true that you have joined yourself to the Lord, see that you put all malice away.

3. CHRISTIANS DESIRE THE SINCERE MILK OF THE WORD.

As a child has an appetite for milk, so should you have an appetite for the pure Word of God, that ye may grow thereby, in faith and in holiness.

How do babes desire milk? By an instinctive appetite. We should be like newborn babes in this. It has often been noticed that God has shown creating wisdom in nothing more wonderfully than in hunger. If He had left us to seek food by our reason, there is no doubt that many, then, would quite forget to take food – for example, those of studious habits – and some would take too much and some too little. But God has not left it to reason. He has put an instinct into us which acts before reason, hunger.

Hunger impels the studious man to leave his books. A blind instinct in itself it drives the savage to seek food, and the little child to seek its mother's breast. It is not moved by an argument. No one tells it, or instructs it, but the indwelling instinct of nature alone impels it. So is it with the child of grace. He is not left to read the Bible according to his own reason. If God had left him to that, many

Tasting and Growing

would forget. But God puts an appetite for it in their soul. They seek the Bible as a child does the breast. They cannot be without it; nothing else will satisfy. Every Christian is impelled to the Word of God by an ever-recurring appetite.

Dear friends, so it will be if you have tasted that the Lord is gracious. Test yourself by this. If you have no love for the Bible you have not tasted. King Alfred copied out the Psalms with his own hand and carried the copy in his bosom.

i. Desire the Sincere Milk.

Many love to read other works who do not love the Bible. Remember, the child loves nothing but the pure milk. So should you. True, it is right to read good books, for they lead you to the Bible. But do not forget the sincere milk.

ii. Why? To Grow Thereby.

Dear Christians, the only true mark of *life* is *growth*. How do you know that the day is dawning? Because it gets lighter and brighter. How do you know that the tide has turned? Because the waves come higher and higher up the shore. Oh! ask the Lord that you may grow: grow in faith, in peace, in holiness. Resolve to know more of Christ, to grow up into Him, to grow more like Him.

36

Built on the Foundation

To whom coming, as unto a living stone, disallowed indeed of men, but chosen of God, and precious, ye also, as lively stones, are built up a spiritual house, an holy priesthood, to offer up spiritual sacrifices, acceptable to God by Jesus Christ (1 Pet. 2:4–5).

IN THESE WORDS, believers are called, firstly, *a temple, or spiritual house*, and secondly, *a holy priesthood*. There is a glorious temple rising day by day in this world. The foundation has long since been laid. Many stones have been perfected and built on it, some are being polished, some are on the way to the building. The eyes of men are engaged with other things, but this is the one grand thing in the universe. When some great monument or temple is rising, it is usual for the people of that city to go often and admire it. How few come to enquire about this one! When it is finished, it will be the admiration of all worlds. What dead stones they are that see no beauty in this rising building, even now! Let us look at it.

1. THE FOUNDATION

   i. PRECIOUS

   This word shows what God thinks of the foundation. Had He taken a jewel out of His crown, you would have said it was precious.

Had He taken all the jewels in the world, or in the mines of heaven, or of the assembled worlds, and made it a foundation, you would have said, Precious! Ah! what do you say of the Jewel out of His own bosom? Oh, if precious to God, how precious should it be to us!

ii. CHOSEN

Great skill is involved in choosing a foundation stone, that it may be able to bear the weight of the building. Who chose this foundation stone? God. God knew the weight of sin, the weight of our weakness. Ah! How assuredly, with what comfort, may we rest on Christ, for He is chosen of God.

iii. DISALLOWED OF MEN

If God chose, and God says, 'Precious', you would have thought all the world would have said, 'Amen.' Ah! No. The holy angels did indeed wonder and adore and said, 'Worthy is the Lamb.' But men hate God, and therefore hate this foundation stone. They see no preciousness in it; they dare not trust themselves on it.

You should apply this to yourselves.

a. *Some think themselves safe enough where they are.* Some rely on the foundation of an innocent life, some on their duties. But 'other foundation can no man lay' than Christ. Whoever stumbles over this foundation stone will be broken (*Luke* 20:18).

b. *Some dare not rest on Christ.*

God has chosen Him, yet they dare not choose Him. You wish to be in that temple, you wish to be Christ's, still you fear to come to a personal relying on Christ, resting all your weight on Him. Ah! Why do you fear? God hath chosen Him. He is as free to you as to any. Whosoever believeth on Him shall not be put to shame.

iv. Living

Other foundation stones are dead, but this is living. He is a living Saviour. All his preciousness is in this, He is the living One. The Mighty God, able to bear the whole weight put upon Him. He was dead and is alive for evermore (*Rev.* 1:18). The weight bruised Him, but He lives now, and will never die any more.

As living, He invites stones to come to Him; He charms, woos, and wins them, gives His Spirit to them. As living, He gives life to all that are in Him, as branches in a vine, they have life from being in Him.

2. THE BUILDING

Living stones are built up on this precious, chosen Foundation.

i. Every Stone Was Once Dead.

The whole Bible shows that a natural man is as dead as a stone. A stone will as soon leap from the bottom of the sea or the depth of the quarry, and fall on some house that is being built, as a natural man of himself will come to Christ. Nothing can be more dead than a stone. Speak to it, it does not hear. Tell it that it is a stone, it does not feel. Tell it that the fire shall devour it, it does not weep. Such are unconverted souls. Nothing is more dead to spiritual and eternal things. How often, by a dying bed, the minister is taught this. He speaks; the stone hears not. Wrath and love melt him not. I may be speaking to someone like this. You are able to live in sins, and yet come into the house of God and to the Lord's Table. You feel nothing of what I am saying just now. You are the very person I mean. You are a dead stone.

ii. Every Stone of the Temple Comes to Him.

a. *In conversion.* When Moses smote the rock, all Israel stood round, men, women and little children. The water gushed out. What a wondrous shout would rise to heaven! So it is with a soul smitten by the rod of God's Spirit. The heart weeps. There is a sense of sin and misery, a sense of Christ neglected. Oh! what a gush of grief! How often do friends and ministers stand amazed.

So it is in awakening. God's Word is a hammer that breaks the rock in pieces. When the Word is in the hand of the Spirit, it must break hearts. Ministers are apt to sleep, and forget the power of God's Word. We are apt to despair. Oh, that we could only believe and wait on God! There may be a breaking-up in this quarry yet! As the water gushed, so, when Christ is received, the soul flows toward Him. Oh, that He would reveal Himself to you! Oh, that you knew His loveliness, His excellence, His glorious freeness! Your hearts would surely melt and run to Him. The fire of His love would melt the hard wax of your hearts.

So every stone that comes to Christ gets life and becomes as living as He is. Before he was dead, but now alive, justified, born again. He lives unto God. Are you living or dead? Is any of the life of Christ in you? Do you have the same Spirit, the same mind? If you have come to Him, you are alive.

iii. Living Stones Are Built Together.

Just as, in Ephesians, the whole body is said to grow up together in all things into Christ, the Head (*Eph.* 4:15), so here the temple or spiritual house is said to be built up in Christ, the One Foundation.

This building is different from all other temples. Every stone is not only built but grows higher, stronger, fuller, more living, in union with Christ and with all the other stones. Is it so with you Christians? Are you daily coming to Christ? Are you daily built up in Him? Are you growing up into Him in all things?

iv. The Whole Temple Is a Spiritual House.

It is obviously not a literal house like the temple of Jerusalem. Indeed it is as much greater as the body after the resurrection is more glorious than this frail body. This is the work of the Spirit, and particularly His indwelling. Only so can there be such a thing as a habitation of God through the Spirit (*Eph.* 2:22). Every stone is filled with the Spirit, and so is the whole together. How glorious and holy! At present the building is unfinished. Building work is going on every day. See what a dwelling God has made for man, and much more for Himself!

Let us learn to be dwelt in by the Spirit, and to cling to all who have the same Spirit.

37

God's Foundation Stone

Wherefore also it is contained in the scripture, Behold, I lay in Zion a chief corner stone, elect, precious: and he that believeth on him shall not be confounded. Unto you therefore which believe he is precious: but unto them which be disobedient, the stone which the builders disallowed, the same is made the head of the corner (1 Pet. 2:6–7).

PETER CONFIRMS WHAT HE HAD SAID out of the Scriptures. He told them they were come to a divine foundation stone and were built up on him, a spiritual house. Now he shows them Scripture warrant for their hope, that they were not wrong in so coming, that he was not wrong in so saying. Oh, it is a happy thing to take our peace out of the Bible, to have Bible warrant for it, to be Bible Christians! It is my desire for you that you would be like the noble Bereans and search the Scriptures to see if these things are so (*Acts* 17:11).

How do I know but that it may be all a dream after all, this coming to Christ and praying and finding peace in Him? The answer is, 'It is contained in the scripture' (verse 6).

What do the Scriptures say of Christ? That God laid Him: 'Behold, I lay . . .' Stand aside, the whole universe, and look on! God comes with His own hand to lay the stone. Oh! if the holy God lays the stone, surely I may rest on Him.

1. WHERE WAS THE STONE LAID?

It was laid in Zion. Christ died there. It was then and there that the foundation was laid. The foundation was laid on the cross, and laid in the grave. Christ was first preached in Jerusalem as a chief corner stone.

2. WHAT IS THE STONE LIKE?

Christ has three names as a stone: THE FOUNDATION STONE; THE CHIEF CORNER STONE; THE HEAD OF THE CORNER. He is all these to his own.

i. THE FOUNDATION STONE

He is the foundation, and there cannot be another. 'For other foundation can no man lay than that is laid, which is Jesus Christ' (*1 Cor.* 3:12).

ii. THE CHIEF CORNER STONE

In a foundation, there was a stone laid at the corner so as to unite the two adjoining walls closely together. Both were to lean on that stone. Christ is this stone, because Jews and Gentiles both rest on Him and are united in Him. 'Barbarians, Scythians, bond and free' – all are one in Him, just as branches are united to one another by being united to the vine. There is nothing that will unite you like being on the same Chief Corner Stone. This will keep you from quarrels with one another.

iii. THE HEAD OF THE CORNER

The stone at the head of the corner of the building used to be beautifully carved and was the glory of the building. This is Christ raised and exalted, though previously men disallowed Him.

God's Foundation Stone

iv. He Is Elect, Precious and Tried.

He is not only chosen by God, but He is a tried stone. Many have rested on Him. Abel was the first. Have you a friend in glory? Did he die in peace, resting on Christ? Follow his faith, then, considering the foundation of that peace, Christ the same yesterday, today and forever. There is certainty in resting on Him. 'He that believeth on him shall not be confounded.'

A believer shows that Christ is precious by forsaking all other hopes. He once prided himself on his goodness. Now he throws that away. He sells all that he had for this pearl, even if there were ten thousand others. He has chosen the way of faith. It is not always the way of light and joy, but Christ is always precious. He is not always present, but when He is not the soul cries, 'I am sick of love.' And he will still cleave to Him when the world despises Him.

3. THE HAPPINESS OF BIBLE CHRISTIANS

The truest peace is when one can turn up the Bible and show the foundation of it: 'Thus it is written'. Be like the Bereans. Meditate, and be like a tree planted by the waters. Hold fast His Word, and then you will not deny His Name. The scoffing world asks, How do you pretend to a divine peace? We answer, 'Thus it is written', and 'Thus saith the Lord.' 'In this Word do I hope', we say. 'I know His Word, and it cannot lie.'

God said, 'I lay.' Behind the death of Christ was the purpose of the Father. We look too often at the 'wicked hands' and not at the 'determinate counsel and foreknowledge of God' (Acts 2:23). Like Isaac bearing the wood, Christ bears His cross. He is bound by the hand of His Father. The Father bids the sword awake against His shepherd (Zech. 13:7). With this foundation, we shall not be confounded.

38

Chosen

But ye are a chosen generation, a royal priesthood, an holy nation, a peculiar people; that ye should shew forth the praises of him who hath called you out of darkness into his marvellous light (1 Pet. 2:9).

GOD HAD DEALT WITH THESE PEOPLE very differently from the way He dealt with others. He rejected others but chose them. They were like Israel of old: 'Only the LORD had a delight in thy fathers to love them, and he chose their seed after them, even you above all people, as it is this day' (*Deut.* 10:15). Other passages testify to the same thing: 'Now therefore, if ye will obey my voice indeed, and keep my covenant, then ye shall be a peculiar treasure unto me above all people: for all the earth is mine: and ye shall be unto me a kingdom of priests, and an holy nation. These are the words which thou shalt speak unto the children of Israel' (*Exod.* 19:5–6).

'But because the LORD loved you, and because he would keep the oath which he had sworn unto your fathers, hath the LORD brought you out with a mighty hand, and redeemed you out of the house of bondmen, from the hand of Pharaoh king of Egypt' (*Deut.* 7:8).

From our text I would observe what Christians are:

Chosen

1. A CHOSEN GENERATION

They were a chosen generation, or a chosen race. Some were left to stumble at Christ and to be crushed by Him when He comes again as the head corner stone (*Luke* 19:17–18), but they were a chosen race, as was ancient Israel. This is the distinguishing mark of all the children of God. They were chosen in Christ before the foundation of the world; but it was not for good in them that they were chosen. When a mason chooses stones for a building, he chooses those that are sound and will answer well. When a recruiting officer is choosing soldiers, he chooses men that will answer his purpose on account of some good qualities he sees in them. But it is not so with God.

Often the worst and meanest are chosen. God chooses His people, and then makes them what He will. It is not because He foresees they will repent and believe. That would be because of some foreseen goodness in them. No, He chooses them, then awakens them, then draws them: 'As many as were ordained to eternal life believed' (*Acts* 13:48). They were ordained to bear fruit. They were chosen to be holy.

i. Jacob and Esau

We have a special instance in the case of these two children in their mother's womb. They had done neither good nor evil. Yet God said, 'Jacob have I loved, but Esau have I hated' (*Rom.* 9:13). He had chosen the one, and left the other. Do you say this is unfair? Ah! that was what God thought you would say and therefore He provided the answer, 'I will have mercy on whom I will have mercy.'

ii. Daily Proofs of Election

God often takes the worst and leaves those that were better. The publicans and harlots were worse than the Pharisees, yet they were taken and the Pharisees left. Our Byrons and Gibbons, men of gigantic genius, are left as pillars of salt when thousands of mean minds are taken. 'Hath not God chosen the poor of this world?'

In the light of this –

a. *Labour to make your election sure.*

Rest simply on Christ, and you will soon feel in yourself that you are made whole, that you have been ordained to eternal life. Add to faith the things mentioned in 2 Peter 1:5–7, and you will know that God has chosen you to be holy. Rejoice, then, that your names are written in the book of life!

b. *Be humble and grateful.*

You were not chosen for the good in you. You were no better than the worst. Look on those that are left. You are no better than they. Love Him who so loved you. He loved you in eternity and passed them by.

iii. THEY ARE A GENERATION.

They are a class born together, or descended from the same ancestor. They are born of God. Learn from this to bear with one another. Do not dishonour your pedigree. Learn, too, why Christians are of a different temper from the world.

2. A ROYAL PRIESTHOOD

They are like Melchisedec who combined the office of priest with that of king (*Heb.* 7:2, 11). In this he was a type of the Lord Jesus Christ, who is a priest upon his throne. He is on his throne, and yet makes intercession for all His people. In believers, too, both of these offices are united. They are kings in that they rule over their own hearts. The natural man is a slave to himself, and to the devil, the cruellest of all masters. Come to Christ and you shall be free; and not only free but a king. Sin shall not reign over you. God's free Spirit is in His people. Is it so with you?

But Christians are kings in their minority. They are heirs to a throne. To him that overcometh, a reign is promised. 'Thou hast made us kings and priests unto God' (*Rev.* 1:6). They shall sit on twelve thrones judging the twelve tribes of Israel. They shall judge angels. They shall reign with Christ on His throne, as the Queen reigns along with her husband, the King. What manner of persons ought we to be, then? Oh, live as those who are to be kings!

They are also priests. In almost everything the priests of old were types of the Christian: in their clothing, their authority, their care of the temple, and their access to God. The priests came every day into the Holy Place. The High Priest came into the Holiest of all. All that are in Christ are now priests and may draw near. Do you seek to draw others near to God?

In their offerings, too, believers resemble priests. Priests used to offer slain beasts. So Christians offer a broken heart. They draw near with a heart bruised and beaten small like the incense. Such an offering He will not despise. The burnt offering went up in the flame to God. So Christians offer their bodies a living sacrifice, melted and flaming to God. As they blessed the people, so we bless others. We carry the names on our breast and come out and bless the people. They also offer praise and prayer. Let us learn, then, to be the priests we are called to be.

3. A HOLY NATION

Every nation ought to be a holy nation. Suppose a colony of holy angels came down to some island of the sea, and one of the bright Principalities of heaven sat over them as king. Who can doubt but they would be a holy nation? Their law book would be the Bible. They would live as a nation only for God. Such is the duty of every nation under heaven. But where is the holy nation? The children of God out of all nations are now the only holy nation.

They have one King and are under the same government. The Lord Jesus reigns over all. In every heart He has a throne. His sceptre is a righteous sceptre.

They have one holy language. It was sin that brought in many languages. In grace there is but one. Do you know it?

Oh, join this nation! There are none so happy as they, none so peaceful. They have a glorious land. They are set apart for God and also become inherently holy through His grace.

4. A PECULIAR PEOPLE

This speaks of the value God sets on them. They are His jewels, His peculiar treasure. It was customary for kings to have not only the public purse, but a private and peculiar treasure, containing the finest and the rarest jewels. Solomon obtained the peculiar treasure of kings from the conquests of his father. God loves His people as a peculiar treasure. He has bought them with blood. He places them in His inmost cabinet. He lavishes His mercies on them, and has a peculiar interest and complacence in them.

Learn to be peculiar, as His people. Christians should be priests, consecrated to His service, washed, anointed and wearing pure robes. As such they should be ready to offer sacrifices, perform His service, keep His temple and bless the people.

39

The People of God

Which in time past were not a people, but are now the people of God: which had not obtained mercy, but now have obtained mercy (1 Pet. 2:10).

HERE THE STATE OF SOULS WITHOUT CHRIST is contrasted with that of souls in Him. The former are not a people. They have not obtained mercy. But souls in Christ are the People of God, and have obtained mercy.

1. THOSE WITHOUT CHRIST ARE NOT A PEOPLE.
'Ye are not my people', as the prophet Hosea has it (*Hos.* 1:9). Moses says the same thing: 'I will provoke them to jealousy with those which are not a people' (*Deut.* 32:21), meaning the Gentiles, who were not recognized by God as being anything. Christless persons are not God's people. 'Ye are not my people, and I will not be your God' (*Hos.* 1:9).

i. THEY DO NOT BELONG TO GOD.
In one sense all the world belongs to Him. He has made all things for Himself. All the creatures, from the dragons to the owls, shall

honour Him (*Isa.* 43:20). But still they are not God's possession. They are not purchased; they are not accepted in the Surety, therefore the blood shed does not stand for them.

He cannot say of them, 'This people have I formed for myself; they shall shew forth my praise' (*Isa.* 43:21).

ii. God Does Not Reign over Them.

In one sense He does reign *over* them, as with a bit and bridle, but He does not reign *in* them. 'Thou couldest have no power at all against me, except it were given thee from above', said Christ to Pilate (*John* 19:11). But God did not reign in Pilate's heart.

iii. They Are Not a People.

They did not constitute a people in God's eyes (*Deut.* 32:21). A Christless soul is a dead soul. A number of them is just a collection of dead souls, not a people, any more than a heap of stones is a people.

They do not love one another. All seek their own interests. I have often looked round a company of such people and thought, If each heart were laid bare, if the flimsy covering of politeness and this world's flattery were taken off, what a loathsome sight would be seen. They would appear what they are, 'hateful, and hating one another' (*Titus* 3:3). God sees this and says, 'Not a people.'

Christians are branches on the same tree, therefore they are one. They are like quicksilver, they run together and are one, as quicksilver runs together. You who are without Christ, alas, you are no people. You are just nothing. How soon you will be swept down by the oncoming current. What a number have died since I came among you.

All that are Christians now, in time past were not a people. Look to the hole of the pit whence ye were digged (*Isa.* 51:1)!

2. THEY ARE MADE THE PEOPLE OF GOD

They are now the people of God. They are God's property. Oh, never forget that you are God's!

God lives in them. They are all one because they are one with God. United with Christ, they are in the vine. This world is just the wall for training up the vine. When its growth is complete, the wall will be taken down.

3. THOSE WITHOUT CHRIST HAVE NOT OBTAINED MERCY.

The word translated 'mercy' is the word used for the love of a father or a mother for a child. Christless persons are out of the love of God. Even the elect children of God are so, as long as they are out of Christ. They are not beloved.

Since Providence has brought this subject before us again, let us look at it once more. The love of God is infinite. To be in Him is life, yet all natural persons are without His mercy. If you are without Christ, 'not beloved' is written upon all you have and all you are. For us to love a thing, it must be according to our mind. It must suit our taste. It must have a certain soundness in it, or at least it must to your mind; but there is no such loveliness in Christless persons.

Consider *the misery of being without mercy*. To want His love is to want the greatest good. I know that natural men have much good in their lot. They have kind friends and many good things and amusements. I will never deny that there is much good in their lot but, alas! they want the greatest good – the love of the Father of all, the love of Him who is the Maker of all and God of all. I think every good thing you taste should make you feel your misery. You taste the honey – how sweet His love must be who made it so. You smile with wonder to see the setting of a summer sun – how sweet must the smile be of Him who made that sun to rise and fall. Poor sinner without the love of thy God, thou art feeding upon husks, thou knowest not what it is to have the great love of His great heart. To want His love takes away the sweetness of everything. Here is the madness of the world, that they can enjoy things outside of His love.

4. THEY OBTAIN MERCY.

Now they have obtained mercy. 'As the heaven is high above the earth, so great is his mercy toward them that fear him'; 'Like as a Father pitieth his children, so the Lord pitieth his children' (*Psa.* 103:11, 13). All that have come to Christ have obtained mercy.

i. It Is Tender Mercy.

It is like the mercy of a Father, the kindness of a mother. He crowns us with lovingkindness and tender mercies. He considers our frailty, that we are dust, and the frailty of our souls. Here is a lesson for weak disciples. He spareth you, as a Father spares his children.

ii. It Is Satisfying Mercy.

'Whosoever drinketh of the water that I shall give him shall never thirst' (*John* 4:14). Nothing else fills the soul. The love of the creatures does not satisfy us. There is so much imperfection, so much deceit, so much vain show. His love is satisfying. The Christian often retires from the esteem of friends and finds rest in the sweet love of God. Oh! 'Come unto me and I will give you rest', says Christ. The soul that believes is like a mote that floats in the sunbeam. It is like the little flower that is filled with dew till it bends its head, or like a flower filled with the sun's glad rays. It is like a bowl dipped into

The People of God

the clear crystal well. The water fills and overfills it. O little children, abide in his love if you wish calmness, a calm, divine and soft gentle peace that sweetens all the world.

iii. It Is Mercy to Body and Soul.

Ah, He loves us altogether! Our dust is dear to Him. He will make your bed in your sickness. He will guard your grave. Though your dust were scattered to the winds of heaven, He would gather every grain to make up the glorious body of the resurrection. When you love a person, you love all about them, their home, their dress, their everything. So it is with God. Whom He loves, He altogether loves.

One might ask, 'How can he love us, defiled with sin?'

The answer is this, He washes you in blood. He looks on you, not in yourself, but in Christ. Then He holds communion with you. He makes Himself known to you as Joseph did to his brethren.

Dear Christians, all these changes have passed upon you. See that you show forth 'the praises of him who hath called you out of darkness into his marvellous light' (*1 Pet.* 2:9).

40

Beseeching God's People

Dearly beloved, I beseech you as strangers and pilgrims, abstain from fleshly lusts, which war against the soul (1 Pet. 2:11).

1. FAITHFUL MINISTERS BESEECH THEIR PEOPLE IN LOVE.

As Peter did here, so do faithful ministers in all ages.

i. They Plead with the Unconverted.

So did Christ. He wept over Jerusalem: 'O Jerusalem, Jerusalem!' Even His severest reproofs were in love; even when He had to say, 'How can ye escape the damnation of hell?' So did Paul: 'Knowing therefore the terror of the Lord, we persuade men' (2 Cor. 5:11). He spoke the truth in love. As an ambassador and a worker together with God, he besought them.

The apostles were fishers of men. Fishers do not frighten the fish, but catch them. One sent back from the dead would not frighten people into faith. A sight of hell would not persuade us of the love of God, or the fulness of Christ. Paul persuaded both Jews and Greeks. He sought to persuade Agrippa. He warned faithfully and taught all who would listen, in meekness instructing them.

ii. They Plead with the Children of God.

So did Christ. He called them not servants but friends, and little children. So did Paul; 'I beseech you', he said (*Rom.* 12:1). 'My little children, of whom I travail in birth again', he said (*Gal.* 4:19). He was gentle among them, like a nurse (*1 Thess.* 2:7). John was like this also, constantly addressing the Christians as 'little children'.

I would say to the unconverted: Learn that it is in love that we beseech you. Am I become your enemy, because I tell you the truth? When we speak of your sins, your lost condition, the wrath that is over you, the hell beneath you, it is in love. We wish to persuade you to flee. Do not look so cold, so sour, so affronted at us. I have often thought, when I have seen the affronted looks of some worldling, how your thought will change the hour you are in another world. In hell you will be convinced that faithful ministers were your only true friends. What do you think it is that makes men spend and be spent in beseeching you, leaving ordinary pleasures and recreations to spend their days in warning you to flee from the wrath to come? It was said of Joseph Alleine that he was insatiably greedy of saving souls.

I would say to the children of God: Bear with the words of your ministers – they are all meant in love. Often they seem harsh to you, and yet you are in our hearts to live and die with you for your furtherance and joy of faith.

2. CHRISTIANS SHOULD ABSTAIN FROM FLESHLY LUSTS.

Because they are strangers and pilgrims on the earth, they should abstain from fleshly lusts. Again, because these fleshly lusts war against their souls, they should abstain from them.

i. FLESHLY LUSTS REMAIN IN CHRISTIANS.

If this were not so, there would be no use in beseeching them to abstain. There is no sin into which a Christian may not fall. It is ever God versus these desires. They are the lusts of the flesh and of the mind, and are like smothered fire. A young Christian expects to be freed from them all, but no, they remain. Why are they not rooted out? To keep the Christian humble. Christians are born of God. They are a chosen generation, a royal priesthood, a peculiar people. He might get proud. He might think he was in himself better than others. But fleshly lust rises in his heart. He finds that he is coarser than a devil, that he has lusts which even devils have not. This keeps him going softly all his days. Again it is to keep him dependent on the Spirit. If there were no lusts, a man would go on forgetting the Comforter. But oh, with what a grief of soul is the man driven to hang his all upon the Comforter! 'Hold me up, or I perish!'

A word to new Christians: Remember it is no proof that you are not a Christian that you are ever tempted. 'The flesh lusteth against the Spirit.' It is a proof that the Spirit of God is in your heart if war is going on. It is a most painful proof, and yet it is one, of grace. Oh! be kept humble by it, and near to God, tremblingly near. God is able to make you stand, but He alone is.

ii. THE COMMAND GIVEN

They are to abstain from fleshly lusts, to keep back from them, to flee from them, to flee the beginnings of them. Sin must not reign in the Christian. It must not be allowed to reign:

a. *Because they are strangers and pilgrims.*

They are in a strange land. 'I am a stranger in the earth', said the psalmist, 'hide not thy commandments from me' (*Psa.* 119:19).

Those who died in faith confessed that they were strangers and pilgrims on the earth and sought a better country. In the meantime they were content to live in tents (Heb. 11:9,13,14).

They are in a land of enemies. Many are watching for their halting. Many are laying snares. They must watch and pray, that they may abstain from fleshly lusts. They belong to another nation, to a peculiar heavenly race. Let them abstain, then! It is for a short time only. Let them fight the good fight of faith! The battle is sore, but it will be short. No lust will be in the pilgrim's heart soon, when he arrives at his Father's house. At a death bed I have often thought, Oh, what good are all thy lusts now?

b. *Because these lusts war against the soul.*

They disable you for holy things. You cannot serve God and mammon. If you indulge in any lust, whether pride or dress, or vanity or for money, or fleshly desire, you disable yourself from faith and prayer and for growing in grace. They war against your true joy. There is no joy like the favour of God felt within the soul, and the joy of the Comforter, but lust and the Comforter cannot dwell together. The holy dove will be frightened away from its home.

They lessen your eternal reward. Christians will differ as one star from another in glory. Some will have an entrance, some an abundant entrance. Every lust indulged is lessening your eternal glory. Oh! will you give away something of heaven for that base lust? They may make you a castaway. I know that if God has begun a good work He will finish it. But if you live in lust, how do you know that God has begun a work? Indeed you may be sure that He has not. Many branches seem to be in the Vine, yet are cast into the burning. Oh! take heed lest you be cast away, and pray for your ministers that, when they have preached to others, they themselves may not be cast away!

41

Christian Behaviour

Having your conversation honest among the Gentiles: that, whereas they speak against you as evildoers, they may by your good works, which they shall behold, glorify God in the day of visitation (1 Pet. 2:12).

1. CHRISTIAN CONDUCT AMONG UNBELIEVERS

In the previous verse Peter emphasized inward holiness. Now he speaks of outward behaviour in the world.

i. Christians Are among the Gentiles.

They are in the world 'as the lily among thorns' (*Song of Sol.* 2:2). There are both tares and wheat in the field, and both good fish and bad in the same net. There is nothing in the Bible to suggest that Christians should be monks and nuns. Generally it is not good for a man to be alone. God has placed him in a family, with friends or relations, in the shop, in the market, having dealing with others. Christians must and ought to mingle with the crowd. Why must this be so?

It shows God's power and love to them. To preserve a sheep in the midst of wolves is far more wonderful than to make it lie down in green pastures. It is like preserving a spark while going through the sea. Christians will be monuments of God's mercy because they will have been brought through fire and water, and upheld amid a world lying in wickedness.

They are there to be witnesses. God calls His people His witnesses. They are like salt in the midst of corruption, or a dew in the desert. They leave all around without excuse.

They are also there to make them like Christ in their compassion for the unconverted. Their being among sinners sometimes makes them realize what hell must be like. It makes them long for heaven, and long to see others brought there too.

2. UNBELIEVERS SPEAK EVIL OF CHRISTIANS.

They did so of Christ. They say they are acting a part, that they are hypocrites, that they are trying to make people think they are good and holy, when really they are wicked. They say they are proud, and think themselves holier than others. They read the Bible and pray so that they may be seen of men. When a Christian falls into sin, they say that that is the way with them all, if we only knew it. They are just as bad as others. They say they are mad, and following a mere craze. Marvel not if they say this of you. They said it of Jesus. He is mad, they said, and hath a devil. It was said of Paul. It has been said, I believe, of every child of God.

I will show you who is acting a part: you that come to the house of God without any work of God, or wish for it. You that stand up at prayer, yet never pray at home. The body is worshipping God, but the soul is worshipping the devil. Is not this hypocrisy? You that offer your children in baptism and promise before God and man to pray for them and with them, yet never do so – is not this hypocrisy? You that come to the Lord's Table and take the bread and wine, yet do not close with Christ – do you not have a deceived heart?

And I will tell you who are mad: you that know you have not come to Christ and yet are happy, though the whole Word of God tells you your soul is over hell. You that go on in sin, that go regularly to the tavern and live in uncleanness, whose heart is a cage of every unclean bird, who know you have not been born again, and that you cannot see the kingdom of God. It is you that are mad.

3. CHRISTIANS SHOULD BE OUTWARDLY COMELY.

First, they should be inwardly holy and keep from inward sin. But remember also to keep from open sin. Pray to be cleansed from secret faults, but also to be kept from presumptuous sin (*Psa.* 19:12-13). David fell into adultery, Peter into cursing. What may you not fall into? I know well that the young believer in his pride will say, Is thy servant a dog, that he should do this great thing? (*2 Kings* 8:13). Be not high minded, but fear.

Let us walk honestly, as in the day. Abstain from fleshly lusts. Be outwardly comely. Let there be no secret Christianity. Most are much to blame for their secrecy. A child in a godless family tries to conceal the work in his heart. This often leads him into painful circumstances and suspicions. Be bold as a lion.

Avoid the appearance of evil. There are many practices which I could name which should be avoided by Christians because they have the appearance of evil. Common honesty should be apparent. 'It is naught, it is naught, saith the buyer: but when he is gone his way, then he boasteth' (*Prov.* 20:14). This should not be among Christians.

Avoid haughtiness toward the unconverted, and severity of speech in handling doubters. Be a Christian everywhere. There should not be a great show of love in church and prayer meeting and with the minister, but in the family, nothing to show that you are a Christian. God's precious Word should fall from your tongue. Your conversation should not savour of foolish jesting. No argument can refute a blameless life. They are happiest who keep furthest from the beginnings of sin. Certain places are to be avoided; also certain times, companies, and games. I do not mean to enter on the question whether games are lawful or not. But to the unconverted I would say at once that they are unlawful, for alas, what is it but sporting over the brink of hell? The great question of salvation has to be settled first. To Christians, I would say your own conscience, enlightened by the Word, should guide you. One thing I insist upon: forsake all games that have an appearance of evil. All that lead to gambling, to unnatural excitement, and to late hours. Walk honestly, as in the day. When the great statesman Sir Francis Walsingham was charged with being melancholy, he replied, 'I am not melancholy. I am serious. All things about us are serious. God is serious.' Does it become us to be carefree and trifling?

Christians should study the common virtues:

i. Politeness
'Be pitiful, be courteous.' A Christian should not be a boor. One that is so often in company of the Highest should have a calm and solemn air, a heavenliness in their common talk, and a concern for others.

ii. Cleanliness
Cleanliness is said to be next to godliness. One that has the fine linen, white and clean (*Rev.* 19:8), should be marked by cleanliness too.

iii. Punctuality
An unpunctual man is a thief of others' time.

iv. Activity

The Christian should not be slothful in business. If he is a shoe-black, he should be the best shoe-black.

v. Temper

One that has the Spirit of Jesus should not have a bad temper. One who has been forgiven should be cheerful. Otherwise some will say, 'Well, if heaven is made of such, I would not wish to be there.' Avoid a ragged temper which jolts one in passing like a rough road. 'A soft answer turneth away wrath.'

4. THE EFFECT OF CHRISTIAN BEHAVIOUR

The worldly will 'glorify God in the day of visitation'. This seems to be a day when the Spirit is outpoured, a day of awakening, such a day as Jerusalem had when Christ preached to them.

Unconverted persons may be led to glorify God in such a day. 'The beast of the field shall honour me . . . because I give water in the wilderness, and rivers in the desert, to give drink to my people, to my chosen' (*Isa.* 43:20); how much more shall men?

Christians should walk honestly and commend the gospel by word and deed.

42

Submit to Earthly Rulers

Submit yourselves to every ordinance of man for the Lord's sake: whether it be to the king, as supreme; or unto governors, as unto them that are sent by him for the punishment of evildoers, and for the praise of them that do well. For so is the will of God, that with well doing ye may put to silence the ignorance of foolish men: As free, and not using your liberty for a cloak of maliciousness, but as the servants of God (1 Pet. 2:13–16).

SOME THINK THAT, because we are God's people, therefore we are free from all restraint. However, you must not use your freedom as a cloak of maliciousness. You are the servants of God.

1. EARTHLY RULERS ARE SENT BY GOD.

The ruler is the ordinance of God. He is the minister of God. God has set up two kinds of ministers on earth. One has the sceptre to curb, restrain, and direct men to Christ. The other has the Word, to win and draw men to Christ. Both should have the same end in view. We do not take our office of preaching on ourselves but are called; so are they. It is our part to seek the good of the souls and bodies of men; it is theirs too. Both are the two great means God has set up in the world for building His temple.

The magistrate has as much to do as the ministry, for both are equally the ministers of God. I know well that many of you do not agree with this, but search the Scriptures, for it is not my word that the ruler is the minister of God (*Rom.* 13:4)!

When I look on a prisoner in a cell I see both types of minister. One minister of God hedges up the sinner's way. The other visits, draws, wins him to Christ. Many are saved thus.

Earthly rulers are sent for the punishment of evildoers and the praise of them that do well. The whole Bible declares it. 'By me kings reign, and princes decree justice' (*Prov.* 8:15). 'The most High ruleth in the kingdom of men, and giveth it to whomsoever he will' (*Dan.* 4:17). 'I gave thee a king in mine anger, and took him away in my wrath' (*Hos.* 13:11). 'Let every soul be subject to the higher powers' (*Rom.* 13:1). History proves this. Even Nebuchadnezzar was sent by God, as was Cyrus: 'I girded thee, though thou hast not known me' (*Isa.* 45:5). Pharaoh was another ruler whom God is said to have raised up. The rulers of the earth are the shields of the earth (*Psa.* 47:9), and they belong to God. How soon was Napoleon Bonaparte hurled from the Empire of the world!

QUESTION: Are wicked kings sent by God?

ANSWER: Yes, Saul was a wicked king, yet God says, 'I gave thee a king in my anger' (*Hos.* 13:11). Nero was a wicked emperor, yet both Paul and Peter say he was ordained by God.

2. CHRISTIANS SHOULD SUBMIT.

Christians should yield cheerful obedience. They should live quiet and peaceable lives, and pay taxes willingly (*Rom.* 13:7). Some people murmur when paying taxes. Some say the burden is too heavy, and why are other countries better off? If you look on the government as God's minister, it will be as pleasant a duty as prayer

Submit to Earthly Rulers

or hearing the Word. You should not speak evil of dignities (*2 Pet. 2:10; Jude 8*). It is common to rail at public men, and for men to take a side and, by falsehood, to run down all that are on the opposite side. It shall not be so among you.

Do not interfere with the duties of government. I know well that, when I arouse your political feelings and sentiments, I arouse a sea of roaring waves which Paul himself could not allay. 'Great is Diana of the Ephesians', they cried. Yet suffer one who, for many years, has ceased, not only to interfere with matters political, but even to study them, to give a word from the Word of God. A good man says, the devil has a thousand baubles and toys to entice sinners from Christ, and that is his one end and aim. Of all his baubles, politics is the chief.

I remember once trembling in a stage-coach when, at a steep and dangerous hill, the horses became unmanageable and ran away. The driver was a skilful man, but the passengers with one consent sprang forward to lay hold upon the reins. 'Off, off,' he cried, 'If I cannot drive them I will give the reins to you.'

My dear friends, unless it be your business to rule, meddle not with rulers. Quite right, if you are electors, to choose a faithful and godly representative, but beyond that, do leave the fever of politics if you would be saved. Oh! that God would persuade you to forsake that rage for newspapers! They are the vehicles of prejudice and falsehood. They are not food for a child of God.

Pray for rulers. Many argue about governments who do not pray for them.

Pray for your ministers. Ah! how can we prevail if you do not hold up our hands! It was well observed by a little child among you when he heard a full and fervent prayer, 'I wonder he did not pray for the minister.' So pray for governments, that the public mind may be enlightened. Some people are proud of petitions, and indeed it is a happy right of the meanest subject; but a happier right is to petition God to give them a right mind. I am persuaded that, if the children of God would pray, it would produce a greater change in our country than any other means.

3. CHRISTIANS ARE FREE, YET SERVANTS OF GOD.

A Christian cannot be a slave. He is free from the curse of a broken law. He is free from the tyranny of the devil. He is free from the tyranny of the world. You are free indeed, but the highest freedom is to serve God!

43

Duties to God and Man

Honour all men. Love the brotherhood. Fear God. Honour the king (1 Pet. 2:17).

IT IS ONE OF THE MOST WONDERFUL QUALITIES of the Bible, that it expresses so much in so little. 'A word spoken in due season, how good is it!' 'A word fitly spoken is like apples of gold in pictures of silver.' 'The words of the wise are as goads.' Philosophers in all ages have had their wise sayings, short, emphatic, portable, easily used. Solomon led the way in this: 'to understand a proverb and the interpretation; the words of the wise, and their dark sayings' (*Prov.* 1:6). Jesus too had His short sayings, for example, 'Ye believe in God, believe also in me.' 'I will have mercy and not sacrifice.' So did the apostles. Here is a case in point: 'Honour all men. Love the brotherhood. Fear God. Honour the king.'

Three of these refer to believers' feelings toward those on earth, one toward our Father in heaven.

1. HONOUR ALL MEN.

Believers should honour all men. There is a peculiar affection to our kindred, 'Honour thy father and thy mother.' There is also a

[289]

peculiar affection to Christians. But here the believer is commanded to have a regard for every man that breathes.

i. Because God Does.

The first reason is that this reflects God's disposition towards them. 'Behold, God is mighty, and despiseth not any' (*Job* 36:5). We are to love our enemies and do good to those who hate us, because our Father 'maketh his sun to rise on the evil and on the good' (*Matt.* 5:44). God sees our infinite loathsomeness as sinners. When He looks on a large city, how much abomination does He behold! He is angry with them every day; and yet He is gentle to all. So should we, if we are to be the children of our Father in heaven.

ii. So That They May Be Saved.

When Paul came to Corinth he saw sights of sin which must have made his blood boil; but Jesus said to him, 'I have much people in this city.' Now He would despise none, for any one might be a chosen vessel of mercy. We should honour all. You must despise none. Do not be proud over any, however vile. They may be chosen by God. Rather, pray for them that they may be saved.

iii. Because Christians Were Once as Bad.

We should be gentle, showing all meekness to all men, for we ourselves also were just like them (*Titus* 3:2–3). Paul had been a blasphemer, proud, injurious, and a persecutor of the church of God. He had been just like his fellow-Jews. Therefore, instead of being proud, his heart's desire and prayer was that they might be saved. So it should be with you. Have you not been as bad? What would you have been this day if free grace had not prevented? Is not your heart as wicked as any? Honour all, therefore. 'Be careful to entertain strangers.' Give to the bad as well as to the good.

Duties to God and Man

The world is not like this. Cain said, 'Am I my brother's keeper?' The world have no esteem or value for one another. All seek their own. A natural heart does not value others a straw. It would be more concerned to lose a little finger than if the whole of China were sunk in the sea with all its millions. When one comes to Christ, he begins to care for men. He begins to look on them with different eyes. He cannot esteem the wicked. In his eyes a vile person is contemned; but he cares for them. They are upon his heart. He remembers that God so loved the wicked world that He gave His Son. We did not love God, but He loved us (1 John 4:10).

2. LOVE THE BROTHERHOOD.

The believer is to care for all the world, but to love the brethren. He is to pray for his enemies, but to be a companion of all them that fear God. 'As we have therefore opportunity, let us do good unto all men, especially unto them who are of the household of faith' (Gal. 6:10).

i. THIS IS CHRIST'S NEW COMMANDMENT.

We are to love them as much as Christ did us. How amazing is the patient love of Christ to His own disciples! They had much infirmity, in our eyes. They slept when Jesus was in agony. They quarrelled who should be the greatest. They all forsook Him and fled. Peter denied Him; and yet He loved them to the end.

So should we love the brethren. They have great imperfections. Some have little faith; some have little peace; some do not see Christ clearly. Some have little holiness; some are bad tempered; some suffer much temptation. Still you are to love them. That is to be Christ-like. His commandment is, 'As I have loved you, that ye also love one another' (John 13:34). This is something more than is seen in the tables of the Law. If man had never fallen, such a love as this would have been unknown. 'These things I command you, that ye love one another' (*John* 15:17).

ii. THE WORLD MAY SEE AND TAKE NOTICE.

'By this shall all men know that ye are my disciples, if ye have love one to another' (*John* 13:35); 'That the world may believe that thou hast sent me' (*John* 17:21) – because all the disciples of Christ are one. Nothing would awaken the world more than the sight of the true vine. So then, to honour all you must love the brotherhood. The sight of the body, all caring for one another, all sweetly tempered, rejoicing with one another and grieving with one another, that would make the world feel that there is one Spirit.

If you saw a great mill, with large wheels and little wheels, ropes and pulleys all acting on one another, and not running into confusion but helping one another, you would say, There is some great mind that has put all these things in order. So when they see true Christians, the world should know that Christ is risen! Show forth the Holy Spirit!

iii. THIS IS THE ONLY WAY TO HOLINESS.

'He that loveth another hath fulfilled the law' (*Rom.* 13:8). 'And the Lord make you to increase and abound in love one toward another, and toward all men' (*1 Thess.* 3:12). It is a constant in all Christians: 'Since we heard of . . . the love which ye have to all the saints' (*Col.* 1:4). It is the first of the fruits of the Spirit (*Gal.* 5:22).

iv. WE SHOULD INCREASE IN LOVE.

If we compare 1 Thessalonians with 2 Thessalonians we will observe an increase in love. In one the apostle beseeches them to abound in love more and more, and in the other he thanks God that they do! We are to let brotherly love continue (*Heb.* 13:1). It is one of the things we are to add to our faith: 'And to brotherly kindness, charity' (*2 Pet.* 1:7).

3. FEAR GOD.

Every natural man fears God with the fear of dread. Adam hid, and said, 'I was afraid.' So men hide themselves still. On seeing the Lord's glory, Isaiah cried, 'Woe is me! for I am undone.' Peter prayed, 'Depart from me.' God is so holy, and man's sins are so many, that he fears God is his Enemy. Every divine manifestation makes him tremble.

A large part of the gospel is, 'Fear not: I bring you good tidings.' Jesus partook of flesh and blood to deliver us from the fear of death. He took the sting away. Now we need no more *dread* God. If His eye be on me, there can be no dread. When a thunderstorm is rolling over our heads, many persons are filled with dread. But when it is past, the dark clouds have been driven past, and the thunder is retiring, all fear is gone. So it is in Christ! 'Thine anger is turned away' (*Isa.* 12:1). Now there arises a new feeling in the breast, a childlike fear, the beginning of wisdom!

The sinner feels himself worthy of God's anger, yet he finds himself seated at God's table. He adores the mercy that has saved him, while he sees the awfulness of Him who would not pardon without blood.

We are fearfully and wonderfully saved. The joy of a Christian is awfully solemn. These still waters run very deep. There is not a sweeter feeling in the world than this fear of God. No angel has it. It lives only in a soul bought by blood. 'Then thou shalt see, and flow together, and thine heart shall fear, and be enlarged' (*Isa.* 60:5). Fear and great joy can well go together (Matt. 28:8).

Fear God. Keep up the freshness of the fear of God. We should be 'of quick understanding in the fear of the LORD' (*Isa.* 11:3). You may have seen a hound running backward and forward seeking the scent of the game. How quickly it catches it and follows it! So it is with one brought nigh. If the Spirit of Christ rests on them, He quickens them. A child observes the least motion of a parent's eye. We should keep this up between the Lord and ourselves, and advance in it, 'perfecting holiness in the fear of God' (*2 Cor.* 7:1), 'walking in the fear of the Lord' (*Acts* 9:31).

4. HONOUR THE KING.

This has been spoken before, yet it is so important that it is repeated here. Some might say, If we are to be lovers of all, and devoted to Christians, and to live as children of God, then we need not be so subject to civil rulers. Ah, no! You must. Though you may be the heir of a throne in heaven, and the earthly king may not be, you are still to honour the king. If you are a child of God, you must be an honest, quiet citizen.

44

Masters and Servants

Servants, be subject to your masters with all fear; not only to the good and gentle, but also to the froward, for this is thankworthy, if a man for conscience toward God endure grief, suffering wrongfully. For what glory is it, if, when ye be buffeted for your faults, ye shall take it patiently? But if, when ye do well, and suffer for it, ye take it patiently, this is acceptable with God. For even hereunto were ye called: because Christ also suffered for us, leaving us an example, that ye should follow his steps: who did no sin, neither was guile found in his mouth: who, when he was reviled, reviled not again; when he suffered, he threatened not; but committed himself to him that judgeth righteously (1 Pet.2: 18–23).

IN THE SOVEREIGN GRACE OF GOD, the servant is often taken, and the master left. Here Peter speaks to Christian servants who have froward masters. When the world chooses its people it chooses the rich, the well-born, the noble, the fair. But God has not chosen many wise, noble or mighty. His choice is to the praise of the glory of His grace. Naaman the Syrian was rich and great. Thousands waited for his nod. His little maid was a captive and a slave, yet he was a leper and she a child of God. Nebuchadnezzar was ruler of the world, Daniel his youthful slave, yet Nebuchadnezzar was driven forth to feed with beasts, while Daniel was a man greatly beloved of God. So it is now. Many a lordly master sits at a feast, while the servant that stands behind and waits has a sweeter feast, pardon and peace with God. Many of you who are servants do not, cannot, envy your masters. Many of you servants know the grace of God in your heart. You sigh to read of our poor Queen spending her Saturday nights at the Opera. Such is grace. Oh! The depth of God's wisdom! Bless God who made you to differ. 'For Jesus hath loved me, I cannot tell why.' What a leveller is the grace of God!

To unconverted servants I would say, How wretched you are if you have not the grace of God! If you have, how wonderful is His free mercy. How great is His kindness in giving so many instructions, so full and precious, as we have here.

1. CHRISTIAN SERVANTS SHOULD BE SUBJECT TO GOOD MASTERS.

They should be obedient to good and gentle masters, with all fear. 'Servants, be obedient to them that are your masters . . . in singleness of your heart, as unto Christ (*Eph.* 6:5). 'Obey in all things your masters' (*Col.* 3:22). Let as many servants as are under the yoke count their own masters worthy of all honour' (*1 Tim.* 6:1). Just as a child should obey its parents, so should a servant his master. The same word is applied to both in the Bible. Some servants think they are not to obey their masters in all things, but only when they please. But Titus 2:9 says 'Please them well in all things.'

Can it really mean in *all* things? In all lawful things. If the command of the master is contrary to the command of God, we ought to obey God rather than men. If the master command you to break the Sabbath, you ought to obey God rather than man. If the master command you to lie, to say, 'Not at home', when the master *is* at home, you ought to obey God rather than man, at whatever risk. 'Ye are bought with a price; be not ye the servants of men.' 'Lie not one to another.' All liars shall have their part in the lake which burneth with fire and brimstone (*Rev.* 21:8). Servants should show all good fidelity, 'not purloining' (Titus 2:10). If you have been bought with blood, you will not steal. God redeemed His people, then said, 'Thou shalt not steal.' 'Let him that stole steal no more: but rather let him labour . . . that he may have to give to him that needeth' (*Eph.* 4:28). 'Not purloining' includes taking small things, odds and ends which will never be missed. If a tree be grafted it will show the change in the smallest leaf. Some caterpillars take the colour of their food and show it in the smallest fibres of their bodies. So if the Spirit of God is in you, He will make you holy to the finger ends, in little things as well as in great.

Obedience to masters is to be 'with fear and trembling, in singleness of your heart as unto Christ. Not with eyeservice' (*Eph.* 6:5–6). In Colossians, it is said, 'Fearing God' (*Col.* 3:22). Here is the great secret of being a good servant, or a good anything: Be in the fear of God, having a single heart. The world has a double heart. We are to be united to Christ in one heart, having the heart of a child in the presence of a sin-pardoning, Christ-delivering Father. He will be a good servant that is thus 'within the veil'. Everything will be made pleasant in the doing of it.

Let me persuade servants to become Christians. You will never be good servants till then. You will never be happy servants till then. You may honour Christ every day, in cleaning the house, in waiting at table – you may do it all to Christ; especially if your master be a child of God. Then you can give him a cup of cold water in the name of a disciple.

2. CHRISTIAN SERVANTS SHOULD BE SUBJECT TO BAD MASTERS.

Some masters are froward, wicked, cruel, capricious. Servants often endure grief, suffering wrongfully. What should they do then? They should take it patiently, not answering again, and so follow in Christ's steps.

i. This Is Thankworthy.

God will reward it. It is a hard thing to be brow-beaten and scolded when we have done nothing amiss, but bear it patiently. God will take notice of it. A child in an ungodly family, among ungodly companions, will surely be treated ill. Remember, this is glorifying to God. He could easily change your place and take all the enemies away. He is Head over all. But He does not. Bear reproaches, then. Endure grief, suffering wrongfully. You often think, if you could preach you would glorify God. But you can glorify Him where you are, and you will not lose your reward. 'Great is your reward in heaven.' There is reason to think that there will be a greater reward for patient suffering than for the boldest doing. It can be easier to preach than to be silent.

ii. It Is Christlike.

He did no sin, yet He was reviled and suffered. He was perfectly holy, as holy as God Himself. He did no sin, not in heart, not in tongue, not in deed. Yet He suffered. He was called a wine-bibber, a devil, a deceiver. He was mocked, buffeted, finally crucified.

Yet He was silent. He committed Himself to God. He prayed for His murderers. Is this your Saviour? Oh, follow His steps. Suffer with Him. Be happy to be like Him. Angels cannot do this. It is only here that you can bear reviling for Him. Be like Stephen who said, 'Lay not this sin to their charge.'

45

Christ Bore Our Sins

Who his own self bare our sins in his own body on the tree, that we, being dead to sins, should live unto righteousness: by whose stripes ye were healed. For ye were as sheep going astray; but are now returned unto the Shepherd and Bishop of your souls (1 Pet. 2:24–25).

CHRIST IS HERE REVEALED TO US in a three-fold character: as a Lamb slain for us; as a good Physician, bending over us, applying the blood from His own stripes; and as a tender and watchful Shepherd.

Believers delight to look on Him in all these ways. It gives peace, joy, and a sense of security. When a child loves a thing, it loves to look at it from all sides. So it is with believers. I would apply the first of these characters to the solid comfort of those who have believed in Jesus, those who have come to close with Him. Who has borne our sins? He Himself. How? In His body. Where? On the tree. Why? That we should be holy. You may see all your sins pressing down on the soul of the Redeemer.

But we see also the miserable case of Christless souls. They remain under the burden of their sins, and under a disease which brings eternal death. They are as sheep which are still going astray.

To the awakened I would say, Would you not like that peace? You, too, are welcome to the Saviour.

It gives peace and solid comfort to the believer at all times to look to Jesus as his Ransom, Physician and Shepherd.

1. CHRIST OUR RANSOM

He Himself bore our sins in His own body on the tree. As long as a man is in his natural state, he bears his own sins, the sin of Adam, his own sinful nature, his own sinful actions. God is angry with him every day.

Most feel no burden because they are insensible to the greatness of the iniquity of sin. They do not remember their sins. They do not believe the Bible when it says that the wrath of God is revealed against them. The dead do not feel the weight of the earth above them. The dead earth does not feel the weight of the Pyramids, the weight of the solid globe. Neither does a dead soul feel the weight of his sins. They do not believe God. They believe their own fancies and hopes sooner than God.

As for the awakened, they feel them. The Word comes in much conviction to them. Their language is, 'My burden is heavier than I can bear.'

The soul that comes to Christ feels that Christ has borne his sins in His own body on the tree, and that this is past. He *bore*, not He *will*. He has carried them all away in His dying.

Believers have sins, some few, some many. Paul was a blasphemer and a persecutor. A woman which was a sinner came to Christ. He has washed us all from all our sins. Believers can say, 'He has borne them. He washed me. He let His blood flow instead of mine, in His own body on the tree.'

See that you hold fast the beginning of your confidence. The devil will try to shake you, saying, Thy sins are too many to be forgiven. The answer is, Many or few, He hath borne them.

Christ Bore Our Sins

He will say, Thy sins are against God, against Christ, against thine own body.

Answer: Still He hath borne our sins.

He will say, Thou hast sinned since believing, against the blood, against the Spirit. Thou hast sinned away Christ.

Answer: Still I am heartily willing that He should be my Surety. I have no other hope. 'He bore our sins.'

He will say, Thou hast sold Him like Judas. Thou hast profaned His sacraments. Thou hast sinned in thy very prayers in the house of God. Thou hast willingly followed the devil instead of Christ.

Answer: Still Christ has died. In myself I am hell-deserving, but He has borne our sins.

To believers I would say:
Christ has borne your sins, feel the comfort of this. Blessed is the man whose sin is forgiven. Feel the peace of this. Feel the joy.

To the unconverted, I would say:
You may have the same. Christ is as free to you as to any that have come to Him. We are to preach the gospel to every creature. These good tidings are to all people. Righteousness of God is unto all that believe.

Why did He do this? That we, being dead to sins, should live unto righteousness; that we, being justified, might be sanctified. Oh! See that it be so. By this you will know if you have been really justified. This is the end of God in choosing, in redeeming, to raise up a race of justified and holy ones to praise Him in eternity, more loudly than angels, but not less purely.

2. CHRIST OUR PHYSICIAN

Man is sick, yet he knows it not. When awakened, he finds out that he is sick. His *conscience* is wounded sore. A gnawing worm is there.

He cannot heal his wounds. He goes to other physicians. All cry out, 'It is not in us to heal you.' A guilty conscience is the most secret of all diseases.

But Jesus draws near. 'I gave my back to the smiters', says He. He shows His stripes – the stripes of angry men, the stripes of an angry God. This heals the conscience. 'Ye were healed.' Is it not in this way that you were healed? Ah, there is no sight like the lacerated back of the Redeemer for healing a lacerated conscience. I do not need to bear stripes, for He has borne them.

Again, when awakened, man finds he is sick in *heart*. The flames of lust burn there. What a palsy of the whole soul! What leprosy! He is all unclean. Ah, what a loathsome disease sin is! In vain you try other physicians. Finally you come to Him who is the bruised balm. As the incense was beaten small before it could give out its fragrance, as some plants must be bruised, like the walnut leaf and the myrtle, so it was with Christ. 'He was wounded for our transgressions, he was bruised for our iniquities' (*Isa.* 53:5). It is looking to His stripes that sanctifies. How? Because doing so gives us confidence to keep near to God.

Conviction makes us see what a dreadful thing sin is. How hateful to God. Dare I sin anymore? It shows us how God has loved us. Shall we not love Him? All natural helps to holiness are very frail, but these stripes bring us near to God. He imputes them to us. He justifies us, and fills us with His Spirit.

Oh! Incomparable Physician! Others use their skill. They take great pains; but Thou usest Thine own pains and sufferings!

Let me ask all who hear, Do you know the virtue that is in the stripes of Christ to heal a burning heart, to quench the flames of lust, to still the rising waves of passion, to hush the whirlwinds of strife and anger and malice, to give activity to the palsied soul, to give purity to the depraved heart? Believer, struggling with thy lusts, often well nigh overcome, use thy bruised Physician more. Go to God by Him and He will say, 'My grace is sufficient for thee.'

3. CHRIST OUR SHEPHERD AND BISHOP

The unconverted are like sheep going astray. Christ compares a lost soul to a lost sheep, not only lost but going further and further astray. Isaiah adds that 'we have turned every one to his own way' (*Isa.* 53:6).

Some of you will not be wakened by any description of what you are. Will it awaken you to think you are every day going more astray? Every day that you swear an oath it becomes easier to you. Every day that you mingle with loose company it becomes more natural to you. You are going astray, like a stone rolling down a hill. Faster and faster see the stone rolling. You are going away from Christ. Every day you hear sermons and heed them not. You are becoming deafer to the voice of Christ. Every new death in your family or friends or neighbourhood that you are hardened to takes you further away. How much further astray you are today than this time last year, further from heaven, nearer to hell!

But when this geat change takes place, you are brought back to 'the Shepherd and Bishop of your souls'. When the soul is ransomed and healed, it needs to be tended. What a sweet office of Christ this is, Shepherd and Overseer of souls. Those that are truly come to Christ know Him as their Shepherd and Bishop. They are come under the care of a watchful Shepherd who has an eye on every one of the flock. He knows your case. He knows your want.

i. He Will Keep Us from Straying.

'Tell me, O thou whom my soul loveth, where thou feedest . . . for why should I be as one that turneth aside by the flocks of thy companions?' (*Song of Sol.* 1:7). May He always keep us from straying! A mother will let her child fall on a soft carpet, but not over a precipice. Though the righteous fall, he shall not be utterly cast down (*Psa.* 37:24). Surely He will bring us back on His shoulder if we stray. We will hear his voice and follow Him.

ii. He Will Supply All Our Secret Needs.

He is the Bishop of our souls, the Overseer, the Visitor of the flock. 'He restoreth my soul.' He is an ever-watchful Saviour. What a privilege in life, and in the valley of the shadow of death! He is the Chief Shepherd, the Great Shepherd of the sheep. The Good Shepherd. His office is to feed the flock. Many look to Christ only as a Surety, but this is wrong. True, our pardon is all found there, but we need more than pardon. We need guidance, protection, food. For this He is a Shepherd and Bishop. Oh! Christians, keep Him as your Shepherd!

a. *Feeding*

He will make us lie down in green pastures. We shall go in and out and find pasture. He is able to supply all our need. He is the Chief Shepherd. He will find us in unlikely places and help us.

b. *Protection*

He takes us out of the greatest dangers, from the very mouth of the lion and the paw of the bear. He will protect us in many a dark and cloudy day.

c. *Guidance*

He leadeth us. His rod and staff comfort us. Oh, then, live under His guidance! Go where He leads. Though it be through sufferings, yet it will be to a crown of glory that fadeth not away. In heaven we shall still follow the Lamb. It is eternal life to be led by Him.

46

Believing Wives

> *Likewise, ye wives, be in subjection to your own husbands; that, if any obey not the word, they also may without the word be won by the conversation of the wives; while they behold your chaste conversation coupled with fear. Whose adorning let it not be that outward adorning of plaiting the hair, and of wearing of gold, or of putting on of apparel; But let it be the hidden man of the heart, in that which is not corruptible, even the ornament of a meek and quiet spirit, which is in the sight of God of great price. For after this manner in the old time the holy women also, who trusted in God, adorned themselves, being in subjection unto their own husbands: Even as Sara obeyed Abraham, calling him lord: whose daughters ye are, as long as ye do well, and are not afraid with any amazement* (1 Pet. 3:1–6).

WE SEE FROM THIS PASSAGE that believing wives may have unbelieving husbands. But they should not marry such. This is contrary to God's Word. Someone may object, Perhaps I will be able to convert them. Ah! but you must not break God's law to convert souls. You must not do evil that good may come. How can you pray, 'Lord I have broken Thy command, but now put thy blessing on my sin'?

God often chooses the wife, and leaves the husband. Two may be in one bed: one may be taken, and the other left. The woman is called the weaker vessel. She may be weaker in body and mind, yet God chooses the weak things of the world.

When God has a work of grace to do in a house, He often begins with the wife.

1. BELIEVING WIVES SHOULD BE IN SUBJECTION.

   i. It Was So in Paradise.

Woman was made from a rib out of Adam's side: not from under his feet, nor from his head, neither to rule nor to be trampled upon, but from his side, to be a helpmeet. Weaker, softer, frailer she may be, yet she is to be cherished. She is to be obedient, to take the man as her head, to lean upon the man. It was so in Sarah, the mother of believers.

   ii. Sin Has Disturbed This Order.

Sin has disturbed the order established in the beginning, before the Fall. Sin has made the woman usurp authority over the man. But this disturbance should be reversed in the case of believers.

Believing wives may have believing husbands.

Remember what is said to servants in 1 Timothy 6, 'Do them service, because they are faithful and beloved, partakers of the benefit' (verse 2). What joy to be subject to one who is one with you in the Lord! There is not a lovelier sight in all this world than a believing husband and wife sheltering and supporting one another, she learning of him, he learning of Christ.

Believing wives may have unbelieving husbands.

But the husband may 'obey not the word'. He withholds belief from the Word. He may hear the gospel in word only. but is not brought under its power. Many will not have divine things pressed upon them. They cannot bear the Word, and least of all from the lips of those they love. Hear they may be won 'without the word'.

What a blessing is a 'chaste conversation, coupled with fear'. Nothing but the Spirit of Christ can give this. By nature the eye is 'full of adultery, and cannot cease from sin'. If we could see into the reaches of natural hearts where God sees, what dark chambers of imagery would we behold. But if the Spirit of Christ dwells in you, He is the Spirit of purity. Your body is a member of Christ. It is the temple of the Holy Ghost. 'Walk in the Spirit, and ye shall not fulfil the lust of the flesh' (*Gal.* 5:16). 'This is the will of God, even your sanctification, that ye should abstain from fornication' (*1 Thess.* 4:3).

Many may be ready to say, 'Is thy servant a dog, that he should do this thing?' But those of you who know the hell that is within will tremblingly keep near to God and say, Lead me not into temptation. Given opportunity on the one hand, and Satan tempting on the other, and the grace of God at neither, where should you and I be?

2. BELIEVING WIVES SHOULD WIN THEIR HUSBANDS.

Wives should lay it to heart to seek to save their unbelieving husbands. The means is not the word but chaste behaviour proceeding from the fear of God. This is of all arguments the strongest. It is the mark of a divine work. Men pay regard to actions more than words.

There is nothing so lovely in all this world as a believing wife filled with that Spirit who is the Holy Spirit, holy in eye and dress and look and word, thinking on the things that are lovely and pure. This is most powerful to gain unbelieving husbands to Christ, and to provoke them to say, 'There must be something in this faith!'

47

Seeing the Unseen

Casting all your care upon him; for he careth for you. Be sober, be vigilant; because your adversary the devil, as a roaring lion, walketh about, seeking whom he may devour: whom resist stedfast in the faith, knowing that the same afflictions are accomplished in your brethren that are in the world (1 Pet. 5:7–9).

IT IS THE GREAT MARK OF A BELIEVER that he 'looks not at the things which are seen' (2 Cor. 4:18). He is engaged with an unseen Friend, and an unseen enemy. Hence the world think him mad. The world believes only what it sees. But we know and believe in unseen powers. Hence arise our conflicts. Many a cloud passes over the believer's brow that the world knows nothing of. Hence also arise our secret joys. There is many a gleam of sunshine that the world never feels. 'The heart knoweth his own bitterness; and a stranger doth not intermeddle with his joy' (*Prov.* 14:10).

I. THE UNSEEN ENEMY

He is here called 'your adversary the devil'. This is his name. He exerts power over the world; however this is not so much an adversary as 'the god of this world' (2 Cor. 4:4); and 'the prince of the power of the air' (*Eph.* 2:2). Men are taken captive by him at his will (*2 Tim.* 2:26). He takes away the seed of the Word when it is sown. He is the strong man armed (*Luke* 11:21). He entered into Judas (*John* 13:27). He filled the heart of Ananias (*Acts* 5:3).

As the strong man armed, he keeps his palace. His goods are at peace, for he keeps all quiet within. He keeps out the light (*2 Cor.* 9:4), since it might disturb the quiet repose of those inside. He works in them (*Eph.* 2:2). Oh, Christless men, ye little know under whose power you are!

i. He Is the Adversary of Believers.

It is against believers that all his strength and rage and cunning are turned. His warfare he carries on in two ways:

a. *He tries to separate between the soul and Christ.*

'I fear, lest by any means . . . your minds should be corrupted from the simplicity that is in Christ' (*2 Cor.* 11:3). To this end are all his wrestlings and wiles and roarings. He tempts, or he persecutes, all to separate us from Christ.

b. *He accuses us before God day and night.*

He moves God to destroy us (*Job* 1:6–12; *Zech.* 3:1; *Luke* 22:31; *Rev.* 12:9–10).

ii. How Is He Described Here?

He is likened to a lion, the king of the forest, the strongest and fiercest beast. He was once the brightest and best of the morning stars, called Lucifer, the Son of the Morning. Now he is the prince of the power of the air, and the god of this world. Consider how great his power must be if he keeps so many eyes blinded and leads so many souls captive. Look at false religion, politics and entertainment and you will see the power of this lion.

a. *His roaring*

The lion roars when it is hungry (*Psa.* 104:21; *Amos* 3:4). If you take away the lion's cubs, he makes the forest resound with his tremendous roar. So Satan is hungry for souls. He is angry at being robbed of his whelps. You were once the whelps of the great lion. You were of your father, the devil. But you were turned from the power of Satan to God. Now he roars. Satan is greatly enraged at believers. He knows his time is short (*Rev.* 12:12).

b. *His walking about*

This suggests his diligence. As the lion, in search of prey, traverses the forest, so does he. The descriptions in Job 1:6 and in Revelation 12:10 are awful. He accuses day and night. He is a sleepless accuser. In heaven, they rest not day nor night. So Satan never rests from his soul-destroying work. Should not this teach you to be working the work of him that sent you? You should be as diligent in seeking your sanctification as Satan is in seeking your destruction.

c. *His attempts to devour*

We have many enemies that do not seek our life, but Satan is a mortal enemy. He hunts for the precious life (see *Prov.* 6:26). He knows that he is to be cast into the lake of fire, and he seeks companions. Nothing short of this will satisfy.

QUESTION: Is Satan ignorant that the saints will persevere?

ANSWER: Perhaps he is. In his dealings with Christ we see that he was ignorant of many things. Perhaps he does not know who are true saints.

We know that he wants to have the sentence of condemnation passed on us. Resist him then! In small temptations, this is his end. Take heed!

2. THE UNSEEN FRIEND

There is One who 'careth for you'. In temptation, the believer cries, 'No man cared for my soul' (*Psa.* 142:4). But it is not so. The hireling flees because he does not care for the sheep, but the Good Shepherd lays down his life for them (*John* 10:13–15). He is our Advocate. If any man sins He pleads on his behalf (*1 John* 2:1). The disciples awoke Christ saying, 'Master, carest thou not that we perish?' But He arose and rebuked the wind and the waves (*Mark* 4:38–41).

Two things in particular burden the soul with care, guilt and weakness.

i. Cast All the Care of Your Guilt upon Him.

Satan accuses you and brings up your old sins: the sins of youth; sins against light; sins since conversion. He moves God to destroy you. He can be overcome only by the blood of the Lamb.

ii. Cast All the Care of Your Weakness upon Him.

Satan tempts, and you feel helpless. Lust is so strong. Look again to Jesus. It pleased the Father that in Him should all fulness dwell. He is faithful and will not suffer you to be tempted above what you can bear, but will make a way of escape for you.

We must be sober and vigilant. These two things are inseparable in a true believer. If you really cast all your care on him, you will be sober and vigilant.

iii. Be Sober.

Be not too much taken up with the griefs of this world. Weep as though you wept not. Satan often takes advantage of inordinate grief. Sit light to both the pleasures and the cares of this life.

iv. BE VIGILANT.

Keep a watch over your own heart. Watch every night how it has acted. Watch for the lion. You are in his country. Watch the prints of his feet. Watch for Jesus. Keep your eye fixed on Him.

v. RESIST THE DEVIL.

Take to you the whole armour of God (*Eph.* 6:11-17). Submit to God, and resist the devil (*James* 4:7). Be like a child in His arms and cry to Him. Draw out the spear (*Psa.* 35:3). Set your back to the Rock, and fight the good fight of faith. 'Without me ye can do nothing', says Christ. And let us say, with Paul, 'I can do all things through Christ which strengtheneth me' (*Phil.* 4:13).

48

New Creatures in Christ

Whosoever committeth sin transgresseth also the law: for sin is the transgression of the law. And ye know that he was manifested to take away our sins; and in him is no sin. Whosoever abideth in him sinneth not: whosoever sinneth hath not seen him, neither known him. Little children, let no man deceive you: he that doeth righteousness is righteous, even as he is righteous. He that committeth sin is of the devil; for the devil sinneth from the beginning. For this purpose the Son of God was manifested, that he might destroy the works of the devil. Whosoever is born of God doth not commit sin; for his seed remaineth in him: and he cannot sin, because he is born of God. In this the children of God are manifest, and the children of the devil: whosoever doeth not righteousness is not of God, neither he that loveth not his brother (1 John 3:4-10).

IT IS INTERESTING TO REMARK that, of all the apostles, John seems to have excelled in two things:

In love, in that gentle, tender, compassionate love that dwelt first in the bosom of Christ;

In hatred of sin; his constant aim seems to have been to persuade believers to forsake their sins. He learned both of these by leaning on the bosom of Christ, and we cannot learn much there without being made like John.

Oh! pray, dear friends, that I may be like John among you, loving your souls and hating your sins, that I may show you this day plainly who are the children of God and who are the children of the devil. The whole object of this searching passage is to show that if any man be in Christ he will be a new creature, and that if a man be not a new creature, then he is not in Christ at all. Sin cannot reign in such a new creature, for several reasons.

1. BECAUSE SIN IS THE TRANSGRESSION OF THE LAW.

The law was first written on the heart of God. During the past eternity it lay there graven in indelible characters on the unseen tablet of God's heart: the pure and holy law of God, His Word and will. When man was created God wrote the law upon his heart. He was made in the image of God. His understanding, affections, will were all a reflection of God's, and this pure and holy law was graven deep in his holy heart.

When man fell the law was broken in pieces. It was erased from the heart of man, although it remained in his conscience still as an accuser. Satan wrote another law in his members, a law of sin and death. When a man is brought into God's family, this is one of the first and sweetest gifts which he receives, the whole law graven in his heart. When our poor Roman Catholic brethren write down the law of God, they pass over one of the commandments because it forbids the worship of images. But the Spirit is a faithful engraver, He omits none of the commandments; when He writes them into the new heart He writes them in full.

Has this been done on your hearts? Once you hated the law of God, you thought it too severe, too strict, too searching. You thought it unjust to put you under a law which you had not strength to obey. You thought it not good, not kind. If God had been kinder, you thought, He would have made a more indulgent law.

New Creatures in Christ

But now you have been brought to Christ and got it written in your heart. Now you say, I delight in the law of God after the inward man. The law is holy, just and good. You feel it would be your supreme joy to keep the whole law of God. This is your constant desire and prayer. How then can sin reign in you? It is not possible. It will live and struggle in you, but it cannot reign.

Is there any of you afraid of being made holy? Do you feel some idol in your heart that you do not wish to part with? You are willing to give God all the rest of your heart, except this little corner where your idol stands. Then you are not come to Christ yet! For when you come to Christ your word will be, What have I to do any more with idols? (*Hos.* 14:8).

2. BECAUSE CHRIST CAME TO TAKE AWAY OUR SINS.

The object for which Christ was manifested was two-fold:

i. To Take Away the Curse of Our Sins.

This He did when He offered himself a sacrifice without spot unto God. 'Behold the Lamb of God, which taketh away the sin of the world' (*John* 1:29). 'Who his own self bare our sins in his own body on the tree' (*1 Pet.* 2:24).

ii. To Take Away the Power of Our Sins.

He 'gave himself for us, that he might redeem us from all iniquity, and purify unto himself a peculiar people, zealous of good works' (*Titus* 2:14). 'Christ . . . suffered for sins, the just for the unjust, that he might bring us to God' (*1 Pet.* 3:18).

Now there are a great many in our day who are contented with the first of these and have no desire for the second. There are a great many willing to be saved from hell by Christ who are not willing to be saved from sin by Christ. And yet there is every reason to believe that the last is the grand object Christ had in dying for us.

It is said in Zechariah 9:16 that His people shall be 'as the stones of a crown, lifted up as an ensign upon his land'. And in Isaiah 62:3, 'Thou shalt also be a crown of glory in the hand of the LORD, and a royal diadem in the hand of thy God.' When Christ came to this world, it was not merely to save souls from hell, but to make them into jewels that would shine in glory. If you are really saved by Christ, He will not only give you peace of conscience, but He will renew your heart and make you shine as a jewel and as a diadem in the hand of our God.

In Isaiah 61:3, Christ says the Father anointed Him to save sinners, 'that they might be called trees of righteousness, the planting of the LORD that he might be glorified'. He came to pluck brands out of the fire. He went into the fire and bore it for them that He might pluck them out, but then it was to plant them as trees of righteousness, that they might glorify God by bearing much holy fruit. If you are really plucked out of the fire, you will also be planted as a tree of righteousness and watered every moment. You will be 'filled with the fruits of righteousness, which are by Jesus Christ, unto the glory and praise of God'. Oh, search and try if this is the case with you! If you are still a rotten branch, I fear you are near the burning.

In Romans 8:29 it is said, 'For whom he did foreknow, he also did predestinate to be conformed to the image of his Son, that he might be the firstborn among many brethren.' This seems to have been the great end of Christ's coming into this world, that He might save a company of hell-deserving souls and make them in His own image, one holy family of which He should be the eldest brother. If you are one of those whom Christ has saved from hell, then He will make you a brother. He will take away your sins and give you His own graces. 'Of his fullness have all we received, and grace for grace' (*John* 1:16). For every grace that is in Christ we receive a corresponding grace; from every fountain of holiness in His heart, a stream flows into our heart.

Oh! then, if you are not thus being saved from your sins, you are none of His. Is there any one who thinks that he is saved from hell, but feels that he is not saved from sins? I fear you know not Jesus!

3. BECAUSE THEY ABIDE IN CHRIST.

Dear friend, there is such a thing as *vital union to Christ*. Every one that is saved by Christ is united to Him for eternity. In Romans 7:4 it is compared to marriage, 'Ye also are become dead to the law by the body of Christ; that ye should be married to another, even to him who is raised from the dead, that we should bring forth fruit unto God.'

In Colossians 2:19 it is compared to the union of the members of the body to the head, 'Not holding the Head, from which all the body by joints and bands having nourishment ministered, and knit together, increaseth with the increase of God.' If the Head be holy, will not the members receive holiness from him?

Do you feel that you have Christ for your Head? Is it from Him that your nourishment proceeds? Then you will hate all sin. I do not say you will be sinless, but you will war against all sin.

In John 15:5, Jesus says, 'I am the vine, ye are the branches: He that abideth in me, and I in him, the same bringeth forth much fruit.' Search and try, dear friends. The branches always bear the same fruit as the stem. Would you not be much surprised if you were to find a tree bearing fine grapes upon one branch and poisonous berries on another? No, it cannot be! Neither can you be united to Christ, and live on in sin.

[317]

'If any man have not the Spirit of Christ he is none of his' (*Rom.* 8:9) – *any man*. If you have had deep convictions of sin; if you have had great light and joy and peace; views of Christ; great engagements in prayer; liberty in relating your experiences; great resemblance in your case to that of other Christians; yet, if you have not the Spirit of Christ, you are none of His!

'If ye live after the flesh, ye shall die' (*Rom.* 8:13). Some people say, 'I have surely been converted. I have undergone a wonderful change of mind. I never attended to divine things before.' But do you live after the flesh? Then you shall die! Do you follow 'the desires of the flesh, and of the mind'? Are you living in avowed sin? Then what need have you of witnesses? You are on the road to hell. 'Whosoever sinneth hath not seen him, neither known him' (*1 John* 3:6).

CASE 1: *I have fallen into open sin: can I be united to Christ?*

ANSWER: Does your sin lead you to Christ? Peter fell by denying his Lord. But the next time he saw his Lord he girded his fisher's coat unto him and swam to Christ. His fall led him to Christ. If yours leads you to cleave closer to Christ than before, then you may have good hope that you are restored.

CASE 2: *I am constantly tormented with one particular lust; it rises up within me; can I be united to Christ?*

ANSWER: Does it lead you to cry to the Lord? You remember Paul had a thorn in his flesh. He besought the Lord thrice that it might depart from him. He received the answer, My grace is sufficient for thee.

CASE 3: *I have felt deep convictions of sin. I have wept and prayed and trembled for my soul. I have been made glad by hearing the preaching of the gospel, and yet I do not feel that my heart is changed. I still love to live in sin.*

New Creatures in Christ

ANSWER: Then you have never seen Christ, nor known Him. Every lost sheep found by the Shepherd, He lifts it upon His shoulder. 'If any man be in Christ, he is a new creature.'

4. BECAUSE HE IS SAVED FROM THE HANDS OF THE DEVIL.

Every natural man is of the devil. He is a child of the devil. It is very awful to hear the gentle lips of Christ using these words, 'Ye are of your father the devil, and the lusts of your father ye will do' (*John* 8:44) And again, 'Ye serpents, ye generation of vipers, how can ye escape the damnation of hell?' (*Matt.* 23:33). It is very worthy of notice that Christ does not say this to publicans and harlots, to open sinners, but to the Pharisees, men who were exceedingly moral in their outward behaviour. There may be many of you who live very decent outward lives who are, in the sight of Christ, children of the devil.

Every natural man is wrought in by the devil – the prince of the power of the air (*Eph.* 2:2). As God's children are dwelt in by the Holy Spirit, so natural men are dwelt in by the devil. 'Greater is he that is in you, than he that is in the world.' There may be some of you, dear friends, at present under the power of Satan.

Every natural man is Satan's house. How can one enter into a strong man's house and spoil his goods, except he will first bind the strong man? Just as the believer's heart is a temple of the Holy Ghost, so the heart of every one of you who is Christless is a palace for the great enemy of souls.

Oh! if you could see behind the scenes, dear friends, if you could see the Mighty One who is in the heart of believers, and the mighty spirit of evil who is in the unconverted, it would make poor sinners cry out in agony.

But Christ came to destroy the works of the devil. Has He done this for you? Has He cast out Satan, and made you sit at His feet, clothed, and in your right mind? Then sin shall not have dominion over you. Christ liveth in you. He is on the throne in your heart. Oh! let Him reign over all.

5. BECAUSE HE IS BORN OF GOD.

Dear friends, have you been born of God? Have you been awakened by the Spirit, drawn to Christ, made alive in divine things? Then it is to you this glorious word is spoken. You do not sin, for God's seed remaineth in you, and you cannot sin.

QUESTION: Is it impossible to sin, after conversion?

ANSWER: It is alas all too possible. David fell into adultery, Peter into denying Christ. The disciples quarelled who should be the greatest. Nay, so far as I understand the Bible and my own heart, there is not a moment of life from the new birth to glory spent without sin. The very imperfection of your faith is infinitely vile in the sight of God. All believers that I know have very imperfect faith, their eyes are only half open. They need to cry, Help my unbelief!

How cold the love of all believers! Our heart is only half melted by the love of Christ. If at any time it is warmed, does not that make you feel how cold it is ordinarily? Take your best moment, believers, when you are nearest the throne, is not your comeliness turned into corruption? Do you not bring the blind and lame and sick for sacrifice?

One dear child of God said that she felt she deserved hell just for the want of humility in her for naming the Name of God. Alas there is nothing but rottenness and corruption in the heart of man. 'I know that in me (that is, in my flesh,) dwelleth no good thing.'

New Creatures in Christ

Yet it is gloriously true that 'everyone that is born of God sinneth not'. 'It is no more I that do it, but sin that dwelleth in me' (*Rom.* 7:20). If you are really in Christ, the Spirit of God will be like a seed of life in your heart, imperishable. He is all for holiness, and your new heart is all for holiness. The old man in you is all for sin, but God and the new heart are all for holiness. If not, then there is nothing but sin in you.

Dear friends, do you have the seed of grace in you? Then it will remain. If the spark from God has been kindled in your heart, then it never can be quenched. You may pass through temptations – still that seed will remain in you. 'Holiness to the Lord' is graven in your forehead. You cannot die. You may be brought through persecutions – still the life of God will be maintained in your soul. You may be carried through the waters of trouble – still they cannot quench it.

Soon, soon you shall be freed from the body of sin also. Then we shall be holy only, without any tendency to sin any more. We shall lose the old heart, and be all the new heart, altogether.